World Atlas CD-ROM

1. Running your *World Atlas* CD-ROM

Your *World Atlas* CD-ROM will run on both PCs with Windows and on Apple Macs. To make sure that your computer meets the system requirements, check the list below.

Minimum system requirements:

Acrobat Reader system requirements:

Windows
- R-class processor
- Microsoft® Windows 98 Second Edition, Windows Millennium Edition, Windows NT 4.0 with Service Pack 5 or 6 (Service Pack 6 recommended), Windows 2000, Windows XP Professional or Home Edition
- 64 MB of RAM
- 30 MB of available hard disk space (an additional 60 MB is needed temporarily during installation)
- Additional 70 MB of hard disk space for Asian fonts (optional)
- Web browser support. The Web browsers within which Adobe PDF files may be viewed are:
  – Internet Explorer 5.0 to 6.0
  – Netscape Navigator 4.5 to 4.77, 6.1
  – America Online 6.0

Macintosh
- PowerPC processor
- Apple® Mac® OS 9.1, 9.2, 9.2.2, 10.1.3, 10.1.5, 10.2
- 64 MB of RAM
- 30 MB of available hard disk space (an additional 60 MB is needed temporarily during installation)
- HFS formatted hard drive
- Additional 70 MB of hard disk space for Asian fonts (optional)
- Web browser support. The Web browsers within which Adobe PDF files may be viewed are:
  – Internet Explorer 5.0
  – Netscape Navigator 4.5 to 4.77, 6.1
  – America Online 6.0

2. Loading your *World Atlas* CD-ROM

To use your *World Atlas* CD-ROM, you will need to install Acrobat Reader if you do not already have it installed on your hard drive.

1. Place the *World Atlas* CD-ROM in your CD drive.

2a. If you have a PC, double click on the 'My Computer' icon, then double click on the 'World Atlas' folder. Double click on the 'Maps' folder and attempt to open one of the maps. If you are successful, you have a compatible version of Acrobat or Acrobat Reader already installed.

2b. If you have a Mac, double click on the 'World Atlas' icon on your desktop. Double click on the 'Maps' folder and attempt to open one of the maps. If you are successful, you have a compatible version of Acrobat or Acrobat Reader already installed.

3. If you cannot open a map, then proceed to the 'Acrobat Reader Installers' folder. On opening it, select your platform (Mac or PC) and proceed through the further folders until you reach the folder covering your operating system.

4. On finding the installer that matches your platform and operating system, double click on the installer and follow the on-screen instructions.

5. If you are unable to find either your platform or operating system, please go to the following website:
http://www.adobe.com/products/acrobat/readstep2.html

3. How to use your *World Atlas* CD-ROM

The *World Atlas* CD-ROM contains 47 world, regional and country base maps. The maps are 'text-free' PDF versions of the maps that appear in the accompanying *World Atlas* book. Lines of latitude and longitude are labelled. The names of physical features, town stamps, country and town names are not featured, allowing these maps to be used as a template for all sorts of homework activities. You can print the maps straight from the CD-ROM, then, using the accompanying *World Atlas* to help you, choose exactly which countries, towns and physical features you wish to label.

4. Contents of your *World Atlas* CD-ROM

The 47 world, regional and country maps are divided into nine folders. The number at the beginning of each file name refers to the page in the accompanying *World Atlas* where you can find the complete version of that map.

THE WORLD
16. The physical world
18. The political world

THE POLES
20. The Arctic Ocean
21. Antarctica

NORTH AMERICA
22. North America
24. Canada
26. Western US
28. Midwestern US
30. Southern US
32. Northeastern US
34. Mexico and Central America
36. The Caribbean

SOUTH AMERICA
38. South America
40. Northern South America
42. Southern South America

EUROPE
46. Europe
48. Northwestern Europe
50. The British Isles
52. The Low Countries
54. France
56. The Iberian Peninsula
58. Germany
60. The Alpine states

62. Italy and Malta
64. Eastern Europe
66. Central Europe
68. Southeastern Europe

AFRICA
70. Africa
72. Northwest Africa
74. Northeast Africa
76. West Africa
78. Central and east Africa
80. Southern Africa

ASIA
84. Asia
86. The Russian Federation
88. West Asia
90. Central Asia
92. South Asia
94. Southeast Asia
96. East Asia
98. Japan and the Koreas

AUSTRALASIA AND OCEANIA
100. Australasia and Oceania
102. Australia
104. New Zealand

THE OCEANS
44. The Atlantic Ocean
82. The Indian Ocean
106. The Pacific Ocean

5. Copyright details and disclaimer

Kingfisher Publications Plc
New Penderel House,
283-288 High Holborn,
London WC1V 7HZ
www.kingfisherpub.com

THE KINGFISHER
WORLD ATLAS

KINGFISHER

Kingfisher Publications Plc
New Penderel House,
283–288 High Holborn,
London WC1V 7HZ
www.kingfisherpub.com

Project Management: Picthall & Gunzi Ltd

For Picthall & Gunzi
Editor: Margaret Hynes
Designer: Dominic Zwemmer
Placename Consultant: Roger Bullen
Editorial Assistant: Carmen Hansen
Indexers: Jan Clark, Gill Cooling, Deborah Murrell

For Kingfisher
Managing Editor: Russell Mclean
Art Director: Mike Davis
Designer: Carol Ann Davis
DTP Manager: Nicky Studdart
Senior Production Controller: Nancy Roberts
Picture Research Manager: Cee Weston-Baker

Maps designed and produced by Anderson Geographics Limited, Warfield, Berkshire

First published by Kingfisher Publications Plc 2003
3 5 7 9 10 8 6 4
3TR/1204/TWP/CLSN(CLSN)/130ENSOMA/F

The publisher would like to thank the following for permission to reproduce their material. Every care has been taken to trace
copyright holders. However, if there have been unintentional omissions or failure to trace copyright holders, we apologise
and will, if informed, endeavour to make corrections in any future edition.

Key: b = bottom, c = centre, l = left, r = right, t = top

6bl Corbis; 8t Lloyd Cuff/Corbis; 8b Lloyd Cuff/Corbis; 9t James A. Sugar/Corbis; 9b Jeff Vanuga/Corbis; 10bc Imagebank/
Getty Images; 10br Imagebank/Getty Images; 11tr Annie Griffiths Belt/National Geographic Image Collection; 12tr Darrell
Gulin/Corbis; 12b Laurence Fordyce/Eye Ubiquitous/ Corbis; 13tr Gary Braash/Corbis; 13bl Wolfgang Kaehler/Corbis;
13bc Wolfgang Kaehler/Corbis; 13br DiMaggio/Kalish/Corbis; 14-15 Bill Ross/Corbis; 14bl Adrian Arbib/Corbis;
14br Richard Bickel/Corbis; 15tc Robert Essel NYC/Corbis; 15tr Paul Almasy/Corbis

The publisher would also like to thank the following illustrators for their contribution to this book:
Richard Bonson 11b; Chris Forsey 7tr, 9tr; Jeremy Gower 10bl; Maltings Partnership 8bl; Janos Marphy 6–7

A CIP catalogue record for this book is available from the British Library.

ISBN 13: 978 0 7534 0813 1
ISBN 10: 0 7534 0813 9

Printed in Singapore

THE KINGFISHER
WORLD ATLAS

KINGFISHER

CONTENTS

PLANET EARTH

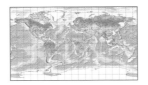

THE WORLD

THE POLES

NORTH AMERICA

SOUTH AMERICA

EUROPE

AFRICA

ASIA

AUSTRALASIA AND OCEANIA

KEY TO MAPS

Settlements

- ■ PARIS   Capital city
- ● Halifax   Administrative region capital
- ○ São Paulo   Major town
- ○ Galway   Other town

Political and cultural regions

MEXICO   Country

Corsica   Dependent territory
(to France)

ARIZONA   Internal administrative region

TUSCANY   Cultural region

Boundaries

International border

Disputed border

Internal administrative boundary

Drainage features

Congo   River

Warrego   Seasonal river

Albert Canal   Canal

Angel Falls   Waterfall

Lake Taupo   Lake

Lake Mackay   Seasonal lake

Topographic features

△ Mont Blanc 4,810 m   Spot height of mountain

▽ –8,605 m   Spot depth below sea level

Balearic Islands   Island / island group

Thar Desert   Landscape feature / region

Seas and oceans

INDIAN OCEAN   Ocean

North Sea   Sea

Guinea Basin   Sea feature

Ice features

Limit of summer pack ice

Limit of winter pack ice

Land height

4,000 m
13,124 ft

2,000 m
6,562 ft

1,000 m
3,281 ft

500 m
1,640 ft

200 m
656 ft

Sea level

THE HOME PLANET

Planet Earth is roughly spherical in shape and measures 40,075 km around the Equator. As far as we know, it is the only planet that can support life. There are two main reasons for this. First, the Earth has an atmosphere that contains oxygen. Second, the planet is the just the right distance from the Sun. Planets closer to the Sun, such as Mercury, are too hot for life. Those further away, such as Mars, are too cold.

The Solar System

The Sun, our nearest star, has powerful gravity which attracts nine major planets, including the Earth, and countless minor planets, called asteroids. These, and other bodies, such as moons and comets, circle the Sun and form its family, or Solar System. The planets of the Solar System were probably created about 4.5 billion years ago from a cloud of gas and dust thrown out by the Sun when it was formed. The smaller planets nearer the Sun are made up of minerals and metals. The outer planets were formed at lower temperatures, and consist of swirling clouds of gases.

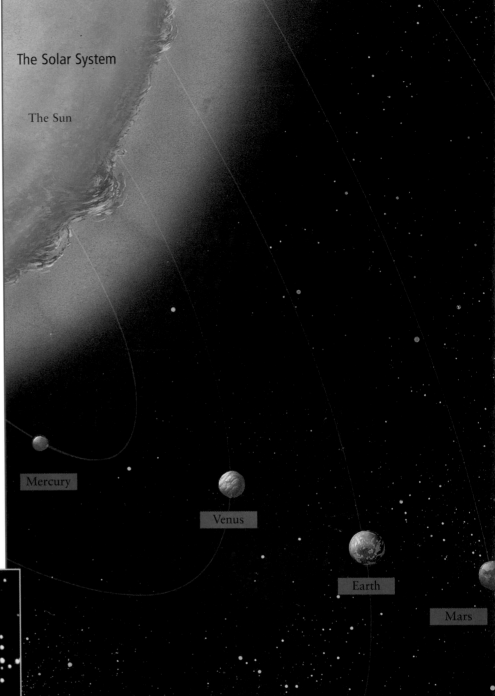

The Solar System

The Sun

Mercury

Venus

Earth

Mars

The Milky Way is an enormous, spiral-shaped galaxy of which our Solar System forms a tiny part. The galaxy contains at least 200 billion stars.

The Earth is the third planet from the Sun (above). It takes 365.25 days for the Earth to complete a full circle of the Sun.

The Sun and Moon

With a diameter of about 1,400,000 km, the Sun is more than 100 times wider than the Earth. Like other stars, the Sun is a great ball of gases. Although it lies about 150 million kilometres from the Earth, the Sun provides the light and warmth needed to make our planet suitable for life. The Moon lies about 384,000 km away from the Earth, and is our planet's closest neighbour in space. Its gravity is weaker than the Earth's, so it cannot hang on to any gases to make an atmosphere. However, the Moon's gravity does pull at our oceans to create tides.

Inside the Earth

Rocky crust

Outer mantle

Inner mantle. It is richer in iron than the outer mantle.

Outer core of molten iron and nickel

Inner core of solid iron and nickel

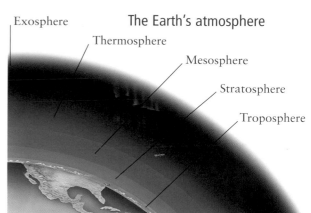

Exosphere   The Earth's atmosphere
Thermosphere
Mesosphere
Stratosphere
Troposphere

Pluto

Neptune

Uranus

Saturn

Jupiter

The Earth's outer structure

The Earth is surrounded by a layer of air roughly 2,000 km thick, called the atmosphere. It contains the air that we breathe, together with water vapour and tiny pieces of dust. Held by the pull of the Earth's gravity, the atmosphere protects us from the dangerous rays of the Sun, and the cold of outer space. The atmosphere is made up of layers. The layer closest to the Earth is the troposphere. It contains most of the gas in the atmosphere, and is the narrowest layer. Above the troposphere is the stratosphere. It extends from 11 km to 50 km above the Earth. The mesosphere lies between 50 km and 80 km above the Earth. If meteors fall into this layer, they burn up, causing shooting stars. A very thick layer of air called the thermosphere extends from about 80 km to 480 km above the ground. Above this is the exosphere, which has no definite upper limit.

The Earth's inner structure

At the centre of the Earth lies a solid core made of iron and a small amount of nickel. Its temperature is about 4,500°C. Around the core is the outer core, formed of liquid iron and nickel at a temperature of about 3,300°C. Outside the core is the mantle, a layer of rock about 2,900 km thick. The temperature reaches about 3,700°C at the bottom of the mantle, but high pressure there keeps the rock solid. There is less pressure on the top part of the mantle, which is relatively soft and can move. We live on the Earth's rocky outer layer, called the crust.

THE CHANGING EARTH

The Earth's crust, which covers the planet's surface, is made up of several sections, called tectonic plates. These plates interlock with each other, like the pieces of an enormous jigsaw puzzle. They are not fixed in position, however, but are moving slowly. As a result, the world's continents have shifted position over millions of years. More than 200 million years ago, the continents made up one single landmass, which gradually split up and moved apart to produce the continent shapes that we see today. The boundaries of the plates are places of huge stress. Sometimes, if plates are drifting apart, new crust is created as hot liquid rock from the mantle below fills the gap. If the plates are pushing towards each other, the land on one side can be pushed upwards, creating mountain ranges.

Earthquakes

Earthquakes occur when two tectonic plates slide past each other and friction is created along the line that lies between them. The friction causes violent vibrations, called tremors, that spread across the ground from the source. Sometimes the crust of the Earth cracks, or is faulted, and the land on one side of the fault line is raised, while on the other side it is lowered.

Sliding plates

The San Andreas Fault extends for over 1,000 km across California. This area is the site of frequent minor earthquakes.

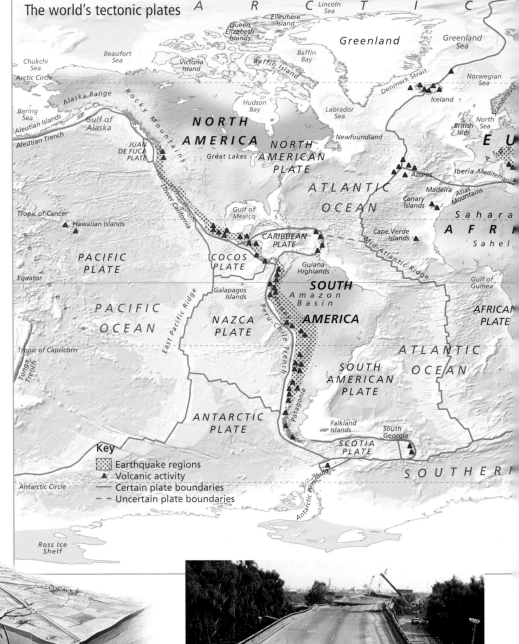

The world's tectonic plates

Key
- Earthquake regions
- ▲ Volcanic activity
- — Certain plate boundaries
- – - Uncertain plate boundaries

Fault line

Area of friction

Vibrations spreading away from the source

The enormous power of an earthquake can pull down buildings and rip apart roads, sometimes causing death and injury in the process.

Lava flowing from volcanoes can reach temperatures of more than 1,000°C, and move at speeds of up to 60 km/h.

Smoke, ash and rock
Volcanic cone
Geyser
Layers of cooled lava
Side vent
An erupting volcano
Magma chamber
Lava flow
Central vent

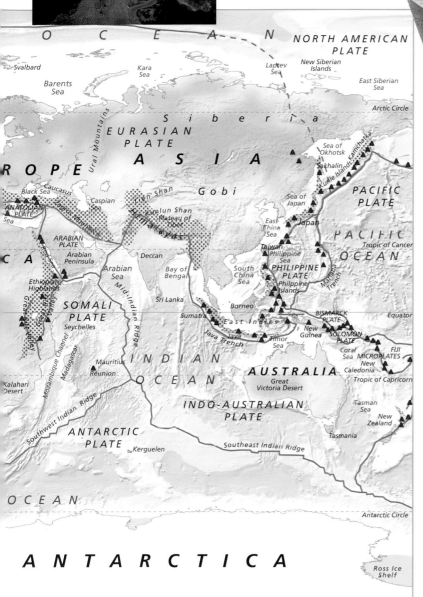

Volcanoes

When hot liquid rock, or magma, from the Earth's mantle escapes to the surface of the Earth, a volcano is created. Sometimes the magma collects in a huge underground chamber, before it rises through a channel called the central vent, or smaller side vents. Once the magma breaks the surface it is called lava. The lava gradually cools to form the shape of the volcano. Some volcanoes are cone-shaped, while others, called shield volcanoes, are more rounded. During a volcanic eruption, gases, ash and rock are often thrown high into the air.

Geysers

Geysers are found in the volcanic regions of New Zealand, Iceland, Chile, eastern Russian Federation and western USA. Pools of water, in underground caverns made of watertight volcanic rock such as rhyolite, are heated by scorching hot magma. The water boils, and some of it turns to steam. Eventually, the pressure in the cavern builds up, and the water and steam is forced upwards through a crevice to the Earth's surface. Here, the water and steam burst out of the ground, and spurt up into the air.

There are less than 1,000 geysers in the world. A number of them erupt very often and extremely regularly. Some geysers are known to reach heights of more than 100 metres.

CLIMATE AND WEATHER

Climate is the average sunshine, wind, rainfall and humidity that an area receives over a long period of time. The major influence on a region's climate is its latitude (the distance it lies north or south of the equator). The equator receives the most direct rays from the Sun, so the climates there are warm. Places near the poles receive less heat from the Sun, so they have colder climates. Other influences on an area's climate include its distance from an ocean, its height above sea level, ocean currents and wind patterns.

The Earth's climate zones

The Earth's climate varies from place to place. Polar and mountainous zones are freezing and dry all year round. Continental regions are cold in winter and warmer in summer. Steppe areas have cold winters and very hot summers, while temperate regions enjoy a milder climate without extremes of temperature. The tropics are mainly hot and wet all year round. Some subtropical zones have hot, dry summers and warm, wet winters. Arid areas are hot with very little rain at all. Savanna regions are hot throughout the year, but they have a rainy season that lasts about three months.

The greenhouse effect

Certain gases in the atmosphere, such as carbon dioxide, are called greenhouse gases because they act like the glass panes in a greenhouse. These gases let the Sun's rays pass through to the Earth, but they restrict the amount of energy that can pass back into space. The heat becomes trapped in the atmosphere, causing the Earth to warm up.

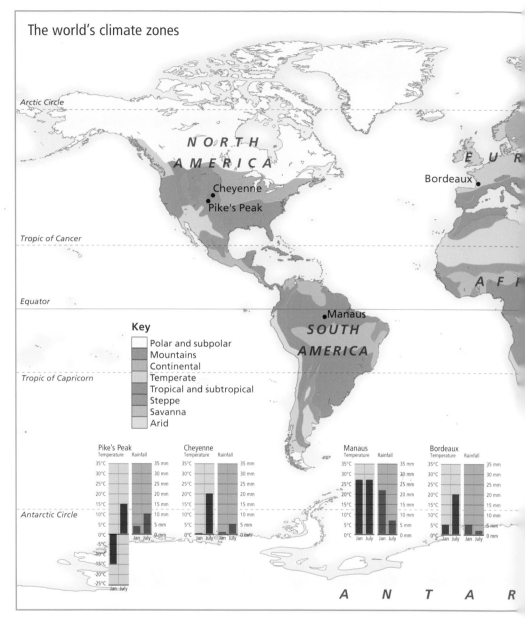

The world's climate zones

Key
- Polar and subpolar
- Mountains
- Continental
- Temperate
- Tropical and subtropical
- Steppe
- Savanna
- Arid

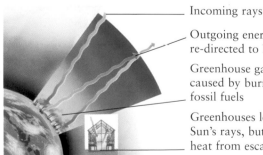

How the greenhouse effect works

- Incoming rays
- Outgoing energy re-directed to Earth
- Greenhouse gases caused by burning fossil fuels
- Greenhouses let in Sun's rays, but keep heat from escaping

Many deserts are so dry that virtually no plants can grow. The Namib Desert, in southern Africa, receives an average rainfall of only 25 mm per year.

Temperatures on Antarctica reach as low as −88.8°C. A few animals, such as penguins, have adapted to the freezing conditions and howling winds.

Tropical areas, such as the coast of Texas, USA, are wet and hot all year round. During storms, the rain falls in torrents and fierce winds lash trees and houses.

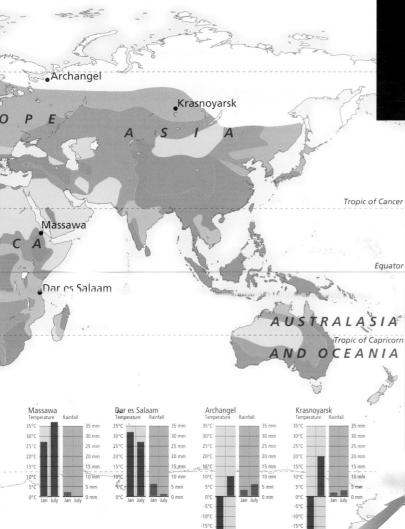

Archangel

Krasnoyarsk

O P E

A S I A

Tropic of Cancer

Massawa

C A

Equator

Dar es Salaam

A U S T R A L A S I A

Tropic of Capricorn

A N D O C E A N I A

Massawa
Temperature Rainfall

Dar es Salaam
Temperature Rainfall

Archangel
Temperature Rainfall

Krasnoyarsk
Temperature Rainfall

C T I C A

Weather

Short-term events in the atmosphere, from showers to hurricanes, make up the world's daily weather. Changes in weather are mainly caused by the movements of large air masses. The temperature and moisture content of these air masses change as they pass over land and water. They also swirl around to produce depressions – bringing cooler, wetter weather – and anticyclones – tending to bring warmer, drier conditions.

The water vapour forms clouds that produce rain or snow

Rivers carry water to the sea

Water runs below the surface of the land to the sea

The water cycle

The continuous movement of water across the Earth and through its atmosphere is called the water cycle. Water in the oceans and the ground evaporates as the Sun heats the Earth. The water vapour rises into the sky where it begins to cool down, forming drops of water within clouds. Eventually, the drops of water become heavy enough to fall back to the Earth as rain or snow. The water soaks into the ground and feeds lakes and rivers. Then the cycle starts all over again.

Moist air is blown towards the land

The Sun heats a body of water, and moisture from its surface evaporates

Water falls back to the land and sea

How the water cycle works

THE NATURAL WORLD

All living things are connected with one another, and rely on each other for food, protection, or even shelter. It is possible to divide the world up into a number of broad zones, in which certain species of plants and animals live together within particular climate conditions. These ecological areas are called biomes.

The harshest habitats

The toughest of the world's biomes are those which have low rainfall, or experience bitterly cold or scorching hot temperatures. Polar regions are permanently covered in ice, so no plants can live in them. Animals, such as the walrus, have developed insulating fat and stocky limbs to survive in the freezing conditions here. With very little soil and large areas of frozen ground, tundra regions are treeless. A few plants, such as lichens and mosses, grow during the summer months. Needleleaf trees, including spruces and pines, are the only type of vegetation that can survive the long, snowy winters in the northern parts of Scandinavia, the Russian Federation and Canada. In mountainous regions, the lower slopes may be forested, but only ground-hugging shrubs can grow above the tree line. Deserts have very little rain. Certain plants and animals are adapted to the extreme temperatures and the lack of water in these regions.

For 50 to 60 days each year, the tundra regions, which are usually frozen, become carpeted with colourful, low-lying plants.

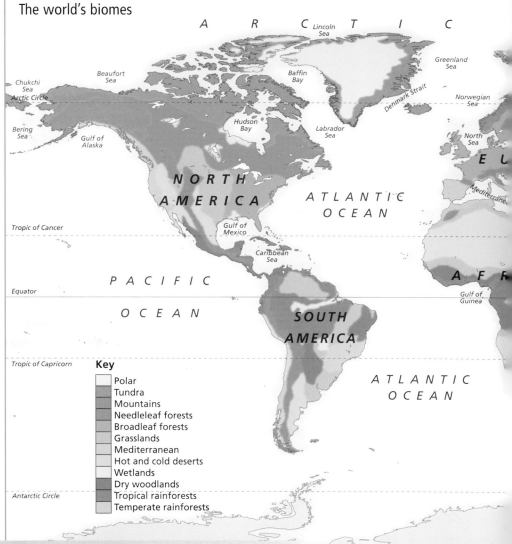

The world's biomes

Key
- Polar
- Tundra
- Mountains
- Needleleaf forests
- Broadleaf forests
- Grasslands
- Mediterranean
- Hot and cold deserts
- Wetlands
- Dry woodlands
- Tropical rainforests
- Temperate rainforests

Mountain peaks are hostile environments. The rocky terrain and thin air at high altitudes make it very difficult for plants and animals to survive.

A wealth of species of trees, ferns and creeping plants are found in tropical rainforests. These regions are also home to various animals, which range from snakes and monkeys to sloths, parrots and countless insects.

Temperate and tropical zones

Much of the northern hemisphere was once covered in broadleaf, deciduous trees, but most of them have now been cleared for settlements. Trees and evergreen shrubs, adapted to dry summers, grow in Mediterranean regions and dry woodlands. The world's major grasslands are found in the centre of the larger continents. These regions are grazed by herbivores, such as bison and zebras. Wetlands are rich feeding grounds for fish and breeding grounds for birds. With plenty of rain and sunshine, the rainforests have the greatest variety of species on Earth.

Biodiversity

The number of plant and animal species, and the variety within each species, make up the Earth's biodiversity. Some plants and animals, such as the kangaroos in Australia, are endemic (found only in one region). Man-made environments, including cities and farms, ruin natural habitats and threaten plant and animal biodiversity. Increasing efforts are now being made to conserve the Earth's wild places.

The grasslands of Africa, with trees dotted here and there, are broad, open habitats where herds of grazing animals range free, while looking out for carnivores such as leopards and lions.

Isolated places have the greatest range of endemic species. Lemurs (above) are only found in Madagascar and Comoros.

The planet's oceans have a huge variety of different species, from enormous whales to the tiniest plankton.

THE HUMAN WORLD

There have been people on planet Earth for over 130,000 years. Humans first evolved in Africa, and they gradually spread across the world. They probably travelled in search of food, either following herds of animals, or looking for fruit. By about 10,000 years ago, people had reached most parts of the globe, and some had started to settle down. Today, there are about six billion people in the world, but they are not distributed evenly. Some areas, including China, India and Europe, are densely populated, while others are not.

Feeding the world

Humans have developed skills to help them survive, and these have had an impact on the Earth. One of the earliest skills was farming. In different parts of the world, people worked out how to raise animals. They also learned how to cultivate crops that grew well in the local environment – from rice in eastern Asia to wheat in North America. Today, almost two-fifths of the planet's land is farmed. Through fishing, we have also changed the oceans. A modern fishing ship can catch entire shoals of fish in one go and some species, such as cod, have suffered badly as a result. Agreements have now been made to reduce the numbers of fish caught, to allow stocks to recover.

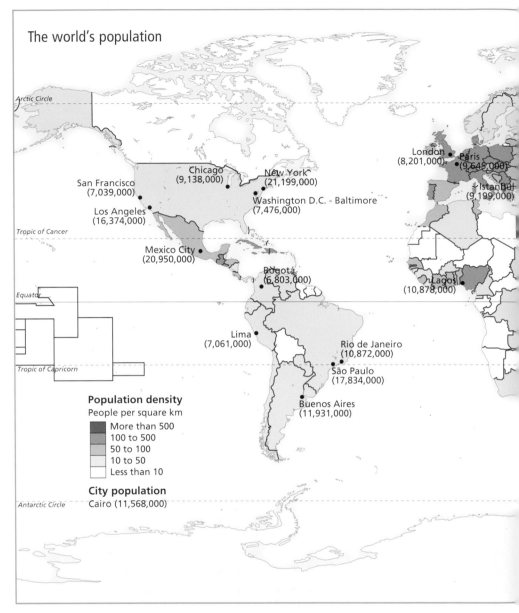

The world's population

Chicago (9,138,000)
New York (21,199,000)
San Francisco (7,039,000)
Washington D.C. - Baltimore (7,476,000)
Los Angeles (16,374,000)
London (8,201,000)
Paris (9,645,000)
Istanbul (9,199,000)
Mexico City (20,950,000)
Bogotá (6,803,000)
Lagos (10,878,000)
Lima (7,061,000)
Rio de Janeiro (10,872,000)
São Paulo (17,834,000)
Buenos Aires (11,931,000)

Arctic Circle
Tropic of Cancer
Equator
Tropic of Capricorn
Antarctic Circle

Population density
People per square km
More than 500
100 to 500
50 to 100
10 to 50
Less than 10

City population
Cairo (11,568,000)

The staple diet of half the world's people, rice has been cultivated for more than 5,000 years. Asia grows 91 per cent of the world's rice.

Traditional fishing methods, shown left, catch enough fish for the local market. But in some places, modern trawlers bring in vast quantities of fish. The catch is usually sold to factories, where it is processed for export.

In 1500, the world's population was about 425 million

In 1600, the world's population was about 545 million

In 1700, the world's population was about 610 million

1500   1600   1700

Cities, such as Tokyo (right), have many amenities, but some are also home to shanty towns (far right) where the very poor live with little or no services.

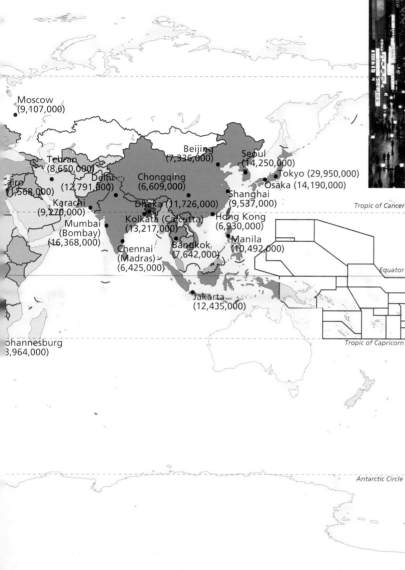

Moscow
(9,107,000)

Beijing
(7,336,000)

Seoul
(14,250,000)

Tehran
(8,650,000)

Cairo
(1,568,000)

Delhi
(12,791,000)

Chongqing
(6,609,000)

Tokyo (29,950,000)

Osaka (14,190,000)

Karachi
(9,270,000)

Dhaka (11,726,000)

Shanghai
(9,537,000)

Mumbai
(Bombay)
(16,368,000)

Kolkata (Calcutta)
(13,217,000)

Hong Kong
(6,930,000)

Chennai
(Madras)
(6,425,000)

Bangkok
(7,642,000)

Manila
(10,492,000)

Jakarta
(12,435,000)

Johannesburg
(3,964,000)

Tropic of Cancer

Equator

Tropic of Capricorn

Antarctic Circle

Rushing to the cities

By 2007, half of the world's population will live in urban environments. This figure is expected to rise to 60 per cent of the total population by 2030. In many developing countries, cities are growing two or three times faster than the overall population. The world's cities are centres of government, education, industry and trade, but they also have problems, including crime, poverty and pollution.

The population explosion

In the second half of the 20th century, death rates in the developing countries of Africa, Asia and Latin America halved, particularly amongst children. This was due to improved public sanitation, better personal hygiene, and advances in medicine. Birth rates, however, did not decrease at the same rate, so there was a rapid rise in the population. By the year 2020, the number of people in the world is likely to reach about 8.6 billion.

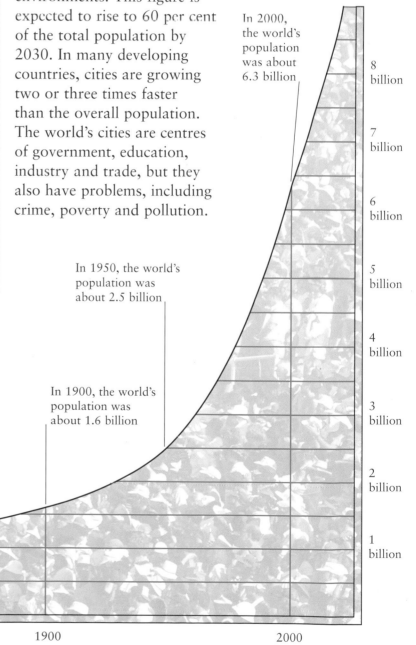

World population growth

In 2000, the world's population was about 6.3 billion

In 1950, the world's population was about 2.5 billion

In 1900, the world's population was about 1.6 billion

In 1800, the world's population was about 900 million

8 billion

7 billion

6 billion

5 billion

4 billion

3 billion

2 billion

1 billion

1800

1900

2000

THE PHYSICAL WORLD

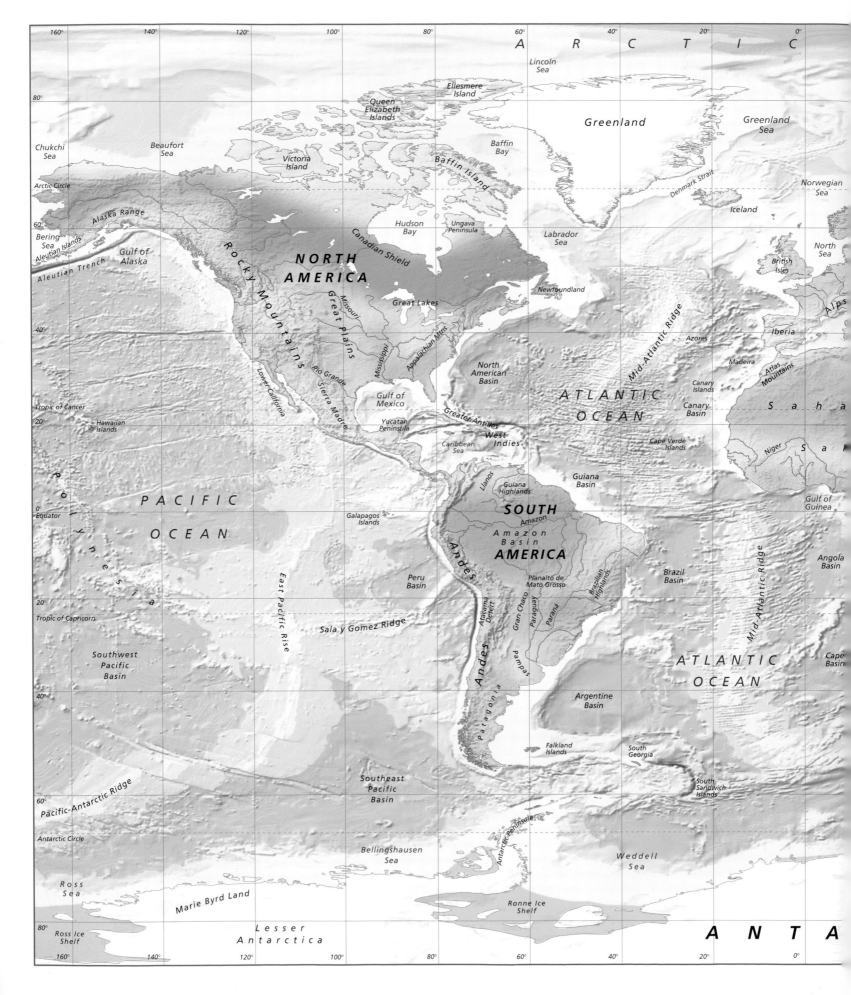

ARCTIC

160° 140° 120° 100° 80° 60° 40° 20° 0°

Lincoln
Sea

Ellesmere
Island

Queen
Elizabeth
Islands

Greenland

Greenland
Sea

80°

Chukchi
Sea

Beaufort
Sea

Victoria
Island

Baffin
Bay

Baffin Island

Denmark Strait

Norwegian
Sea

Arctic Circle

Iceland

60°

Alaska Range

Hudson
Bay

Ungava
Peninsula

Labrador
Sea

North
Sea

British
Isles

Bering
Sea

Aleutian Islands

Gulf of
Alaska

Rocky Mountains

NORTH
AMERICA

Canadian Shield

Newfoundland

Alps

Aleutian Trench

40°

Great Plains

Missouri

Great Lakes

Appalachian Mtns

North
American
Basin

ATLANTIC
OCEAN

Mid-Atlantic Ridge

Azores

Iberia

Madeira

Atlas
Mountains

Sahara

Mississippi

Canary
Islands

Tropic of Cancer

Lower California

Rio Grande

Sierra Madre

Gulf of
Mexico

Yucatan
Peninsula

Greater Antilles

Canary
Basin

20°

Hawaiian
Islands

West
Indies

Cape Verde
Islands

Niger

S a

Equator
0°

PACIFIC

OCEAN

Galapagos
Islands

Caribbean
Sea

Llanos

Guiana
Highlands

Guiana
Basin

Gulf of
Guinea

SOUTH

Amazon

Andes

Amazon
Basin

AMERICA

Peru
Basin

Brazil
Basin

Angola
Basin

Polynesia

Planalto de
Mato Grosso

Brazilian
Highlands

Mid-Atlantic Ridge

20°

Tropic of Capricorn

Sala y Gomez Ridge

East Pacific Rise

Atacama Desert

Gran Chaco

Paraguay

Paraná

pampas

ATLANTIC
OCEAN

Cape
Basin

40°

Southwest
Pacific
Basin

Andes

Patagonia

Argentine
Basin

Falkland
Islands

South
Georgia

60°

Pacific-Antarctic Ridge

Southeast
Pacific
Basin

South
Sandwich
Islands

Antarctic Circle

Antarctic Peninsula

Bellingshausen
Sea

Weddell
Sea

80°

Ross
Sea

Ross Ice
Shelf

Marie Byrd Land

Lesser
Antarctica

Ronne Ice
Shelf

ANTA

160° 140° 120° 100° 80° 60° 40° 20° 0°

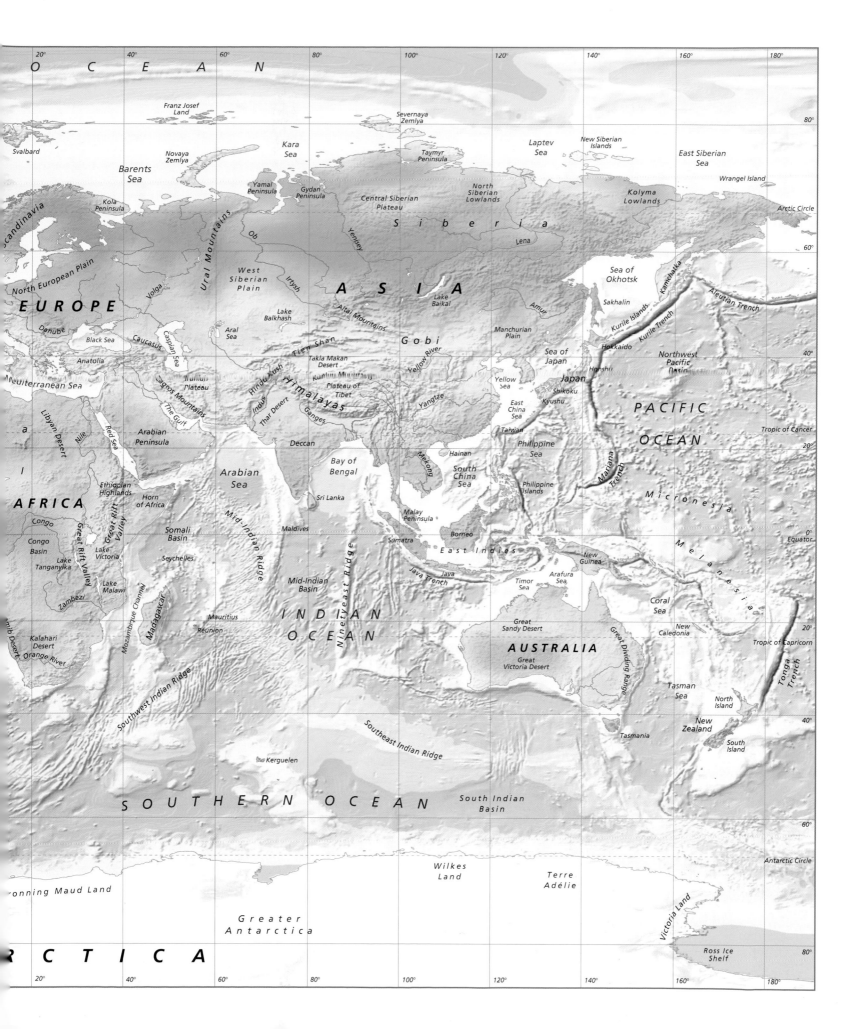

OCEAN

Svalbard

Franz Josef
Land

Kara
Sea

Novaya
Zemlya

Barents
Sea

Scandinavia

Kola
Peninsula

Yamal
Peninsula

Gydan
Peninsula

Severnaya
Zemlya

Taymyr
Peninsula

Central Siberian
Plateau

North
Siberian
Lowlands

Laptev
Sea

New Siberian
Islands

East Siberian
Sea

Wrangel Island

Arctic Circle

Kolyma
Lowlands

80°

North European Plain

Ural Mountains

Ob

West
Siberian
Plain

Irtysh

Yenisey

S i b e r i a

Lena

Sea of
Okhotsk

Kamchatka

Aleutian Trench

60°

EUROPE

Volga

A S I A

Lake
Baikal

Amur

Sakhalin

Kurile Islands

Kurile Trench

Danube

Caucasus

Caspian Sea

Lake
Balkhash

Altai Mountains

Gobi

Manchurian
Plain

Hokkaido

Northwest
Pacific
Basin

Black Sea

Aral
Sea

Tien Shan

Sea of
Japan

Honshu

Anatolia

Zagros Mountains

Iranian
Plateau

Takla Makan
Desert

Yellow River

Yellow
Sea

Japan
Shikoku
Kyushu

PACIFIC

40°

Mediterranean Sea

The Gulf

Hindu Kush

Kunlun Mountains

Plateau of
Tibet

Himalayas

Yangtze

East
China
Sea

Indus

Thar Desert

Ganges

Taiwan

OCEAN

Tropic of Cancer

a

Nile

Libyan Desert

Red Sea

Arabian
Peninsula

Deccan

Mekong

Hainan

South
China
Sea

Philippine
Sea

Mariana Trench

M i c r o n e s i a

20°

l

Ethiopian
Highlands

Horn
of Africa

Arabian
Sea

Bay of
Bengal

Sri Lanka

Philippine
Islands

AFRICA

Congo

Great Rift Valley

Somali
Basin

Mid-Indian Ridge

Maldives

Malay
Peninsula

Borneo

E a s t   I n d i e s

M e l a n e s i a

Equator

0°

Congo
Basin

Lake
Victoria

Sumatra

New
Guinea

Lake
Tanganyika

Seychelles

Lake
Malawi

Ninetyeast Ridge

Java Trench

Java

Timor
Sea

Arafura
Sea

Coral
Sea

Zambezi

Mid-Indian
Basin

New
Caledonia

20°

Namib Desert

Kalahari
Desert

Orange River

Mozambique Channel

Madagascar

Mauritius

Réunion

I N D I A N

OCEAN

Great
Sandy Desert

AUSTRALIA

Great
Victoria Desert

Great Dividing Range

Tropic of Capricorn

Tonga Trench

Tasman
Sea

North
Island

New
Zealand

South
Island

40°

Southwest Indian Ridge

Southeast Indian Ridge

Tasmania

Kerguelen

S O U T H E R N   O C E A N

South Indian
Basin

60°

Dronning Maud Land

Antarctic Circle

G r e a t e r
A n t a r c t i c a

Wilkes
Land

Terre
Adélie

Victoria Land

ARCTICA

Ross Ice
Shelf

80°

20°   40°   60°   80°   100°   120°   140°   160°   180°

THE POLITICAL WORLD

Abbreviations
B&H — BOSNIA & HERZEGOVINA
CRO. — CROATIA
LIE. — LIECHTENSTEIN
LUX. — LUXEMBOURG
MAC. — MACEDONIA
RUSS. FED. — RUSSIAN FEDERATION
SAN. — SAN MARINO
SWITZ. — SWITZERLAND
SERB. & MONT. — SERBIA & MONTENEGRO

A R C T I C

Greenland
(to Denmark)

Jan Mayen
(to Norway)

Arctic Circle

UNITED STATES
OF AMERICA
(ALASKA)

ICELAND

Faeroe Islands
(to Denmark)

C A N A D A

A T L A N T I C

UNITED
KINGDOM   DENMARK
REPUBLIC OF   Isle of Man   NETHERLANDS
IRELAND   (to UK)
BELGIUM
Channel Islands   LUX.
(to UK)   LIE.
SWITZ.
FRANCE
MONACO

O C E A N

St Pierre &
Miquelon
(to France)

UNITED STATES
OF AMERICA

ANDORRA

PORTUGAL   SPAIN

Bermuda
(to UK)

Azores
(to Portugal)

Gibraltar
(to UK)

Madeira
(to Portugal)

MOROCCO

ALGERIA

Tropic of Cancer

MEXICO

BAHAMAS

Canary Islands
(to Spain)

WESTERN
SAHARA
(occupied by Morocco)

CUBA   Turks &
Caicos Is. (to UK)
Navassa   Virgin Is.   British
Cayman Is.   Island   (to US)   Virgin Is. (to UK)   Anguilla (to UK)
(to UK)   (to US)   DOMINICAN   Montserrat (to UK)
HAITI   REPUBLIC   ANTIGUA & BARBUDA
Puerto Rico   Guadeloupe (to France)
JAMAICA   (to US)   DOMINICA
Martinique (to France)
ST KITTS   ST LUCIA
& NEVIS   BARBADOS
Netherlands   ST VINCENT & THE GRENADINES
Aruba   Antilles (to Neth.)   GRENADA
(to Neth.)   TRINIDAD & TOBAGO

MAURITANIA

MALI

BELIZE

GUATEMALA   HONDURAS
EL SALVADOR   NICARAGUA

CAPE VERDE

SENEGAL

GAMBIA

GUINEA-BISSAU   GUINEA

SIERRA LEONE

BURKINA

BENIN

GHANA

TOGO

NIGERIA

Hawaiian Islands
(to US)

Johnston Atoll
(to US)

COSTA
RICA   PANAMA

VENEZUELA

LIBERIA   IVORY
COAST

EQUATORIAL GUINEA

Clipperton Island
(to France)

GUYANA

French
Guiana
(to France)

COLOMBIA

SURINAM

SÃO TOMÉ
& PRINCIPE

P A C I F I C

Kingman Reef (to US)
Palmyra Atoll (to US)

Equator

Galapagos Islands
(to Ecuador)

ECUADOR

Jarvis Island
(to US)

KIRIBATI

O C E A N

B R A Z I L

PERU

Ascension
Island
(to St Helena)

American
Samoa
(to US)

Cook
Islands
(to NZ)

BOLIVIA

St Helena
(to UK)

Niue
(to NZ)

French Polynesia
(to France)

PARAGUAY

A T L A N T I C

Tropic of Capricorn

Pitcairn Islands
(to UK)

Easter Island
(to Chile)

Juan
Fernández Islands
(to Chile)

CHILE

ARGENTINA

URUGUAY

O C E A N

Tristan da Cunha
(to St Helena)

Gough Island
(to Tristan da Cunha)

Falkland Islands
(to UK)

Bouvet Island
(to Norway)

South Georgia
(to UK)

South Sandwich Islands
(to UK)

Antarctic Circle

S O U T H

Peter I
Island
(to Norway)

A N T A R C T I C A

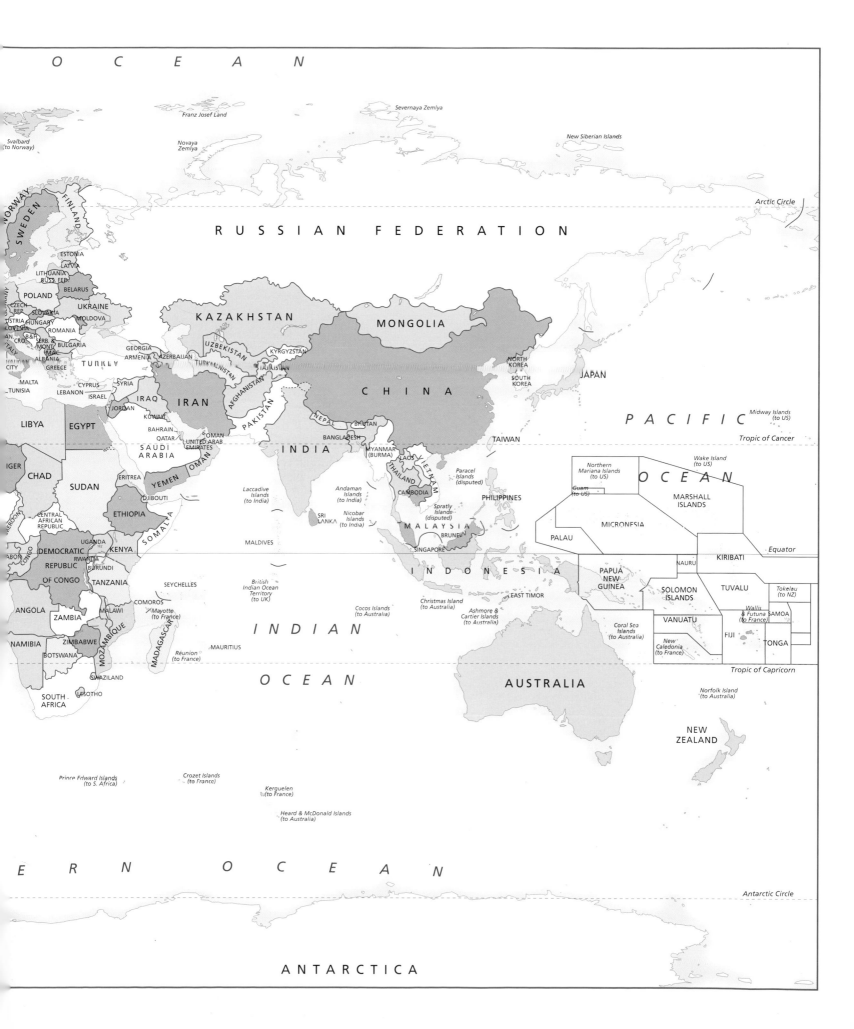

O C E A N

Franz Josef Land

Severnaya Zemlya

New Siberian Islands

Svalbard
(to Norway)

Novaya
Zemlya

Arctic Circle

NORWAY
SWEDEN
FINLAND

RUSSIAN FEDERATION

ESTONIA
LATVIA
LITHUANIA
RUSS. FED.
POLAND
BELARUS
UKRAINE
CZECH
REP.
SLOVAKIA
MOLDOVA
AUSTRIA HUNGARY
SLOVENIA
ROMANIA
AN.
CRO.
B.&H.
SERB. &
MONT. BULGARIA
MAC.
ITALY
ALBANIA
GREECE
VATICAN
CITY
MALTA
TUNISIA

KAZAKHSTAN

MONGOLIA

GEORGIA
ARMENIA AZERBAIJAN
UZBEKISTAN
KYRGYZSTAN
TURKEY
TURKMENISTAN
TAJIKISTAN

NORTH
KOREA
SOUTH
KOREA
JAPAN

CYPRUS
LEBANON
SYRIA
ISRAEL
IRAQ
IRAN
AFGHANISTAN
PAKISTAN
CHINA

JORDAN
KUWAIT
NEPAL
BHUTAN
TAIWAN

PACIFIC

Midway Islands
(to US)

LIBYA
EGYPT
BAHRAIN
QATAR
SAUDI
ARABIA
UNITED ARAB
EMIRATES
OMAN
INDIA
BANGLADESH
MYANMAR
(BURMA)
LAOS

Tropic of Cancer

NIGER
CHAD
SUDAN
ERITREA
YEMEN
OMAN
DJIBOUTI
ETHIOPIA

THAILAND
VIETNAM
CAMBODIA

Paracel
Islands
(disputed)

Wake Island
(to US)

Northern
Mariana Islands
(to US)

O C E A N

Guam
(to US)

MARSHALL
ISLANDS

CAMEROON
CENTRAL
AFRICAN
REPUBLIC
GABON
CONGO
UGANDA
DEMOCRATIC
REPUBLIC
OF CONGO
RWANDA
BURUNDI
KENYA
SOMALIA

Laccadive
Islands
(to India)
SRI
LANKA
Andaman
Islands
(to India)
Nicobar
Islands
(to India)
PHILIPPINES
Spratly
Islands
(disputed)
MALAYSIA
BRUNEI
SINGAPORE

MICRONESIA

PALAU

Equator

MALDIVES

NAURU

KIRIBATI

TANZANIA
SEYCHELLES

British
Indian Ocean
Territory
(to UK)

I N D O N E S I A
PAPUA
NEW
GUINEA
SOLOMON
ISLANDS
TUVALU
Tokelau
(to NZ)

ANGOLA
ZAMBIA
MALAWI
COMOROS
Mayotte
(to France)

Cocos Islands
(to Australia)
Christmas Island
(to Australia)
EAST TIMOR
Ashmore &
Cartier Islands
(to Australia)

Coral Sea
Islands
(to Australia)

VANUATU
New
Caledonia
(to France)
Wallis
& Futuna
(to France)
SAMOA
FIJI
TONGA

NAMIBIA
ZIMBABWE
BOTSWANA
MOZAMBIQUE
MADAGASCAR
Réunion
(to France)
MAURITIUS

I N D I A N

O C E A N

SOUTH
AFRICA
LESOTHO
SWAZILAND

Tropic of Capricorn

AUSTRALIA

Norfolk Island
(to Australia)

Prince Edward Islands
(to S. Africa)
Crozet Islands
(to France)
Kerguelen
(to France)

NEW
ZEALAND

Heard & McDonald Islands
(to Australia)

E R N   O C E A N

Antarctic Circle

A N T A R C T I C A

THE ARCTIC OCEAN

The Poles, at the Earth's northern and southern tips, are the planet's coldest places, where temperatures can fall as low as −80°C in winter. At the North Pole is the Arctic Ocean. With an area of 15,100,000 sq km, it is the smallest ocean on the planet. The Arctic is made up of two large basins divided by three underwater ridges, the greatest of which is the Lomonosov Ridge. Its waters are mainly covered with pack ice. When this ice breaks up, it forms enormous blocks of floating ice, called icebergs. The Arctic is fringed by the northernmost parts of North America, the Russian Federation and Europe.

Despite the region's harsh climate, it has been inhabited for thousands of years by people such as the European Lapps, the Russian Nenet and North American Inuit.

These peoples make their living from herding, hunting and fishing. There are stocks of cod, plaice and haddock in the unfrozen Arctic waters, but numbers have fallen over the years. Now there are restrictions on the amount of fish that people can take from the ocean. The peoples of the Arctic region must import foods, such as grains and vegetables, from elsewhere.

The Arctic is rich in oil, gas and coal, but because of the bitterly cold climate and severe landscape, extracting these resources is difficult and expensive. There are mines and wells in the coastal regions, but these cause pollution and threaten the area's unique wildlife. These industries have also damaged the traditional lifestyles of many of the Arctic region's native peoples.

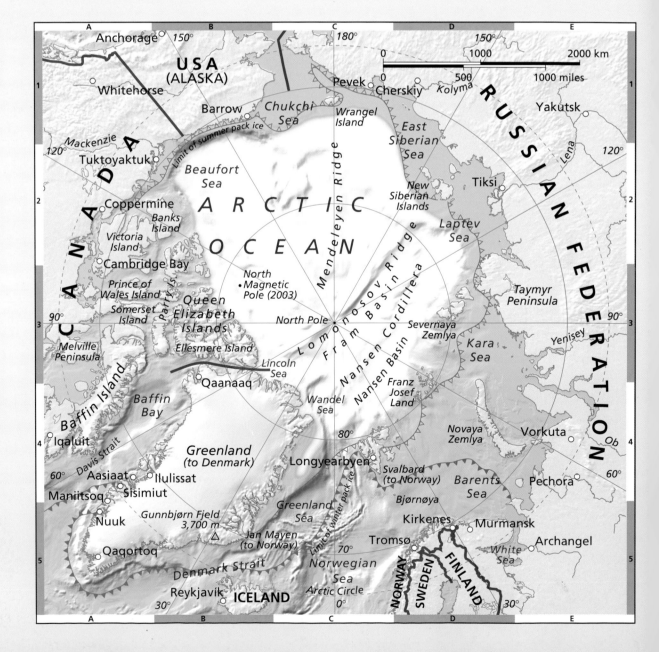

ANTARCTICA

Antarctica, at the Earth's southern tip, is the planet's coldest and smallest continent. It is a frozen world where the land lies beneath a thick layer of ice. Nearly half of the Antarctic coastline is surrounded by ice shelves, which float on the sea. There are two distinct parts to Antarctica. Lesser Antarctica is a series of ice-covered, mountainous islands, which are joined together by ice. Greater Antarctica is a high plateau.

No people live permanently in Antarctica, but teams of scientists visit this region of environmental importance, and stay in research stations for months at a time. These scientists observe the region's wildlife and even study the ice itself. By analyzing chemicals in the ice they can find out how the Earth's atmosphere has changed over the

years. Antarctica is governed by Argentina, Brazil, Chile, the United Kingdom, Norway, France, Australia and New Zealand. All these countries have agreed that the continent should only be used for peaceful work.

Colonies of penguins breed along the continent's coastal regions, and there are whales, seals and many fish species living in the surrounding waters. Antarctica has rich mineral reserves, such as gold, iron and coal, and there is natural gas in the seas. The harsh conditions in the region mean that the mining of these resources is too costly and difficult. Each year, between 2,000 and 3,000 tourists visit the Antarctic region. They come to view the unique wildlife and dramatic landscape from the decks of cruise liners.

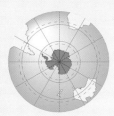

NORTH AMERICA

The continent of North America is shaped like a triangle, stretching from the frozen Arctic in the north to the tropics in the south. In the north, there are two huge countries, Canada and the USA. Smaller countries lie in the south and in the Caribbean Sea. The northern part of the continent has many different types of landscapes. The towering Rocky Mountains to the west give way to the Great Plains, where fertile soils help farmers to grow millions of hectares of crops. To the east are the vast Great Lakes, major rivers such as the Mississippi, and the lower mountains of the Appalachians. Further south, the Rocky Mountains continue into Mexico and southern North America, where they are called the Sierra Madre. This region also contains high plateaux and low-lying tropical forests, lagoons and mangrove swamps.

North America has a variety of climates, from the frozen wastes and pine forests of northern Canada to the baking deserts of Arizona and Mexico. Areas like these can support few people, but the northeast and west coasts are more densely populated, and North America is home to some of the world's biggest cities – New York, Los Angeles, Chicago and Mexico City.

Politically, there is a marked difference between northern and southern North America. The USA and Canada have stable administrations in which the central government shares power with the individual states and provinces. The nations of southern North America have been less peaceful, and dictators ruled some countries, such as Nicaragua and Haiti, for many years.

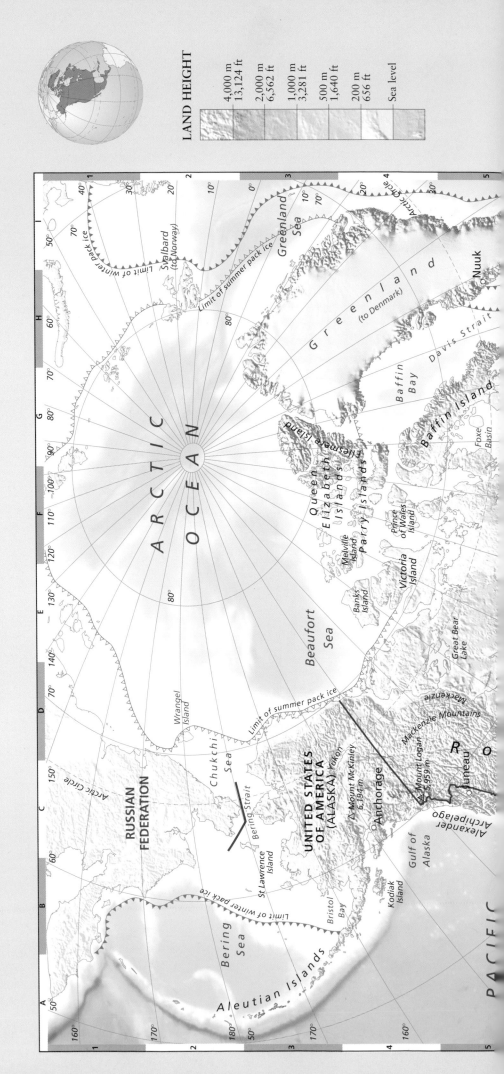

LAND HEIGHT

| 4,000 m 13,124 ft | 2,000 m 6,562 ft | 1,000 m 3,281 ft | 500 m 1,640 ft | 200 m 656 ft | Sea level |

PACIFIC OCEAN

ATLANTIC OCEAN

Labrador Sea

Cape Farewell

Hudson Strait

Cape Chidley

Ungava Peninsula

Southampton Island

Belcher Islands

James Bay

Hudson Bay

Labrador

Smallwood Reservoir

Newfoundland

Laurentian Highlands

Gulf of St Lawrence

St Pierre & Miquelon (to France)

Cape Breton Island

CANADA

Reindeer Lake

Lake Athabasca

Saskatchewan

Saskatoon

Edmonton

Calgary

Peace

Coast Mountains

Queen Charlotte Islands

Vancouver Island

Vancouver

Seattle

Portland

Columbia

Mount Rainier 4,392 m

Rocky Mountains

Great Basin

Great Salt Lake

Mount Whitney 4,418 m

Death Valley -86 m

Colorado Plateau

Grand Canyon

Las Vegas

Colorado

San Francisco

San Jose

Los Angeles

San Diego

Coast Ranges

Winnipeg

Lake Winnipeg

Lake Nipigon

Lake Superior

Great Lakes

Great Plains

Missouri

Minneapolis

Saint Paul

Milwaukee

Lake Michigan

Chicago

Lake Huron

Detroit

Lake Erie

Cleveland

Lake Ontario

Toronto

OTTAWA

Québec

Montréal

St Lawrence

Halifax

Boston

Cape Cod

Long Island

New York

Philadelphia

Baltimore

WASHINGTON D.C.

Appalachian Mountains

Charlotte

Columbia

Cape Hatteras

UNITED STATES OF AMERICA

Denver

Kansas City

Oklahoma City

Arkansas

Saint Louis

Indianapolis

Columbus

Nashville

Memphis

Jackson

Baton Rouge

New Orleans

Mississippi Delta

Atlanta

Jacksonville

The Everglades

Miami

Tampa

Straits of Florida

Fort Worth

Dallas

Austin

Houston

Gulf of Mexico

San Antonio

Monterrey

Rio Grande

Ciudad Juárez

El Paso

Phoenix

Hermosillo

Gulf of California

Lower California

Sierra Madre Occidental

Sierra Madre Oriental

Sierra Madre del Sur

Guadalajara

León

MEXICO CITY

Popocatépetl 5,452 m

Pico de Orizaba 5,700 m

MEXICO

Acapulco

Yucatan Peninsula

BELIZE

BELMOPAN

GUATEMALA

GUATEMALA CITY

EL SALVADOR

SAN SALVADOR

HONDURAS

TEGUCIGALPA

NICARAGUA

MANAGUA

Lake Nicaragua

SAN JOSE

COSTA RICA

PANAMA

PANAMA CITY

ATLANTIC OCEAN

BAHAMAS

NASSAU

Turks & Caicos Islands (to UK)

CUBA

HAVANA

Cayman Islands (to UK)

Greater Antilles

JAMAICA

KINGSTON

HAITI

PORT-AU-PRINCE

DOMINICAN REPUBLIC

SANTO DOMINGO

Puerto Rico (to US)

Lesser Antilles

West Indies

Caribbean Sea

Netherlands Antilles (to Netherlands)

Aruba (to Netherlands)

TRINIDAD & TOBAGO

SOUTH AMERICA

Bermuda (to UK)

Tropic of Cancer

Limit of winter pack ice

Equator

2000 km

1000 miles

1000

500

1000

1. ST KITTS & NEVIS
2. ANTIGUA & BARBUDA
3. DOMINICA
4. ST LUCIA
5. BARBADOS
6. ST VINCENT & THE GRENADINES
7. GRENADA

CANADA

The second-largest country in the world, Canada covers a vast area just north of the USA. This nation has quite a small population of just over 30 million, most of whom live in the south. Some of the people are Native Americans, members of tribes such as the Inuit, Algonquin and Cree. Others are descendants of the Europeans who settled here from the 16th century onwards, especially the French and British.

The landscape of Canada varies greatly. There are mountains in the west and east, and between these two regions is the Canadian Shield. This is a vast area of ancient rocks, low hills, thousands of lakes and huge tracts of forest. In the north, the Arctic regions are cold all year round, and the areas of tundra experience only a slight rise in temperature during summer. Further south, where most of the cities lie, the climate is a little warmer, although winter in many places is long, cold and snowy.

Canadians work in all sorts of businesses, from mining and farming to high-tech industries. The country is rich in minerals such as zinc and iron ore, and it has huge reserves of oil, coal and natural gas. There are good fishing waters off the east and west coasts, and large areas of forest make Canada the world's biggest exporter of timber products. Wheat, which grows well on fertile plains just west of the Canadian Shield, is exported to many countries.

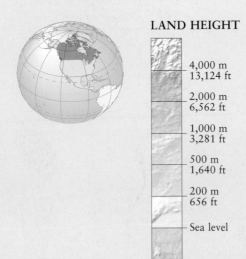

LAND HEIGHT

4,000 m	13,124 ft
2,000 m	6,562 ft
1,000 m	3,281 ft
500 m	1,640 ft
200 m	656 ft
Sea level	

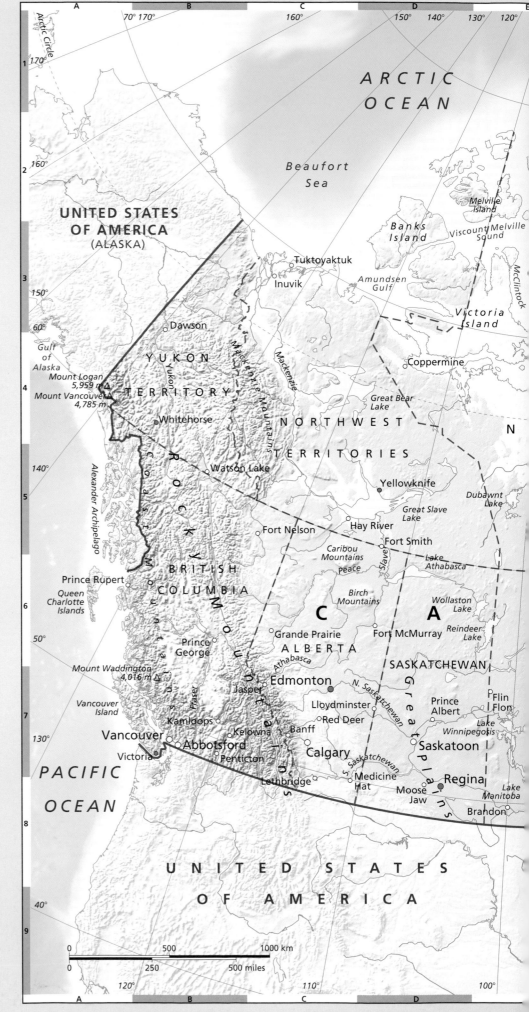

Canada

F 100° 90° 80° 70° 60° **G** 50° 40° **H** 30° **I** 20° **J** 10° **K**

Ellesmere Island

Axel Heiberg Island

Queen Elizabeth Islands

Parry Islands

Devon Island

Lancaster Sound

Somerset Island

Prince of Wales Island

Gulf of Boothia

Boothia Peninsula

Arctic Circle

Greenland (to Denmark)

ICELAND

Baffin Bay

Denmark Strait

Davis Strait

Baffin Island

Melville Peninsula

Prince Charles Island

Foxe Basin

Nettilling Lake

Amadjuak Lake

● Iqaluit

Labrador Sea

ATLANTIC OCEAN

N U N A V U T

Southampton Island

Hudson Strait

Ungava Bay

Cape Chidley

Ungava Peninsula

Hudson Bay

○ Churchill

Churchill

Granville Lake

Nelson

Labrador

NEWFOUNDLAND & LABRADOR

○ Port Hope Simpson

C A N A D A

Belcher Islands

Smallwood Reservoir

Happy Valley-Goose Bay

Labrador City

M A N I T O B A

Lake Winnipeg

C a n a d i a n   S h i e l d

James Bay

Q U É B E C

Manicouagan Reservoir

Laurentian Highlands

Corner Brook

○ Havre-St-Pierre

Newfoundland

Gander ●

● St John's

Cape Race

O N T A R I O

Lake Nipigon

Sept-Îsles ●

St Lawrence

Gulf of St Lawrence

St Pierre & Miquelon (to France)

PRINCE EDWARD ISLAND

Sydney ●

Cape Breton Island

○ Winnipeg

Jonquière ●

NEW BRUNSWICK

Charlottetown ●

NOVA SCOTIA

○ Thunder Bay

Wawa ○

North Bay ○

Québec ●

Trois-Rivières ●

Laval

Fredericton ●

Moncton ●

St John ●

Halifax ●

Lake of the Woods

Lake Superior

Sudbury ●

Sault Ste Marie ○

■ **OTTAWA**

Montreal ●

Drummondville ●

Sherbrooke ●

Bay of Fundy

Yarmouth ○

Cape Sable

ATLANTIC OCEAN

Lake Huron

Georgian Bay

Kingston ●

Oshawa ○

Toronto ●

Lake Ontario

Kitchener ○

St Catharines ○

London ○

Hamilton ○

Lake Michigan

Lake Erie

Windsor ○

90° 80° 70° 60°

F **G** **H** **I** **J** **K**

1 2 3 4 5 6 7 8 9

20° 60° 30° 40° 50° 50° 40° 60°

40° 30°

WESTERN UNITED STATES

The western states have some of the most dramatic scenery in the USA. All of these states are partly mountainous, and much of the region is arid. In the west, the Central Valley separates the Sierra Nevada mountains from California's Coast Ranges. The area east of the Sierra Nevada contains mountain ranges, river basins, deserts and salt lakes. Off the southwest coast is a chain of volcanoes that emerge from the Pacific Ocean as the Hawaiian islands.

A break in the Earth's crust, known as the San Andreas Fault, runs through California. It is the site of frequent earthquakes. Most of the west has dry, hot summers and to the south of the region, the Sonoran Desert and California's Death Valley are two of the hottest places on Earth. In winter, while the Pacific coast is wet and warm, the temperature inland, in states such as Utah and Idaho, drops dramatically.

With large areas of forest, Oregon and Washington are the USA's major timber-producing states. Alaska is rich in oil and natural gas. In other areas farming is important. There are cattle ranches in Nevada, and the heavily irrigated land of California produces half of the USA's fruit and vegetables.

Manufacturing industries, from aircraft building to clothing, employ many people in this region. The western states' best-known products are the computers and other electronic goods that are made in the famous 'Silicon Valley', just south of San Francisco, California. Tourism is another major industry. Some people come to visit the spectacular physical features, such as the Grand Canyon, while others are lured by the sunny beaches of Hawaii and California.

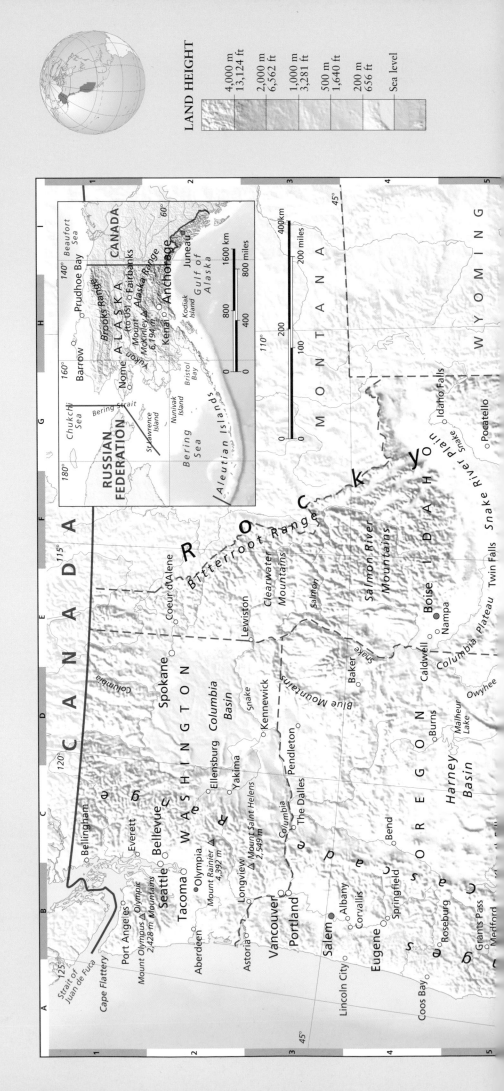

LAND HEIGHT

| 4,000 m / 13,124 ft | 2,000 m / 6,562 ft | 1,000 m / 3,281 ft | 500 m / 1,640 ft | 200 m / 656 ft | Sea level |

United States
of America

COLORADO

NEW MEXICO

M o u n t a i n s

C O L O R A D O

U T A H

Roan Plateau

Uinta Mountains

Brigham City
Ogden
Bountiful
Salt Lake City
Tooele
Orem
Provo

Great Salt Lake

Great Salt Lake Desert

Sevier Lake

Salina

Cedar City

Colorado Plateau

Lake Powell
Glen Canyon

Painted Desert

Little Colorado

Mexican Hat

Grand Canyon

Fagstaff

Prescott

A R I Z O N A

Glendale
Phoenix
Mesa
Tempe
Chandler

Casa Grande

Tucson

Nogales

Salt

Gila

M   E   X   I   C   O

UNITED STATES OF AMERICA

Great Basin

N E V A D A

S i e r r a   N e v a d a

C A L I F O R N I A

Elko

McDermitt
Humboldt
Winnemucca
Pyramid Lake
Reno
Sparks
Carson City
Lake Tahoe

North Las Vegas
Las Vegas
Henderson

Indian Springs

Mount Whitney
4,418 m

Death Valley

Independence

Hoover Dam

Lake Mead

Lake Havasu City

Colorado

Yuma

Sonoran Desert

Gila

Brawley

Salton Sea

Palm Springs

Yucca Valley

San Bernardino
Riverside

Escondido
Oceanside

Chula Vista

San Diego

Mojave Desert

Palmdale

Santa Clarita

Pasadena
Glendale
Los Angeles
Long Beach
Huntington Beach

Anaheim
Santa Ana
San Clemente

Bakersfield

Delano

Fresno

Merced

Stockton
Modesto

Sacramento

Vacaville
Napa
Vallejo
Concord
Berkeley
Oakland
San Francisco
Fremont
Sunnyvale
San Jose

Santa Cruz
Monterey Bay
Monterey

Salinas

Central Valley

Sacramento

Chico
Red Bluff
Redding

Mount Shasta
4,316 m

Ashland
Alturas

Crescent City

Cape Mendocino
Eureka

C o a s t   R a n g e s

Pit

Santa Rosa

Santa Maria

Oxnard

Point Conception

Santa Rosa

Channel Is.

San Clemente

San Clemente

P A C I F I C   O C E A N

P A C I F I C   O C E A N

H A W A I I
(to US)

Kauai
Oahu
Honolulu
Molokai
Maui
Kihei
Red Hill
3,055 m
Mauna Kea
4,205 m
Hilo
Hawaii
Mauna Loa
4,169 m

200 km
100 miles
0
0

40°

35°

40°

35°

30°

30°

20°

110°

115°

120°

155°

160°

MIDWESTERN UNITED STATES

In the heart of the USA is a large area of land known as the Midwest. To the west, it is bordered by the Rocky Mountains, a huge chain of peaks running all the way from Alaska to New Mexico. Few people live in this rugged landscape, but many of those who do are involved in the mining industry, because the Rockies are rich in coal, natural gas and many metals.

To the east of the Rocky Mountains, much of the Midwest is covered by the Great Plains. These plains were once natural grasslands, where native peoples such as the Crow and Cheyenne hunted buffalo. Today, the plains contain many large cattle ranches and cereal farms. Food processing is a major industry in the cities. Far inland, the plains have quite low rainfall and are hot in summer, so the USA's second-longest river, the Missouri, is a vital source of water for farming. This river is also used to generate electricity and for transporting heavy goods.

Not all of the plains are covered with rich grasslands. In the north are the Badlands. The land here is dry, and few plants and animals can survive in the arid conditions. Storms have washed away the soil to reveal a harsh, stony landscape covered with multi-coloured rocks, such as shales and limestones. This striking terrain makes parts of the Badlands popular with tourists.

LAND HEIGHT

4,000 m	13,124 ft
2,000 m	6,562 ft
1,000 m	3,281 ft
500 m	1,640 ft
200 m	656 ft
Sea level	

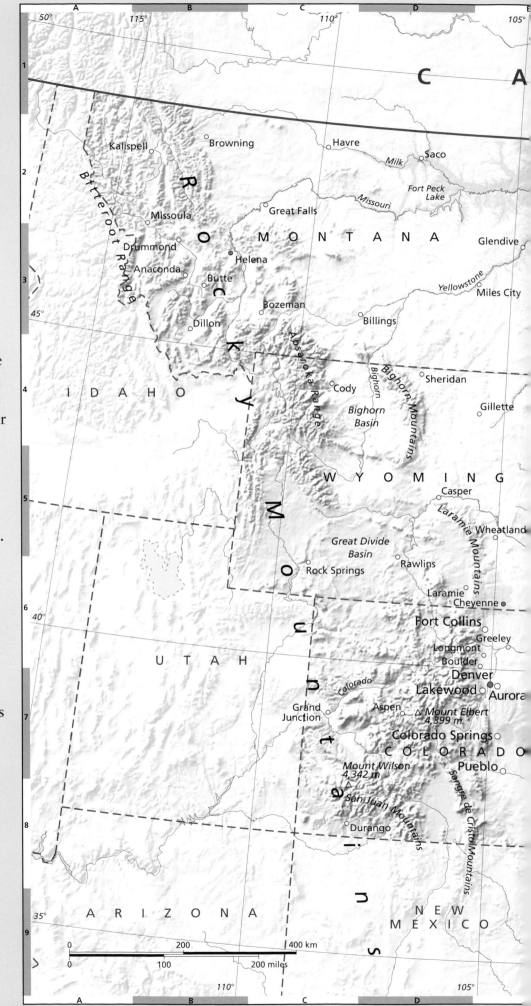

United States
of America

SOUTHERN UNITED STATES

This region of the USA is home to many Native American peoples, such as the Cherokee, Creek and Choctaw. To the south of the area is the large Gulf Coastal Plain. It is drained by many rivers, including the Mississippi, which flows south to a huge swampy delta on the coast of Louisiana. Elsewhere, the landscape ranges from the deserts and mountains of New Mexico to the Everglades, which are southern Florida's swamplands. Further north are uplands, including the Appalachian and Ouachita Mountains. The southern states have a warm climate with mild winters. Summer is generally hot, and the southeastern part of the region can be very humid.

Crops such as peanuts and citrus fruit grow well in the south, while the west contains large cattle ranches and wheat farms. Another typical crop is cotton, which was grown on plantations worked mainly by slaves until the mid-19th century. Many of this region's cities are industrialized, and the states of Texas and Oklahoma are major sources of oil and natural gas. As well as manufacturing and engineering, this area has high-tech computer and aerospace industries. Florida's unique scenery and warm climate make it a favourite tourist destination. People from all over the world come to visit its attractions, including the Everglades National Park.

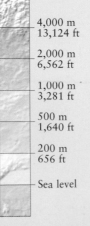

LAND HEIGHT

4,000 m
13,124 ft

2,000 m
6,562 ft

1,000 m
3,281 ft

500 m
1,640 ft

200 m
656 ft

Sea level

United States
of America

95°

WISCONSIN

MICHIGAN

CANADA

PENNSYLVANIA

90°

85°

80°

75°

40°

1

IOWA

ILLINOIS

OHIO

NEW
JERSEY

DELAWARE

2

MISSOURI

INDIANA

WEST
VIRGINIA

MARYLAND

VIRGINIA

KENTUCKY

Appalachian Mountains

Greensboro

Durham NORTH
CAROLINA

3

Clarksville

Morristown

Winston-
Salem

Raleigh

Wilson

35°

Oak Ridge

Cape
Hatteras

Fayetteville

Pocahontas

Nashville

Knoxville

Asheville

Jacksonville

Murfreesboro

Blue Ridge

Gastonia

Muskogee

ARKANSAS

TENNESSEE

Tennessee

Charlotte

Fayeteville

Arkansas

Memphis

Chattanooga

Greenville

SOUTH
CAROLINA

Wilmington

Fort Smith

Florence

Anderson

North Little Rock

Huntsville

Cape Fear

Ouachita Mountains

Little
Rock

Decatur

Chattahoochee

Athens

Columbia

4

Hot Springs

Mississippi

Piedmont

Orangeburg

Pine Bluff

Birmingham

Anniston

Atlanta

Augusta

North Charleston

ED STATES

Columbus

Macon

Charleston

Greenville

Tuscaloosa

OF

MISSISSIPPI

ALABAMA

Columbus

GEORGIA

Savannah

ATLANTIC

Meridian

Selma

Montgomery

Savannah

AMERICA

Jackson

Tombigbee

Albany

OCEAN

5

Sabine

Monroe

Alabama

Brunswick

30°

Tyler

Shreveport

Valdosta

Alexandria

Coastal

Dothan

Jacksonville

If

Hattiesburg

Plain

LOUISIANA

Mobile

Tallahassee

Gainesville

Beaumont

Baton
Rouge

Biloxi

Pensacola

Panama City

Daytona Beach

Lake
Charles

Metairie

Gulfport

Cape
San Blas

Deltona

6

Houston

Port Arthur

New Orleans

Lafayette

Orlando

Cape Canaveral

Pasadena

FLORIDA

Melbourne

Galveston

Mississippi
Delta

Clearwater

Lakeland

Freeport

Saint Petersburg

Tampa

Bradenton

Sarasota

Lake
Okeechobee

West Palm Beach

7

Cape Coral

Hialeah

Fort Lauderdale

Naples

The
Everglades

Hollywood

25°

Miami

Key Largo

Gulf

Cape Sable

Florida Keys

Straits of Florida

BAHAMAS

of

Mexico

8

CUBA

9

20°

MEXICO

5°

90°

85°

80°

F

G

H

I

J

K

NORTHEASTERN UNITED STATES

Along the eastern coast of this area are rocky headlands and sandy beaches, with flooded river valleys that make ideal harbours. Inland, beyond the coastal plain, are the Appalachians, an ancient chain of mountains covered in woods. Still further to the west is part of the huge Mississippi basin, with the Great Lakes to the north.

For thousands of years the region was home to native peoples, such as the Iroquois and Delaware. They were expert farmers and fishers. In the 17th century, some of North America's first European settlers arrived here and the native peoples showed the settlers how to grow local crops. In the 19th century, millions of immigrants passed through New York before settling in the region, and today it is still densely populated. The northeast contains major cities such as New York, the country's financial centre, Chicago and Washington D.C., the capital of the USA.

Many farmers in the northeast grow maize or fruit, or raise livestock. Some areas, such as Detroit and the state of Pennsylvania, have for many years been centres of heavy industry, from mining and steel production to manufacturing. Although these are still important, newer, high-tech industries, producing electronic goods, have developed in Massachusetts and New Jersey.

LAND HEIGHT

4,000 m
13,124 ft

2,000 m
6,562 ft

1,000 m
3,281 ft

500 m
1,640 ft

200 m
656 ft

Sea level

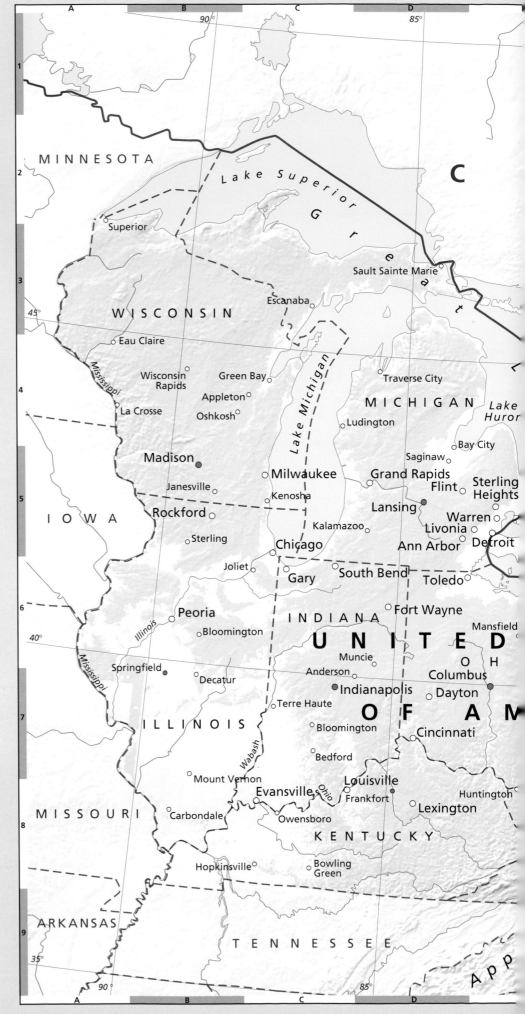

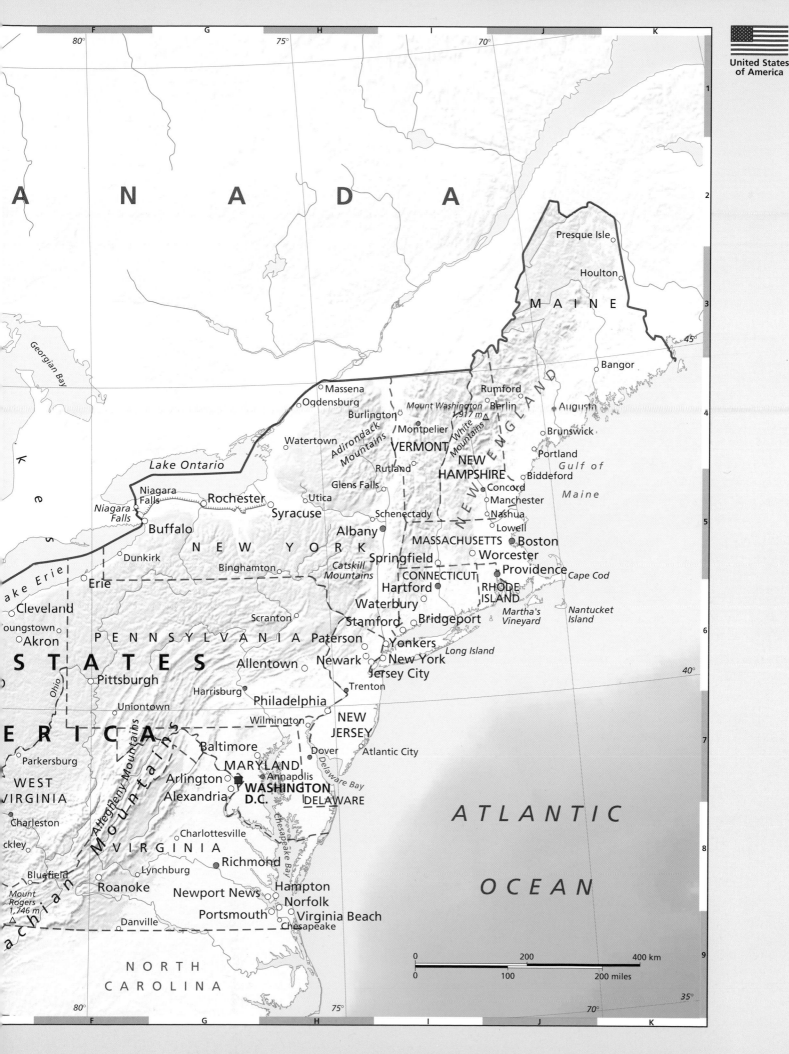

United States
of America

C A N A D A

Presque Isle

Houlton

M A I N E

Bangor

Massena
Ogdensburg   Rumford
Burlington   Mount Washington Berlin   Augusta
Watertown   Montpelier   1,917 m△   Brunswick
                    Adirondack   VERMONT   White   Portland
                    Mountains   Mountains   Biddeford
                            Rutland   NEW   Gulf of
Lake Ontario   HAMPSHIRE   Maine
                    Glens Falls   Concord
Niagara   Utica   Manchester
Falls   Rochester   Schenectady   Nashua
Niagara   Syracuse   Lowell
Falls   Albany   MASSACHUSETTS   Boston
    Buffalo   Worcester
        N E W   Y O R K   Springfield   Providence   Cape Cod
Dunkirk   Catskill   CONNECTICUT   RHODE
Erie   Binghamton   Mountains   Hartford   ISLAND   Martha's   Nantucket
Cleveland   Waterbury   Vineyard   Island
oungstown   Scranton   Stamford   Bridgeport
Akron   Paterson   Yonkers
    P E N N S Y L V A N I A   Newark New York   Long Island
S T A T E S   Allentown   Jersey City
    Pittsburgh   Trenton
                Harrisburg
Uniontown   Philadelphia
                        Wilmington   NEW
ERICA'S   JERSEY
Parkersburg   Baltimore   Dover   Atlantic City
WEST   Arlington MARYLAND Annapolis
VIRGINIA   Alexandria WASHINGTON   DELAWARE
Charleston   D.C.
ckley   A T L A N T I C
    Charlottesville
Bluefield   VIRGINIA
Mount   Roanoke Richmond
Rogers   Lynchburg   O C E A N
1,746 m△ Newport News   Hampton
        Portsmouth   Norfolk
    Danville   Virginia Beach
                Chesapeake

N O R T H
C A R O L I N A

Georgian Bay

Lake Erie

Ohio

Allegheny Mountains

Appalachian Mountains

Chesapeake Bay

Delaware Bay

0   200   400 km
0   100   200 miles

MEXICO AND CENTRAL AMERICA

A chain of mountains, broken by fertile river valleys, forms the backbone of Mexico and Central America. Lowlands run along the east coast, widening to form Mexico's Yucatan Peninsula and Nicaragua's Mosquito Coast. In the south, Costa Rica and Panama form a narrow neck of land that measures less than 100 km across in some places. The Panama Canal, which was completed in 1914, provides a shipping link between the Atlantic and Pacific Oceans.

Most of the inhabitants of this area are descended from native peoples – such as the Maya and Aztec – and Europeans, especially the Spanish, who conquered the region in the 15th and 16th centuries. They are mainly farmers, either producing corn and beans for local use, or growing crops such as coffee, cotton and bananas for export. The area's major industries include mining, manufacturing and construction.

The population of Mexico and Central America is rising rapidly. Millions of people, unable to make a living from farming, have moved to the towns. Some cities have grown very quickly, and have poor housing, health and education services. The air quality in these urban areas is often low due to pollution from cars and factories. As the cities grow, large areas of tropical forest are being cut down to clear land for building.

LAND HEIGHT

4,000 m	13,124 ft
2,000 m	6,562 ft
1,000 m	3,281 ft
500 m	1,640 ft
200 m	656 ft
Sea level	

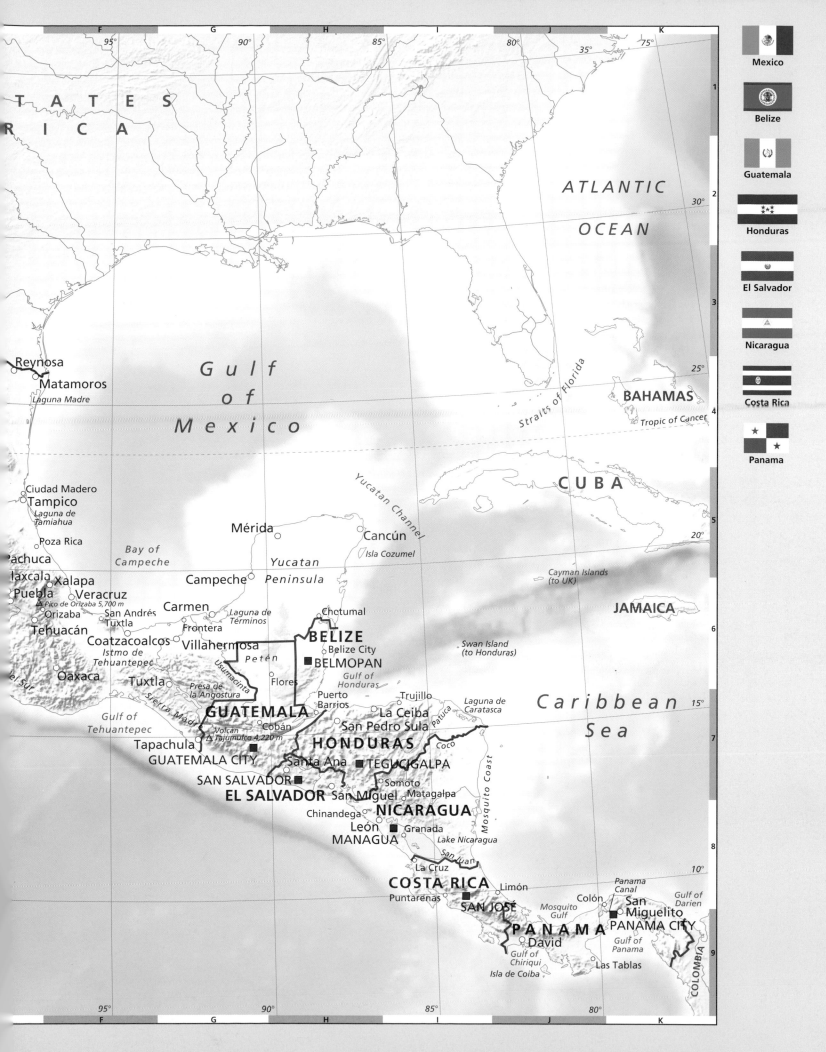

F   G   H   I   J   K

95°   90°   85°   80°   35°   75°

Mexico

Belize

Guatemala

Honduras

El Salvador

Nicaragua

Costa Rica

Panama

STATES
RICA

1

ATLANTIC

OCEAN

2

30°

3

Reynosa

Matamoros
Laguna Madre

G u l f

o f

M e x i c o

25°

Straits of Florida

BAHAMAS

4

Tropic of Cancer

Ciudad Madero
Tampico
*Laguna de
Tamiahua*

Poza Rica

Pachuca

Mérida

Yucatan
Cancún
Isla Cozumel

CUBA

20°

5

Tlaxcala Xalapa
Puebla Veracruz
△ Pico de Orizaba 5,700 m
Orizaba San Andrés
Tehuacán Tuxtla

Campeche *Peninsula*

Yucatan

Cayman Islands
(to UK)

JAMAICA

Carmen
Frontera

*Laguna de
Términos*

Coatzacoalcos
Villahermosa
*Istmo de
Tehuantepec*

Oaxaca Tuxtla

Petén

Flores

BELIZE
Belize City
BELMOPAN

Swan Island
(to Honduras)

6

del Sur

*Presa de
la Angostura*

Usumacinta

Puerto
Barrios

Trujillo

*Laguna de
Caratasca*

C a r i b b e a n

15°

*Gulf of
Tehuantepec*

Sierra Madre

GUATEMALA
Cobán

La Ceiba

San Pedro Sula

Patuca

S e a

7

Tapachula

Volcán
△ Tajumulco 4,220 m

GUATEMALA CITY

SAN SALVADOR

EL SALVADOR

HONDURAS

Santa Ana

TEGUCIGALPA

San Miguel

Somoto

Matagalpa

Coco

Mosquito Coast

Chinandega

León

MANAGUA

NICARAGUA

Granada

Lake Nicaragua

San Juan

La Cruz

8

10°

COSTA RICA

Puntarenas

SAN JOSÉ

Limón

*Mosquito
Gulf*

Colón

*Panama
Canal*

San
Miguelito

PANAMA CITY

*Gulf of
Darien*

David

PANAMA

*Gulf of
Chiriqui*

Isla de Coiba

Las Tablas

*Gulf of
Panama*

COLOMBIA

9

95°   90°   85°   80°

F   G   H   I   J   K

THE CARIBBEAN

In the Caribbean Sea there are two mountain ranges, called the Greater and Lesser Antilles, which run from Florida to Trinidad. For part of their length, these mountains are hidden underwater, but where they break the surface they form the islands of the Caribbean. Many of these islands are small and mountainous, but two larger ones, Cuba and Hispaniola (which is divided into Haiti and the Dominican Republic), have a more varied landscape. On Cuba, the mountains are broken up by plains, while on Hispaniola, valleys divide the uplands.

The Caribbean is well known for its warm, sunny climate, but during the hottest months between July and October, violent storms and hurricanes blow in from the Atlantic Ocean and lash the islands. These winds reach up to 250 km/h and they can flatten everything in their path.

The people of the Caribbean are mostly descendants of Africans, Europeans and Asians who settled here over the years, or were brought to the area as slaves. In the past, nearly everyone lived by farming, and these islands still produce large amounts of crops, such as sugar cane and bananas. Today, the Caribbean's warm weather and sandy beaches attract millions of visitors from North America and further afield. Tourism has had a damaging effect on the environment, but it has also brought much-needed money into the region.

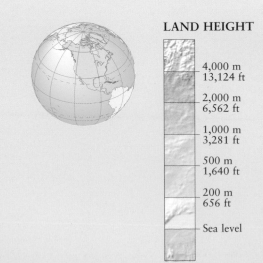

LAND HEIGHT

	4,000 m 13,124 ft
	2,000 m 6,562 ft
	1,000 m 3,281 ft
	500 m 1,640 ft
	200 m 656 ft
	Sea level

ATLANTIC

OCEAN

West Indies

250 km
500 km
125
250 miles

25°

20°

Acklins
Island

Great
Inagua

Turks & Caicos Islands
(to UK)

Windward Passage

Port-de-Paix
Cap-Haïten
Gonaïves
Santiago
St Marc
La Vega
Pico Duarte
3,175m
HAITI *Hispaniola*
PORT-AU-PRINCE
SANTO
DOMINGO
Jacmel
Cayes

**DOMINICAN
REPUBLIC**

San Francisco
de Macorís
La Romana
San
Pedros de
Macorís

Mona Passage

A n t i l l e s

Puerto Rico
(to US)
Bayamón
Mayagüez
Caguas
Ponce

San Juan

*Virgin Islands
(to US)*

British
Virgin Islands
(to UK)

Anguilla
(to UK)

Leeward Islands

St Martin
(to France & Netherlands)
St Barthélémy (to France)

*Netherlands
Antilles
(to Netherlands)*

BASSETERRE
St Kitts
Nevis

**ST KITTS
& NEVIS**

Barbuda

ANTIGUA & BARBUDA
ST JOHN'S
Antigua

Montserrat
(to UK)

Guadeloupe Passage
Grande Terre
Basse Terre
Guadeloupe
(to France)

Basse Terre

DOMINICA ROSEAU

Martinique Passage

15°

Martinique
(to France)
Fort-de-France

ST LUCIA
CASTRIES

St Vincent Passage

KINGSTOWN St Vincent
**ST VINCENT &
THE GRENADINES**

The Grenadines

BARBADOS
BRIDGETOWN

Windward Islands

L e s s e r   A n t i l l e s

ST GEORGE'S
GRENADA

Aruba
(to Netherlands)
Oranjestad
Netherlands Antilles
(to Netherlands)
Willemstad
Bonaire
Curaçao

Tobago

PORT-OF-SPAIN
Arima
Point Fortin

**TRINIDAD
& TOBAGO**
Trinidad

10°

V E N E Z U E L A

70°
65°
60°

Bahamas

Cuba

Haiti

Dominican Republic

Jamaica

Antigua & Barbuda

St Kitts & Nevis

Dominica

St Lucia

**St Vincent & the
Grenadines**

Barbados

Grenada

Trinidad & Tobago

SOUTH AMERICA

The continent of South America is shaped like a triangle. It tapers from the warm Caribbean coasts of Colombia and Venezuela to the cold waters of the Southern and Pacific Oceans at the southern tips of Argentina and Chile. Three very different types of landscape dominate the continent. In the west, the Andes stretch for 7,250 km along the entire Pacific coast. These towering mountains reach more than 6,900 m in height. In the hot and humid regions of the northeast, the Amazon, covers an area of 6.5 million sq km. The mighty Amazon river

flows through this region. Further south, there are great open plains of grass and scrub.

Hundreds of years ago, the native peoples of South America built up powerful civilizations, but later, between the 16th and 19th centuries, much of the continent was ruled by the Spanish and Portuguese. As a result, the official language in Brazil is Portuguese, while Spanish is spoken in most of the other countries. The Spanish and Portuguese also developed South America's cities, building on the Atlantic coast for easy access to Europe. Today, most South

Americans still live on the coast, in places such as Rio de Janeiro, Montevideo and São Paulo, which is one of the world's largest cities.

South America has rich mineral deposits and fertile farming lands, and most of the countries export goods, including oil and foodstuffs. Many people are desperately poor, and large sections of the population cannot read or write. A number of South America's countries have borrowed money from wealthier nations and are struggling to repay their debts.

LAND HEIGHT

| 4,000 m 13,124 ft | 2,000 m 6,562 ft | 1,000 m 3,281 ft | 500 m 1,640 ft | 200 m 656 ft | Sea level |

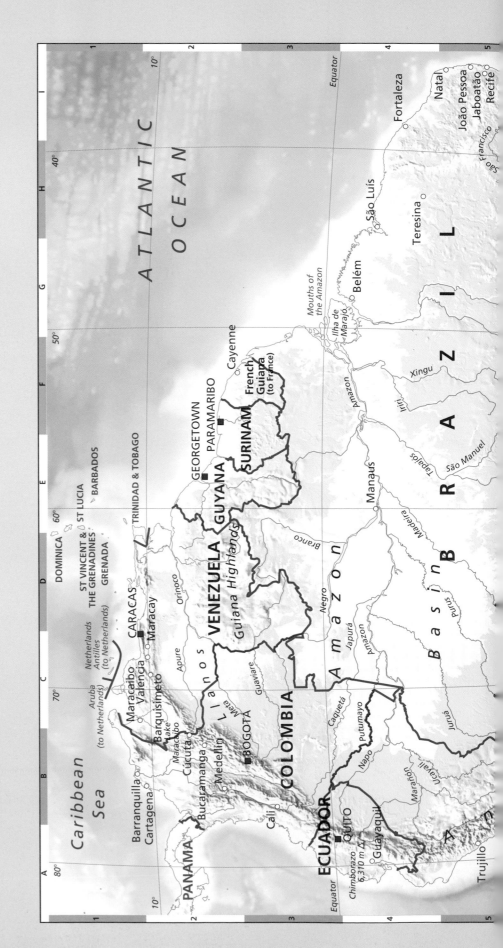

PERU

BOLIVIA

PARAGUAY

BRAZIL

URUGUAY

ARGENTINA

CHILE

ATLANTIC OCEAN

PACIFIC OCEAN

Maceió
Salvador
Represa de Sobradinho
Tocantins
Brazilian Highlands
BRASÍLIA
Goiânia
Belo Horizonte
Ribeirão Prêto
Nova Iguaçu
São Gonçalo
Rio de Janeiro
Uberlândia
Campinas
São Paulo
Guarulhos
Rio Grande
Campo Grande
Curitiba
Araguaia
Planalto de Mato Grosso
Guaporé
Pantanal
Paraná
Serra Geral
Porto Alegre
Lagoa dos Patos
Lagoa Mirim
Juruena
Madre de Dios
Beni
Guaporé
Santa Cruz
Cochabamba
SUCRE
LA PAZ
Lake Titicaca
Altiplano
Nevado Sajama 6,542 m
Arequipa
Callao
LIMA
Atacama Desert
Ojos del Salado 6,880 m
Aconcagua 6,960 m
San Miguel de Tucumán
Salado
Laguna Mar Chiquito
Córdoba
Rosario
BUENOS AIRES
Lomas de Zamora
La Plata
MONTEVIDEO
Río de la Plata
Mar del Plata
Bahía Blanca
Punta Rasa
Río Negro
Gulf of San Matías
Gulf of San Jorge
Bahía Grande
Strait of Magellan
Terra del Fuego
Cape Horn
Isla de Chiloé
Archipiélago de los Chonos
Isla Wellington
Archipiélago Reina Adelaida
Patagonia
Pampas
Mesopotamia
Gran Chaco
Paraguay
ASUNCIÓN
Pilcomayo
Paraná
Uruguay
SANTIAGO
Falkland Islands (to UK)
Stanley
East Falkland
West Falkland
South Georgia (to UK)
Juan Fernandez Islands
Islas de los Desventurados

Tropic of Capricorn

1000 km
500 miles
500
250
0
0

10°
20°
30°
40°
50°
50°
70°
80°
90°

NORTHERN SOUTH AMERICA

The northern part of South America is fringed by uplands – the Guiana Highlands in the north, the Andes in the west and the Brazilian Highlands in the south. This region has many amazing physical features. Lake Titicaca, on the border between Peru and Bolivia, is South America's largest lake. It is also the highest navigable lake in the world. The Angel Falls in Venezuela is the world's highest waterfall. Across the middle of this region is the basin of the Amazon, a river so vast that it carries about one-fifth of the world's fresh water.

Few people live in the interior areas. Most of this region's huge population lives in coastal cities, working in the industries that have grown up around them. These include oil production and metal refining in Venezuela, and chemical and textile industries in Brazil. Mining occurs in most countries. The Amazon region has a thriving timber industry, but loggers are steadily cutting away the rainforest. Large areas of trees have been cleared by farmers for cropland and cattle ranches. Plans to build new oil pipelines and roads across the region will also lead to deforestation. Every year, about eight million hectares of forest disappear from the Amazon, and as about half of the world's known plant and animal species live here, environmentalists are fighting to preserve this important area.

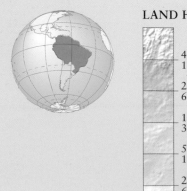

LAND HEIGHT

	4,000 m 13,124 ft
	2,000 m 6,562 ft
	1,000 m 3,281 ft
	500 m 1,640 ft
	200 m 656 ft
	Sea level

BOLIVIA'S TWO CAPITALS
LA PAZ – legislative and administrative capital
SUCRE – legal captial

Galapagos Islands
(to Ecuador)
0   100 km
0   50 miles

ATLANTIC
OCEAN

ATLANTIC
OCEAN

Colombia

Venezuela

Guyana

Surinam

Brazil

Ecuador

Peru

Bolívia

GRENADA
Isla de
Margarita
TRINIDAD
& TOBAGO
Maturín
Ciudad Guayana
Ciudad Bolívar
Embalse
de Guri
GUYANA
GEORGETOWN
PARAMARIBO
Angel
Falls
Highlands
Essequibo
SURINAM
French
Guiana
(to France)
Cayenne
Boa Vista
Branco
Negro
Represa de
Balbina
Macapá
Mouths of
the Amazon
Baía de Marajó
Isla de
Marajó
Amazon
Manaus
Amazon
Santarém
Tapajós
Belém
Baía de São Marcos
São Luís
Parnaíba
Sobral
Fortaleza
Teresina
Imperatriz
Cabo de
São Roque
Mossoró
Natal
Juazeiro do Norte
Campina
Grande
João Pessoa
Jaboatão
Olinda
Caruaru
Recife
Juàzeiro
Maceió
Arapiraca
Aracaju
Madeira
Pôrto Velho
B R A Z I L
Iriri
Xingu
São Manuel
Juruena
Guaporé
Santa Cruz
Corumba
Pantanal
Represa de
Tucuruí
Tocantins
Araguaia
Rio das Mortes
Parnaíba
Represa de
Sobradinho
Taguatinga
Feira de Santana
Alagoinhas
Salvador
Jequié
São Francisco
Vitória da
Conquista
Ilhéus
Planalto de
Mato Grosso
Cuiabá
BRASÍLIA
Goiânia
Anápolis
Montes Claros
Brazilian
Highlands
Teófilo Otoni
Uberlândia
Paranaíba
Uberaba
Linhares
Franca
Divinópolis
Belo Horizonte
Vitória
Rio Grande
Campo
Grande
Ribeirão Prêto
Juiz de Fora
Campos
Dourados
Marília
Campinas
Guarulhos
São Gonçalo
Paraná
PARAGUAY
Londrina
Nova
Iguaçu
Rio de Janeiro
Maringá
São Paulo
Cascavel
Santos
Ponta Grossa
Serra Geral
Curitiba
Joinville
Lages
Florianópolis
Uruguay
N T I N A
Passo Fundo
Santa Maria
Porto Alegre
Bagé
Lagoa
dos Patos
Rio Grande
Lagoa Mirim
URUGUAY

0   500   1000 km
0   250   500 miles

Equator

Tropic of Capricorn

SOUTHERN SOUTH AMERICA

The southern part of South America is made up of Paraguay, Uruguay, Argentina and Chile. The Andes Mountains run from the north to the south, forming the backbone of the region. The Atacama Desert, the driest place on Earth, lies in the northwest. To the east are the forests and grasslands of Gran Chaco, the grasslands of the Pampas, and Patagonia, a high, cold plateau in southern Argentina. The southwest has a dramatic landscape of icy fjords, jagged mountain peaks, U-shaped valleys and frozen glaciers. Further south are the windy islands of Tierra del Fuego.

Most of the people in southern South America live in cities, particularly in the capitals. Buenos Aires, for example, is home to over one-third of Argentina's population. The majority of those who live in this region speak Spanish, the language of the people who ruled the area until the 19th century. In some places, small groups of people still speak the native languages.

The big cities of Chile, Argentina and Uruguay are centres for heavy industries, and some of these have polluted the larger rivers, such as the Paraná and its tributaries. Argentina is famous

for raising cattle on its rich grasslands, and beef from its ranches is exported worldwide. Some of this meat is processed into products such as corned beef in factories in Córdoba and Buenos Aires. Paraguay grows wheat and other crops for its own use, while cotton, coffee, tobacco and oilseeds such as soya, are the country's major export crops. Uruguay's main export is wool. The Chilean Andes, with their deposits of copper, are mined heavily. A wide range of fruits and more specialized crops such as walnuts, and grapes for wine, are grown in Chile's fertile Central Valley.

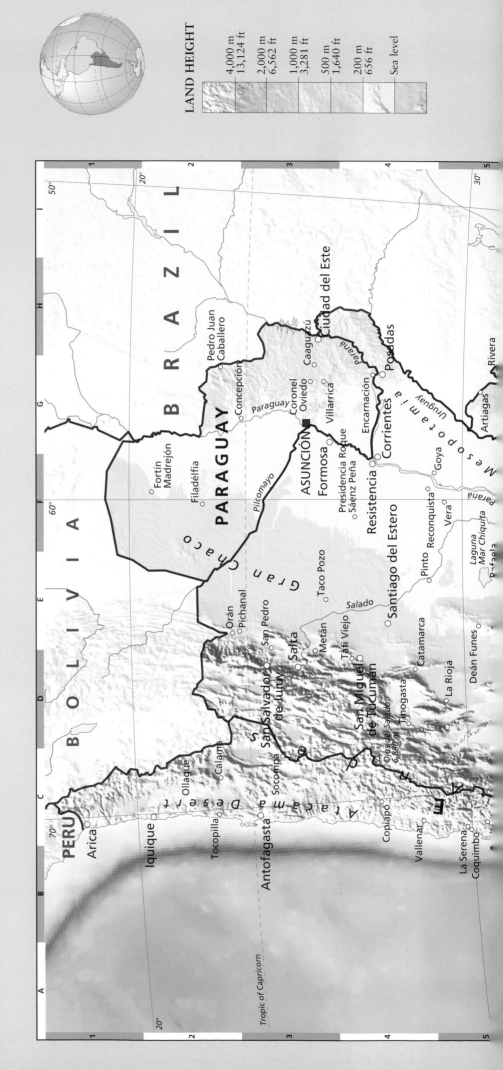

LAND HEIGHT

| 4,000 m 13,124 ft | 2,000 m 6,562 ft | 1,000 m 3,281 ft | 500 m 1,640 ft | 200 m 656 ft | Sea level |

Chile

Paraguay

Argentina

Uruguay

ATLANTIC OCEAN

PACIFIC OCEAN

URUGUAY

ARGENTINA

CHILE

Falkland Islands
(to UK)

West
Falkland

East
Falkland

Stanley

600 km

300 miles

300

150

0

Lagoa
Mirim

Tacuarembó
Salto
Concordia
Paysandú
Paraná
Santa
Fé
San
Francisco
Córdoba
San Juan

Melo
Durazno
Florida
San José de Mayo
Mercedes
Fray Bentos
Gualeguaychu
Rosario
Venado Tuerto
Rufino
Villa María
Río Cuarto
San Luis

MONTEVIDEO
Minas
Las Piedras
San Nicolás de Los Arroyos
Pergamino
Junín
BUENOS AIRES
Lomas de Zamora
Mercedes

La Plata
Río de la Plata
Punta Norte
Azul
Olavarría
San Rafael
Mendoza
Godoy Cruz
San Bernardo
SANTIAGO
Aires
Rancagua
Pichilemu
Viña del Mar
Valparaíso
Malargüe
Talca
Constitución
Chillán
Talcahuano
Concepción
Lebu
Los Angeles
Temuco
Valdivia

Aconcagua
6,960m/...ft
Central Valley

Mar del Plata
Necochea
Tres
Arroyos
Coronel
Pringles
Punta Alta
Bahía
Blanca
Bahía Blanca
Río Colorado
Colorado
Salado
Chos Malal
Neuquén
Zapala
San Carlos
de Bariloche
Osorno
Puerto Montt
Isla de
Chiloé

Punta Rasa
Viedma
Río Negro
General Roca
San Antonio Oeste

Gulf of
San Matías
Península
Valdés

Rawson
Chubut

Esquel
Corcovado
Puerto Aisén
Coihaique

Nueva
Lubecka
Sarmiento
Deseado
Comodoro Rivadavia
Gulf of
San Jorge
Fitz Roy
Cabo Tres Puntas
Puerto Deseado

Puerto San Julián
Chico
Gobernador
Gregores
Puerto Santa Cruz
Santa
Cruz
El Calafate
Puerto Natales

Río Gallegos
Bahía
Grande
Strait of Magellan
San Sebastián
Punta Arenas
Río Grande
Tierra del Fuego
Ushuaia

Cape Horn
Isla de los
Estados

Archipiélago
Reina Adelaida
Isla
Wellington
Gulf of
Penas
Taitao
Peninsula
Archipiélago
de los Chonos

PARAGUAY

THE ATLANTIC OCEAN

Covering about one-fifth of the planet's surface, the Atlantic is the world's second-largest ocean. To the west are the Americas, and Europe and Africa lie to the east. The Earth's longest mountain chain, the Mid-Atlantic Ridge, dominates the ocean's underwater landscape. In places, the ridge rises above the water as volcanic islands, such as Iceland and the Azores. The deepest part of the Atlantic, the Puerto Rico Trench, plunges to −8,605 m.

Since Portuguese and Spanish explorers began to cross the ocean from Europe to America in the 15th century, the Atlantic has been one of the world's major transport routes. Today, ships carry bulk goods, such as oil, grain and iron, between the ocean's many international ports.

The Atlantic is rich in natural resources. The shallow areas along the coasts have deposits of oil and gas, and in recent years, offshore oil and gas reserves have been exploited in the Gulf of Mexico, the Niger Delta and the North Sea. Sand, gravel and shell deposits are mined by the USA and the United Kingdom for use in the construction industry. The ocean is also a vital source of food. Most of the Atlantic's coastal countries fish in its waters, but in the north Atlantic, stocks of cod, herring and haddock have been reduced by overfishing. The ocean's environment is also threatened by pollution. Oil is discharged into the water by ships and drilling rigs. Industrial waste, fertilizers and sewage enter the Atlantic at the coasts, particularly in the Mediterranean, Baltic and North Sea regions, and off the USA, southern Brazil and eastern Argentina. A number of countries are trying to reach agreements to tackle some forms of pollution.

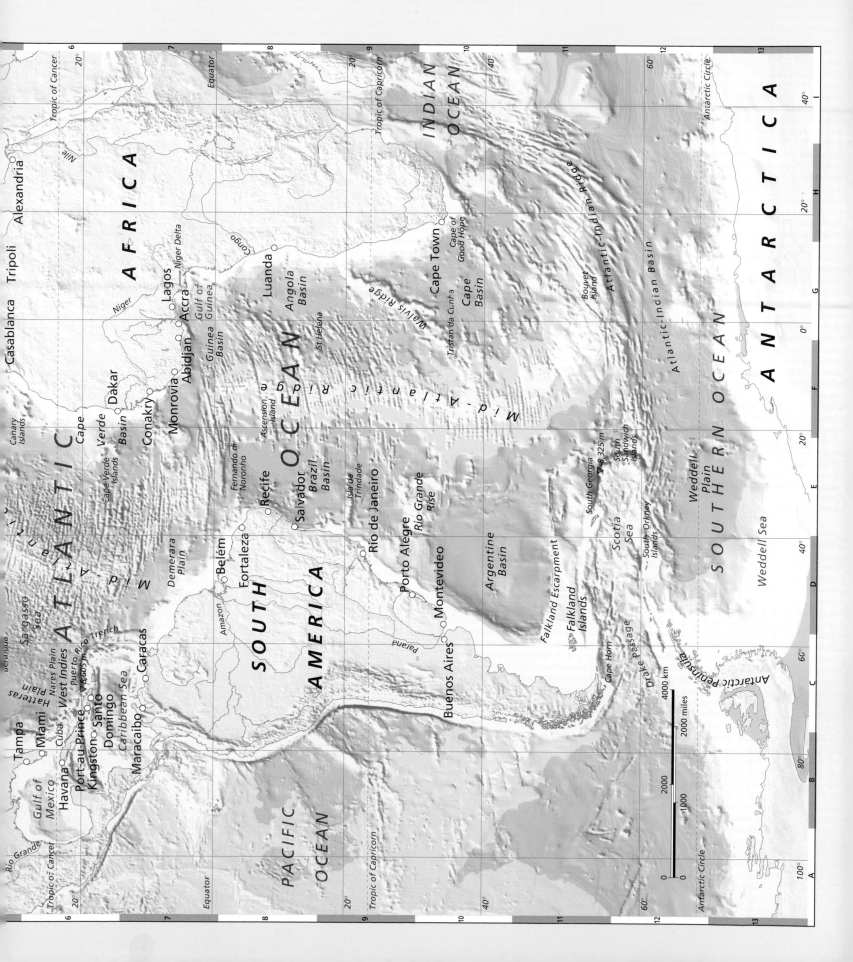

THE ATLANTIC OCEAN . 45

AFRICA

Tripoli
Alexandria
Casablanca

Nile

Niger Delta
Lagos
Accra
Niger
Abidjan
Monrovia
Conakry
Dakar
Cape Verde
Basin

Gulf of
Guinea

Congo

Luanda
Angola
Basin
Guinea
Basin

St Helena

INDIAN
OCEAN

Cape Town
Cape of
Good Hope
Cape
Basin

Tropic of Cancer

Equator

Tropic of Capricorn

Walvis Ridge

Bouvet
Island

Atlantic-Indian Ridge

Atlantic-Indian Basin

ANTARCTICA

Antarctic Circle

Canary
Islands
Cape
Verde
Islands

Cape Verde
Islands

Fernando de
Noronho

Ascension
Island

O C E A N

M i d - A t l a n t i c   R i d g e

Tristan da Cunha

SOUTHERN OCEAN

A N T A R C T I C A

Recife
Salvador
Brazil
Basin
Isla da
Trindade

Rio de Janeiro
Rio Grande
Rise

South Georgia
8,325 m
South
Sandwich
Islands
Weddell
Plain

Demerara
Plain

Belém
Fortaleza

Amazon

Porto Alegre
Montevideo
Argentine
Basin

Falkland Escarpment

Scotia
Sea
South Orkney
Islands

Weddell Sea

A T L A N T I C

Sargasso
Sea

M i d - A t l a n t i c   R i d g e

S O U T H

A M E R I C A

Paraná

Buenos Aires

Falkland
Islands

Cape Horn

Drake Passage

Antarctic
Peninsula

Bermuda
Hatteras
Plain
Nares Plain
West Indies
Cuba
Puerto Rico Trench
8,605 m
Caribbean Sea
Caracas

Tampa
Miami
Havana
Port-au-Prince
Kingston
Santo
Domingo
Maracaibo

Gulf of
Mexico

Rio Grande

PACIFIC
OCEAN

Equator

Tropic of Capricorn

Antarctic Circle

4000 km
2000 miles
2000
1000

0
0

Tropic of Cancer

EUROPE

The continent of Europe extends from the Ural Mountains in the east to the Atlantic Ocean in the west, north to the Arctic Ocean and south to the Mediterranean Sea. There are a number of mountain ranges, including the Alps, which rise to more than 4,800 m, and lesser ranges, such as the Carpathians, Pyrenees and Apennines. Most of the continent's population lives between these uplands on the North European Plain. The plain's rich, fertile soil and temperate climate help farmers to grow a variety of crops, such as wheat, fruit and vegetables, and raise both dairy and beef cattle.

During the Industrial Revolution of the 18th and 19th centuries, Europe developed heavy industries, such as iron and steel-making. Today, in western Europe, these businesses are being replaced by high-tech industries and financial services. In the east, however, many old-fashioned factories remain. These cause terrible environmental pollution in some places.

Many of Europe's countries have existed for hundreds of years and some, such as the United Kingdom and France, had large empires. Although these empires no longer exist, the countries that ran them still play a major role in world affairs. In the 20th century, many of western Europe's countries came together to form the European Union. The union is working towards bringing its members closer politically and economically.

LAND HEIGHT

	4,000 m 13,124 ft
	2,000 m 6,562 ft
	1,000 m 3,281 ft
	500 m 1,640 ft
	200 m 656 ft
	Sea level

Barents Sea

North Cape

Vesterålen
ofoten

Murmansk

Novaya Zemlya

Arctic Circle

Ural Mountains

ASIA

Pechora

Kola Peninsula

White Sea

Archangel

Northern Dvina

S W E D E N

FINLAND

Oulu

Tampere

Lake Onega

R U S S I A N

Perm

Kirov

Izhevsk

F E D E R A T I O N

Turku (Abo)

HELSINKI

Lake Ladoga

St Petersburg

Ufa

Gulf of Bothnia

TOCKHOLM

TALLINN

Gulf of Finland

ESTONIA

Yaroslavl

Ivanovo

Kazan

Kama

Naberezhnyye Chelny

Gotland

LATVIA

RIGA

Tver

Nizhniy Novgorod

Öland

Western Dvina

Volga

MOSCOW

Oka

Simbirsk

Tolyatti

Orenburg

Baltic Sea

LITHUANIA

Vitsyebsk

Ryazan

Samara

Ural

RUSS. FED.

VILNIUS

Smolensk

Tula

Penza

dansk

Kaliningrad

MINSK

Bryansk

Saratov

Volga

N o r t h

BELARUS

Kursk

Lipetsk

Voronezh

Poznan

WARSAW

Homyel

Vistula

Lodz

KIEV

Don

Volgograd

Wroclaw

Rivne

Astrakhan

Oder

POLAND

UKRAINE

Krakow

Lviv

Kharkiv

Caspian Depression

SLOVAKIA

Dniester

Krivyy Rih

Dnipropetrovsk

Caspian Sea

BRATISLAVA

Carpathian Mountains

Cluj-Napoca

Iasi

MOLDOVA

Donetsk

Rostov-na-Donu

Tisza

BUDAPEST

CHISINAU

Stavropol

UNGARY

Timisoara

ROMANIA

Odesa

Dnieper

Sea of Azov

Krasnodar

Grozhyy

ROATIA

BELGRADE

BUCHAREST

Crimean Peninsula

Elbrus
△5,642 m

OSNIA & RZEGOVINA

Danube

Constanta

Sevastopol

Caucasus

SARAJEVO

SERBIA & MONTENEGRO

BULGARIA

Black Sea

Pristina

SOFIA

Burgas

SKOPJE

MACEDONIA

Plovdiv

Istanbul

TIRANA

Thessaloniki

ALBANIA

GREECE

Aegean Sea

ASIA

onian Sea

Patra

ATHENS

Rhodes

Irakleio

Crete

Mediterranean Sea

0		500		1000 km
0	250		500 miles	

NORTHWESTERN EUROPE

Denmark, Norway and Sweden, in the far northwest of Europe, are together known as Scandinavia. These countries have similar languages and for part of their history shared the same rulers. Out at sea to the west lies Iceland. Finland is in the east. Until 1917, Finland was a province of the Russian Empire, so it has a very different language and culture to Scandinavia. All of these countries are highly industrialized and have a high standard of living.

Iceland has a unique landscape. Icy and rocky, it is dotted with volcanoes and dramatic hot springs, some of which are tapped to heat buildings. Much of the rest of northwestern Europe is rugged, mountainous and wooded. The landscape is harsh, and most of the population live in the flatter southern areas, where lakes were scraped out by glaciers thousands of years ago. The soil in the south is more fertile than in the north, allowing farmers to grow crops and lush grass for dairy farming. The western coasts have been eroded by the sea and ice into deep inlets known as fjords. The climate in this part of the region is wet, but mild, and many of the people who live here work in fishing and fish-processing. Further east, the climate is much colder and drier. A great number of those who live inland are employed in the timber industry.

The countries of northwestern Europe produce very little pollution. Most of the region's power is generated from clean hydro-electric stations that harness the fast-flowing mountain streams to produce electricity. However, pollution from elsewhere in Europe blows north and falls as acid rain. This rain poisons forests and lakes, killing the plants and animals living in them.

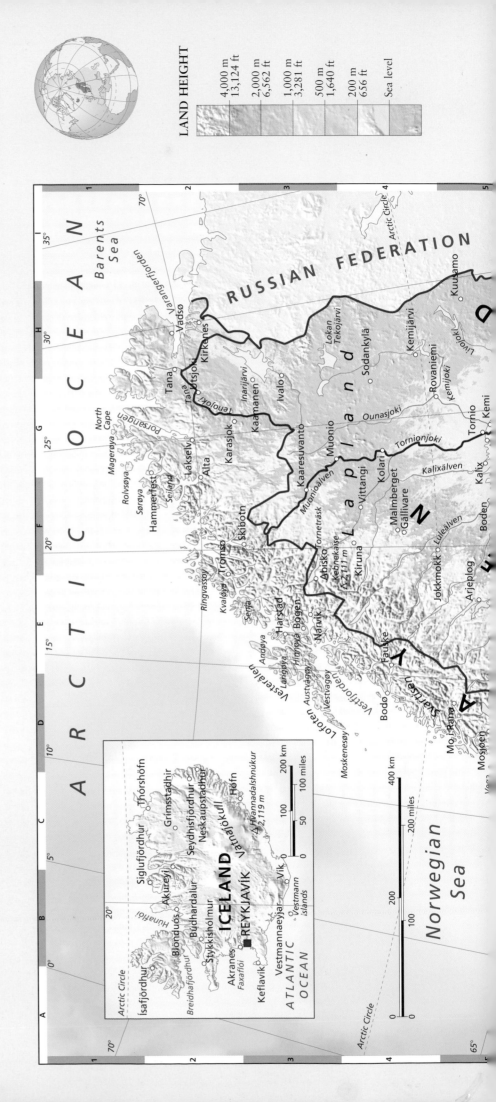

LAND HEIGHT

| 4,000 m 13,124 ft | 2,000 m 6,562 ft | 1,000 m 3,281 ft | 500 m 1,640 ft | 200 m 656 ft | Sea level |

Iceland   Norway   Sweden   Finland   Denmark

RUSSIAN FEDERATION

BELARUS

ESTONIA

LATVIA

LITHUANIA

RUSSIAN FEDERATION (KALININGRAD)

POLAND

GERMANY

Gulf of Finland

Gulf of Riga

Baltic Sea

Gotland

Öland

Bornholm

North Sea

Skagerrak

Kattegat

Suomussalmi
Kuhmo
Kontiomäki
Sotkamo
Kajaani
Nurmes
Pielinen
Joensuu
Orivesi
Parikkala
Oulu
Kempele
Raahe
Pyhäjoki
Oulujärvi
Iisalmi
Kuopio
Siilinjärvi
Varkaus
Mikkeli
Saimaa
Imatra
Lappeenranta
Kotka
Kokkola (Karleby)
Jakobstad (Pietarsaari)
Lapua
Äänekoski
Jyväskylä
Keuruu
Päijänne
Keitele
Lahti
Kouvola
Porvoo
HELSINKI
Vaasa (Vasa)
Seinäjoki
Avus
Mokia
Hämeenlinna
Riihimäki
Hyvinkää
Vantaa
Espoo
Salo
Närpes
Kankaanpää
Parkano
Tampere
Kristinestad
Noormarkku
Pori
Rauma
Turku (Åbo)
Skiftet Kihti
Mariehamn (Maarianhamina)
Åland
Ålands hav

Piteå
Skellefteå
Skellefteälven
Umeå
Holmsund
Örnsköldsvik
Härnösand
Sundsvall
Hudiksvall
Söderhamn
Gävle
Norrtälje
Uppsala
Täby
STOCKHOLM
Sollentuna
Södertälje
Mälaren
Nyköping
Norrköping
Linköping
Katrineholm
Askersund
Mariestad
Vetlanda
Borgholm
Färjestaden
Visby

Storuman
Vilhelmina
Lycksele
Umeälven
Dorotea
Hoting
Angermanälven
Strömsund
Östersund
Storsjön
Ratan
Svenstavik
Ange
Timrå
Kramfors
Ljusnan
Ljusdal
Bollnäs
Rättvik
Dalälven
Falun
Avesta
Sala
Västerås
Nora
Örebro
Katrineholm
Jönköping
Oskarshamn
Växjö
Kalmar
Karlskrona
Kristianstad

Storman
Namsen
Steinkjer
Verdalsora
Røros
Borgefjella
NORGE
Vikna
Namsos
Hell
Heimdal
Støren
Roros
Oppdal
Lillestrøm
Sandvika
Skien
Holmestrand
Fredrikstad
Sarpsborg
Halden
Strömstad
Åmål
Mellerud
Vänersborg
Uddevalla
Trollhättan
Vänern
Tun
Falköping
Borås
Kungsbacka
Varberg
Ljungby
Laholm
Halmstad
Helsingborg
Lund
Malmö
Ystad
Trelleborg
Rønne

Trondheim
Trondheimsfjorden
Hitra
Frøya
Smøla
Kristiansund
Averøya
Molde
Åndalsnes
Dovrefjell
Dombås
Ringebu
Gol
Geilo
Eidfjord
Voss
Jotunheimen
Galdhøpiggen 2,469 m
Glittertind 2,452 m
Lågen
Gjøvik
Lillehammer
Hamar
Mjøsa
Glomma
Hønefoss
OSLO
Drammen
Kongsberg
Moss
Setesdal
Hardangervidda
Bergen
Leirvik
Haugesund
Stavanger
Sandnes
Egersund
Kvinesdal
Kristiansand
Arendal
Evje
Sognefjorden
Boknafjorden
Floro
Jostedalsbreen
Hermansverk
Haukeligrend

DENMARK
Hjørring
Frederikshavn
Ålborg
Thisted
Holstebro
Viborg
Randers
Herning
Hobro
Silkeborg
Århus
Varde
Esbjerg
Billund
Vejle
Kolding
Odense
Nyborg
Svendborg
Jutland
Fyn
Zealand
COPENHAGEN
Helsingør
Ringsted
Nykøbing
Store Bælt
Lolland
Falster
Nakskov
Rødbyhavn
Bornholm

SVERIGE
FINLAND

THE BRITISH ISLES

Located in the northwest of Europe, this group of islands contains two countries: the United Kingdom and the Republic of Ireland. The United Kingdom includes the national regions of England, Wales and Scotland, and the province of Northern Ireland. Britain and Ireland are the British Isles' largest islands.

In the north and west of Britain are uplands, fringed by rocky, jagged coasts. To the south and east of the island are lowlands. They range from the flat fens of the east to the rolling hills of the southeast. Ireland has a low-lying plain

in its centre, which is covered by numerous lakes, peat bogs and grassy hills. The plain is surrounded by low coastal mountains.

Sheep and cattle are raised in Britain's uplands, and cereal crops are grown in the east. The flatter areas of the island, such as central England, produce fruit and vegetables. Dairy products and beef are important sources of income for the Republic of Ireland.

In the late 18th century, the United Kingdom began to develop heavy industries, and by the

early 20th century, the country was a world leader in mining, steel production and textiles. Recently, many of these heavy industries have been replaced by high-tech businesses and financial services. Computer hardware and software companies employ a great number of people in Ireland, Scotland and southern England, while tourism is an important industry throughout the islands. The move away from heavy industry has helped to reduce pollution in the area, but the British Isles is a small, densely populated region with high numbers of cars, so poor air quality is a big problem in large cities.

LAND HEIGHT

| 4,000 m 13,124 ft | 2,000 m 6,562 ft | 1,000 m 3,281 ft | 500 m 1,640 ft | 200 m 656 ft | Sea level |

Republic of Ireland

United Kingdom

THE LOW COUNTRIES

Luxembourg, Belgium and the Netherlands are known as the Low Countries because most of their land is flat and low-lying. Nearly one-third of the Netherlands lies below sea level. The Dutch reclaimed this land from the sea by building dykes to enclose areas of shallow water, which were then drained into canals by pumps. Regions such as these are called polders, and they need constant care to stop them from flooding. Rising to heights of 500 m, the forested hills of the Ardennes, in southern Belgium and Luxembourg, are the Low Countries' only uplands. Two major rivers –

the Meuse and the Rhine – flow through the region on their way to the North Sea.

The reclaimed areas, plus flat plains such as Flanders in northern Belgium, have fertile soils, and provide good conditions for agriculture. Barley, potatoes and flax are the main crops. The Netherlands also produces cut flowers and bulbs, which are exported all over the world. Beef, dairy and pig farming take place in the higher inland parts of this region. Luxembourg is a major centre for banking, and Belgium has a great number of factories. Brussels, which is

the capital of Belgium, is also the administrative capital of the European Union.

Many people work in chemical companies, engineering, the textile industry, and in the new high-tech businesses that are springing up in this region. The majority of people live in towns or cities and the largest urban area is known as *Randstad Holland.* This is a densely-populated, built-up region between Amsterdam and Rotterdam. Most people have a comfortable lifestyle in the cities, but large numbers of cars and factories cause serious air pollution.

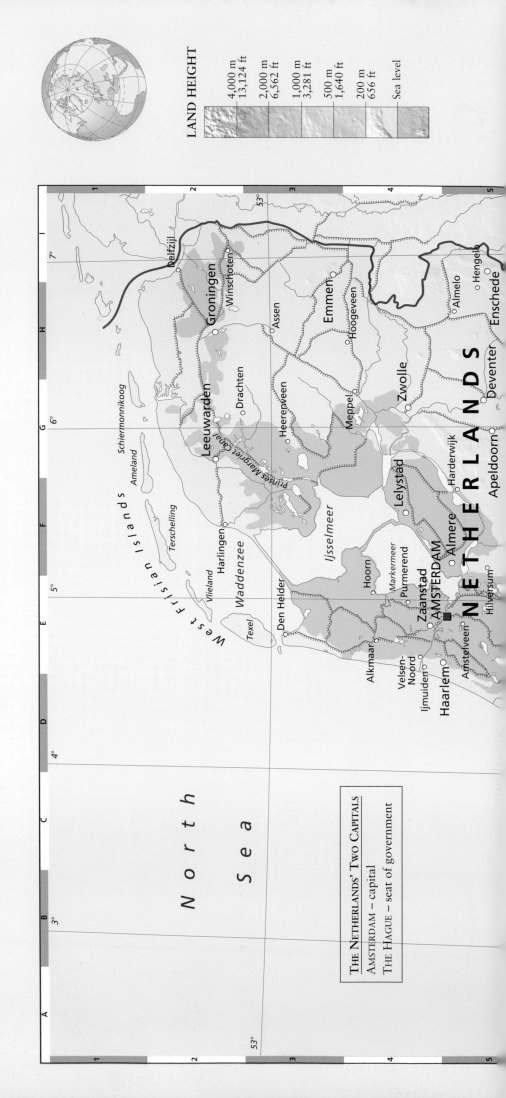

LAND HEIGHT

| 4,000 m 13,124 ft | 2,000 m 6,562 ft | 1,000 m 3,281 ft | 500 m 1,640 ft | 200 m 656 ft | Sea level |

THE NETHERLANDS' TWO CAPITALS
AMSTERDAM – capital
THE HAGUE – seat of government

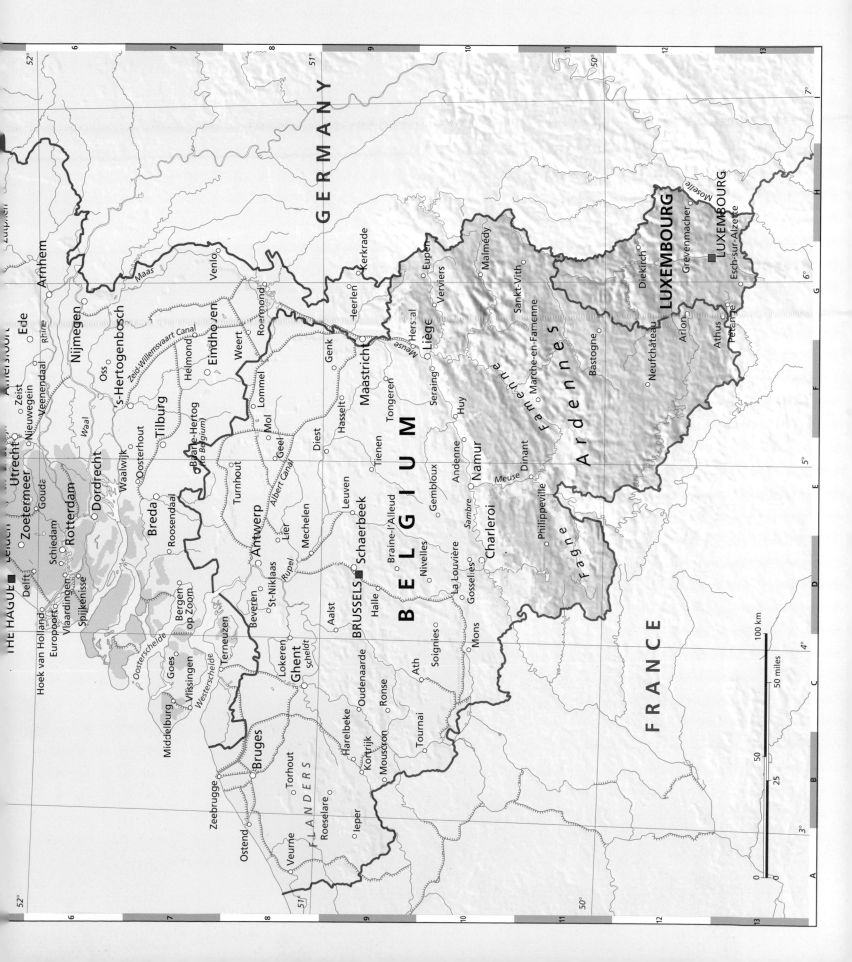

Netherlands
Belgium
Luxembourg

GERMANY

52°
51°
50°
52°
51°
50°

6 7 8 9 10 11 12 13

7°
6°
5°
4°
3°

THE HAGUE
Zoetermeer
Delft
Hoek van Holland
Europoort
Vlaardingen
Spijkenisse
Schiedam
Rotterdam
Gouda
Utrecht
Nieuwegein
Zeist
Veenendaal
Ede
Amersfoort
Rhine
Zoeterwoude
Waal
Arnhem
Nijmegen
Oss
Maas
Venlo
Roermond
's-Hertogenbosch
Eindhoven
Helmond
Weert
Zeid-Willemsvaart Canal
Tilburg
Oosterhout
Waalwijk
Dordrecht
Breda
Roosendaal
Baarle-Hertog
(to Belgium)
Bergen
op Zoom
Goes
Middelburg
Vlissingen
Oosterschelde
Westerschelde
Terneuzen
Zeebrugge
Ostend
Bruges
Torhout
Roeselare
Ieper
Veurne
FLANDERS
Ghent
Lokeren
Scheldt
Ronse
Oudenaarde
Harelbeke
Kortrijk
Mouscron
Aalst
Halle
BRUSSELS
Schaerbeek
Beveren
St-Niklaas
Antwerp
Lier
Mechelen
Rupel
Turnhout
Geel
Mol
Lommel
Albert Canal
Diest
Hasselt
Genk
Maastricht
Heerlen
Kerkrade
Tongeren
Tienen
Leuven
BELGIUM
Braine-l'Alleud
Nivelles
La Louvière
Gosselies
Soignies
Ath
Tournai
Mons
Charleroi
Gembloux
Andenne
Namur
Huy
Philippeville
Dinant
Meuse
Sambre
Seraing
Liège
Hers:al
Meuse
Verviers
Eupen
Malmédy
Sankt-Vith
Marche-en-Famenne
Famenne
Bastogne
Fagne
Ardennes
Neufchâteau
Diekirch
Moselle
LUXEMBOURG
LUXEMBOURG
Grevenmacher
Arlon
Athus
Pétange
Esch-sur-Alzette

FRANCE

100 km
50
25
0

50 miles
25
0

FRANCE

One of the largest countries in western Europe, France has a variety of landscape types, which fall into two main areas. In the north and west are flat plains and low hills. The plains are drained by three great rivers, the Seine, the Loire and the Garonne. These rivers form basins with rich soils. To the south and east are the uplands – the high plateau of the Massif Central and two mountain ranges, the Pyrenees and the Alps. The Pyrenees form a natural border with Spain. The Alps are crossed by high passes that lead into Italy and Switzerland.

Fertile soils and a temperate climate make France a successful food producer. Wheat and vegetables are grown in the north, and corn and fruit are produced in the south. The lowlands make good dairy pasture and grapes for wine are grown in many areas. France is also highly industrialized. It exports a vast range of products, from cars to clothing. Both the northern and southern coasts suffer from industrial pollution, but because France generates about 75 per cent of its electricity in nuclear power stations, the country is less polluted by the use of fossil fuels than other industrialized nations.

From the 18th–20th centuries, France was a colonial power, with an empire in Africa, Asia and North America. Almost all of its colonies are now independent. Today, France plays a leading role in the European Union.

LAND HEIGHT

	4,000 m 13,124 ft
	2,000 m 6,562 ft
	1,000 m 3,281 ft
	500 m 1,640 ft
	200 m 656 ft
	Sea level

France

Monaco

Strait of Dover
2°
Dunkerque
Calais
Boulogne-sur-Mer
Lille
Béthune
Lens
Arras
Abbeville
Tourcoing
Roubaix
Valenciennes

BELGIUM

4°
6°
8°
10°
50°

Dieppe
Somme
Amiens
St-Quentin
Oise
Beauvais
Laon
Charleville-Mézières
Compiègne
Creil
Reims
Pontoise
Évreux
Argenteuil
PARIS
Versailles
Créteil
Melun
Chartres
Seine
Sens
Troyes
Chaumont

LUXEMBOURG

Thionville
Metz
Forbach
Haguenau
Châlons-en-Champagne
Nancy
Strasbourg
Bar-le-Duc
St-Dié
Épinal
Colmar

GERMANY

Rouen
Seine

CHAMPAGNE
Meuse
Marne
Moselle
Rhine

Vosges
48°

Orléans
Olivet
Blois
Tours
Cher
Auxerre
Langres
Mulhouse
Belfort
Vesoul
Montbéliard
Dijon
Besançon

Clamecy
Morvan
BURGUNDY
Loire
Saône

LIECHTENSTEIN
AUSTRIA
SWITZERLAND

Bourges
Nevers
Châteauroux
Montceau-les-Mines
Chalon-sur-Saône
Moulins
Mâcon
Bourg-en-Bresse
Vichy
Roanne
Lyon
Villeurbanne
Annecy
Annemasse
Thonon-les-Bains
Lake Geneva

RANCE
Creuse
Montluçon
Vienne

Jura
Alps
46°

Clermont-Ferrand
Limoges
Puy de Sancy △ 1,885 m
St-Étienne
St-Chamond
Chambéry
Grenoble
Mont Blanc △ 4,810 m
Chamonix

Massif
Central
Isère
Les Ecrins 4,102 m △

érigueux
Brive-la-Gaillarde
Dordogne
Le Puy
Valence

ITALY

Cévennes
Rhône
Montélimar
Gap
Digne

Alps
44°

Cahors
Lot
Mende
Rodez
Tarn
Orange
Avignon
Tarascon
Arles
Camargue
Montauban
Albi
Nîmes
PROVENCE

Durance
Maritime Alps

MONACO
MONACO
Nice
Antibes
Cannes
Fréjus
St-Tropez
Aix-en-Provence
Toulouse
Castres
Montpellier
Béziers
Sète
Marseille
Toulon
La Seyne-sur-Mer
Îles Côte d'Azur d'Hyères

Canal du Midi
Carcassonne
Narbonne
Foix
Gulf of Lion
Cap Corse
Bastia
8

Perpignan
ANDORRA
e e s

Mediterranean Sea

Corsica
42°

Ajaccio
Aléria
Sartène
Bonifacio
Strait of Bonifacio
10°

2°
4°
6°
8°

THE IBERIAN PENINSULA

The Iberian Peninsula is separated from the rest of Europe by the Pyrenees mountains. To the west is the Atlantic Ocean, while the Mediterranean Sea lies in the east. Spain and Portugal occupy most of this large landmass, together with the tiny mountainous state of Andorra, and Gibraltar, a small British territory. The centre of the peninsula is dominated by a vast plateau, which is enclosed by the Cordillera Cantábrica to the north, and the Sierra Morena to the south.

Wheat and barley are Iberia's main crops, but in the south, farmers irrigate the dry land to grow citrus fruits, especially oranges and lemons. Both Spain and Portugal make wines and these two countries also produce two-thirds of the world's cork.

Spain's industries, which are concentrated in the north of the country, make cars, machinery, steel and chemicals. Portugal exports textiles, clothing, shoes and processed fish, and tourism is an important source of income for this entire region.

Soil erosion, which is caused when forests are cleared for farmland, has affected much of the peninsula. High-rise hotels along the Mediterranean coast have spoilt the character of this area, and popular beaches here are extremely overcrowded.

LAND HEIGHT

	4,000 m 13,124 ft
	2,000 m 6,562 ft
	1,000 m 3,281 ft
	500 m 1,640 ft
	200 m 656 ft
	Sea level

Spain

Andorra

Portugal

F   G   H   I   J   K

2°   0°   2°   4°   44°

F R A N C E

*Gulf of
Gascony*

Santander

San Vicente
de Barakaldo

Bilbao   Donostia-   Irún
              San Sebastián

PAÍS VASCO

Vitoria-Gasteiz   Pamplona

NAVARRA   Jaca   **ANDORRA**

                              Aneto 3,404 m △   **ANDORRA LA VELLA**   Llívia *(to Spain)*

Burgos   Huesca   Figueres   Roses

LA RIOJA   Logroño   Ripoll

VIEJA   Girona

              Soria   Monzón   *CATALONIA*   *Costa Brava*

Aranda
de Duero   Ebro   Lleida   Manresa
              Duero   Mataró

Sistema Central   Zaragoza   Terrassa
                                        Sabadell   Badalona

              Calatayud   *ARAGÓN*   L'Hospitalet de   Barcelona
                                              Llobregat

Guadalajara   Daroca   Reus
                        *Embalse
Alcobendas   de Mequinenza*   Tarragona   Alcañiz

MADRID   Tortosa
Getafe   Teruel   Amposta   *Balearic Islands*   Ciutadella
                                                                de Menorca
Aranjuez   Cuenca   Castelló   Vinarós   Mahón
                        de la Plana   Alcúdia   *Menorca
Sistema Ibérico   (Minorca)*

              Utiel   *Costa del Azahar*   Palma de Mallorca
Alcázar de   Paterna   Sagunto   Andratx   Manacor
San Juan   Villarrobledo   Torrente   Mallorca   Santanyí
              La Roda   *Júcar*   Valencia   *(Majorca)*
                                        *Gulf of
LA MANCHA   Valencia*
Manzanares   Albacete   Alzira   Gandía   San Antonio   *Eivissa
                                                Abad   (Ibiza)*
Valdepeñas   Denia   *Cabo de
                Alcoy   la Nao*   Eivissa (Ibiza)

                Hellín   Elda   Benidorm   *Formentera*
              Elche   Alicante
Linares   (Elx)
              Orihuela   *Mediterranean
Jaén   Murcia   Torrevieja   Sea*

Béticos   Huéscar   *Costa Blanca*
              Lorca   Cabo de Palos
                        Cartagena
Baza
                Aguilas

Granada   Huércal-Overa

Sierra Nevada
Mulhacén
3,478 m   Almería

Motril   Adra   *Cabo
                        de Gata*
el Sol

A L G E R I A

*Gulf
of Lion*

Segre

42°

40°

38°

36°

Melilla
(to Spain)

2°   0°   2°   4°

1

2

3

4

5

6

7

8

9

GERMANY

Germany lies in the very heart of Europe. There are flat plains in the northern part of the country, and in the south are forests and the Alps. Two of Europe's greatest rivers flow through Germany. The Rhine runs from the south, where it forms a natural border with France, to the north. It is an important transport link between many industrial centres. To the south, the Danube rises in the Black Forest and flows east on its course to the Black Sea.

Germany's northern plains make good farmland – cattle and pigs are raised here, and cereal crops are grown. Livestock farms are located in the south, but the uplands here are often more suited to growing vegetables. Grapes for Germany's successful wine industry also grow well in the mountainous regions, and vineyards cover the slopes surrounding the Rhine and its tributaries. The chemicals industry, car manufacturing and engineering employ many people in and around major cities, especially in Berlin, and in the Ruhr, Rhine and Main valleys. Germany also has strong high-tech industries, producing goods such as computers and telecommunications equipment.

In 1945, Germany was defeated in World War II and the country was divided. East Germany became part of communist Europe. Many people worked in old-fashioned heavy industries, and salaries and working conditions were poor for most people. West Germany made a rapid recovery following the war, and became one of Europe's richest and most powerful countries. In 1990, the two states joined again, and since then, the German goverment has been trying to unite the country economically and politically. Germany is also an important member of the European Union.

LAND HEIGHT					
4,000 m 13,124 ft	2,000 m 6,562 ft	1,000 m 3,281 ft	500 m 1,640 ft	200 m 656 ft	Sea level

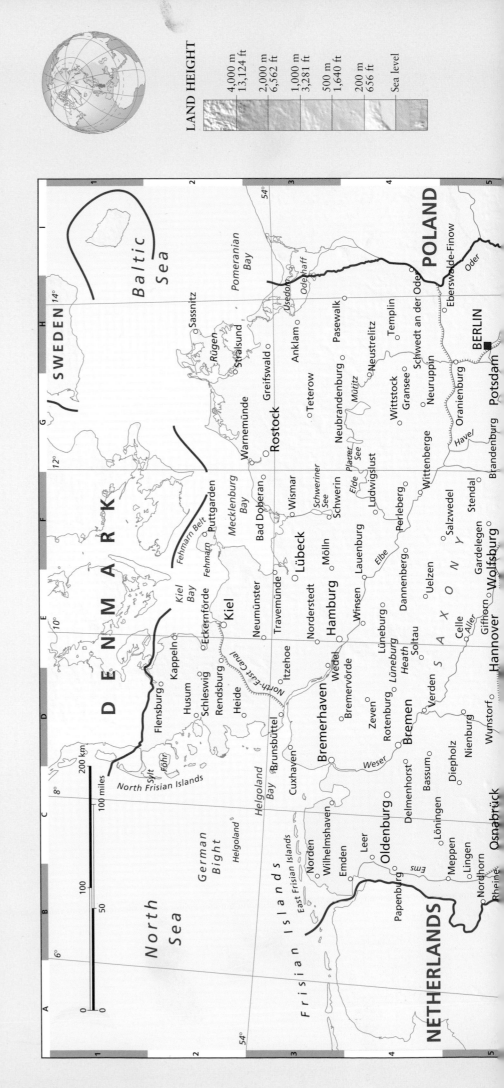

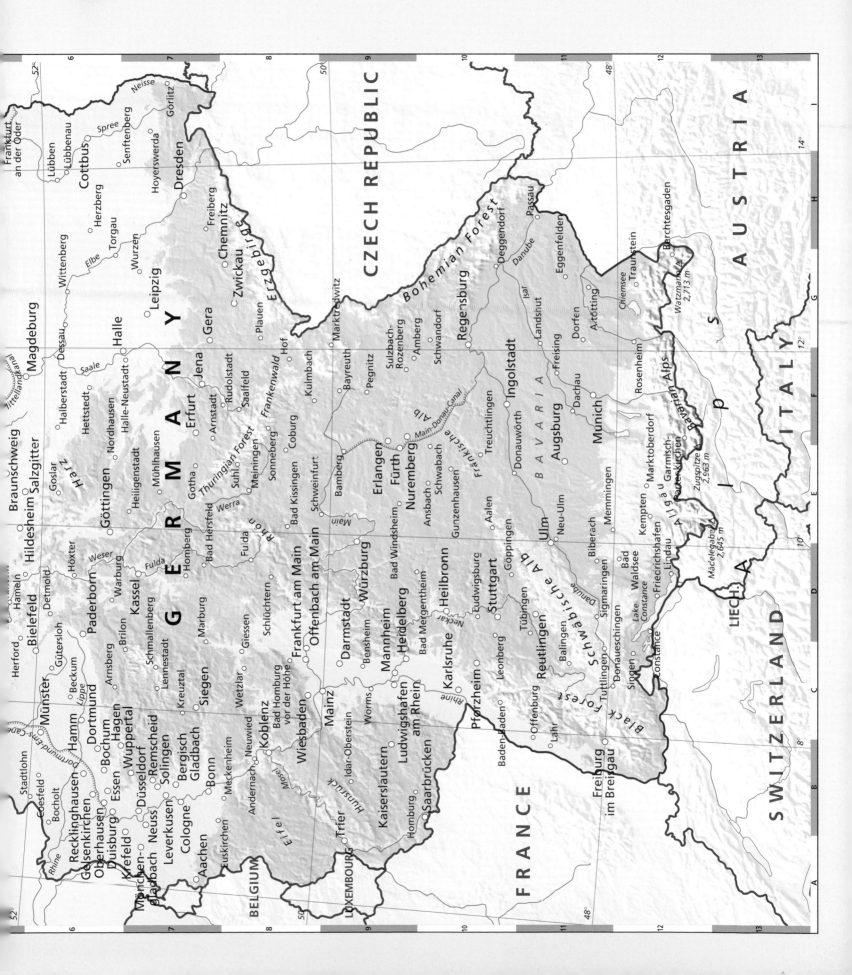

Germany

THE ALPINE STATES

The Alps, Europe's tallest range of mountains, stretch across the Alpine states – Austria, Liechtenstein, Switzerland and Slovenia. This region in central Europe has a landscape of jagged snow-topped peaks, deep valleys and lakes that were scooped out by glaciers over 20,000 years ago. The mountainous terrain of the Alpine states limits the amount of land that can be cultivated by farmers, although the rich pastures of the lower slopes are used to graze both beef and dairy cattle.

Switzerland and Liechtenstein have few raw materials, so these countries concentrate on producing high-quality goods, including pharmaceuticals and watches. They also act as international centres for banking. Austria is heavily industrialized, and all four countries have strong tourist industries. People from many parts of the world come to the Alpine states to ski and to admire the mountain scenery. The vast numbers of visitors, and the buildings needed to house them, put a strain on the environment. This region lies on the main trading routes across the Alps, so air pollution caused by passing lorries is another environmental problem.

Switzerland takes a neutral position in wars and other conflicts. This policy makes the country an ideal base for a number of important international organizations, including the Red Cross and various agencies of the United Nations.

LAND HEIGHT

4,000 m	13,124 ft
2,000 m	6,562 ft
1,000 m	3,281 ft
500 m	1,640 ft
200 m	656 ft
Sea level	

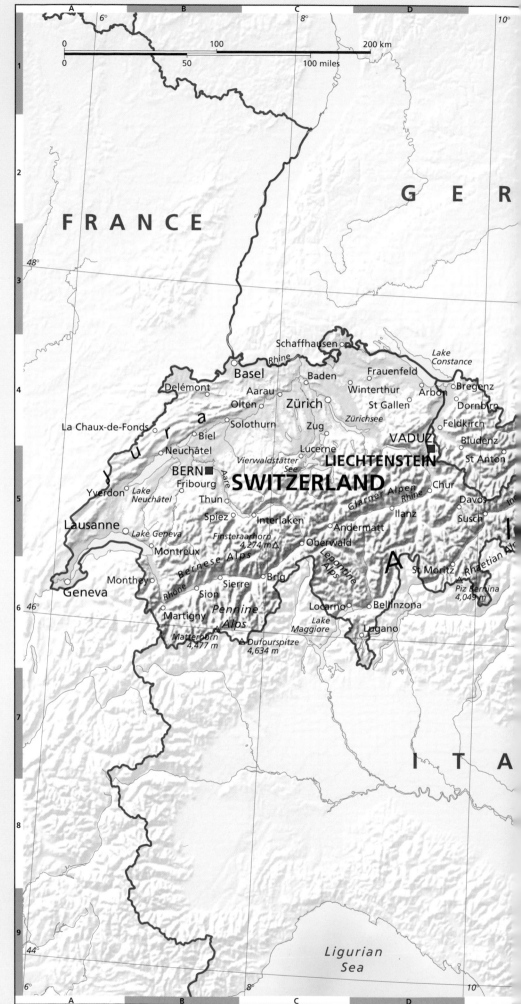

Austria

Switzerland

Liechtenstein

Slovenia

CZECH REPUBLIC

SLOVAKIA

G E R M A N Y

M A N Y

Gmünd

Mistelbach

Hollabrunn

Krems an der Donau

Danube Tulln

■ VIENNA

Linz

Salzach Wels St Pölten Amstetten Mödling

Vocklabruck Steyr Baden *Neusiedler See*

Attersee Gmunden Waidhofen an der Ybbs Wiener Neustadt Eisenstadt

Traunsee

Salzburg **AUSTRIA**

Hallein Bad Ischl Neunkirchen

Liezen *Enns* Mürzzuschlag

Kufstein Rottenmann

Wörgl Bischofshofen Bruck an der Mur

Zugspitze 2,963 m Kitzbühel Radstadt Knittelfeld

Bavarian Alps Schwaz *Niedere Tauern* Judenburg **Graz**

T I R O L Telfs Mittersill *Mur* Köflach Wildon **HUNGARY**

andeck Innsbruck *Hohe Tauern* St Michael im Langau *Raab*

Wildspitze 3,774 m S *Grossglockner 3,797 m* Wolfsberg

A l p *Ötztaler Alpen* Lienz St Veit an der Glan Leibnitz *Mur*

Spittal-an der Drau Völkermarkt Murcka Sobota

Drau Villach Klagenfurt **Maribor**

Karnische Alpen *Karawanken* Ptuj *Drava*

Triglav 2,864 m Jesenice Celje

Tolmin *Julian Alps* Kranj

Sava Trbovlje

I T A L Y Nova Gorica LJUBLJANA ■ Krsko

SLOVENIA

Postojna Novo Mesto

Ribnica Kocevje

Koper Kozina

CROATIA

BOSNIA & HERZEGOVINA

Adriatic Sea

ITALY AND MALTA

This region stretches from the Alps in the north to the Mediterranean islands of Malta in the south. Much of the Italian peninsula is mountainous, with the Apennines extending along almost the whole length of Italy, and the Dolomites in the northeast. In the south are volcanoes, such as Etna and Vesuvius. This area also experiences earthquakes.

The northern and southern halves of the region are different from each other in several ways. The north, which has a milder climate than the south, is more developed. Big cities, including

Turin, Milan and Genoa, are centres of industry. Here, manufacturing companies make cars, engines and other products. There are also high-tech businesses, and design studios specializing in everything from clothing to furniture. The north is a popular tourist destination, luring many people with its stunning scenery, fine food and historical cities including Venice, Florence and Rome. Lake Garda and Lake Como also attract many visitors. In the north are two tiny countries. The Vatican City, a small area of Rome, is the headquarters of the Catholic

Church. The ancient independent state of San Marino is located near the Adriatic coast.

In the south, the climate is hotter, the towns are generally smaller, and industry is less well developed. The dry soils often have to be irrigated, but some crops, such as olives, citrus fruits, grapes and tomatoes, grow well in the baking sun. Still further south are Sicily and Malta, which have an even hotter climate. Sicily is part of Italy, while the islands of Malta form a separate nation. Tourism and shipping are Malta's major sources of income.

LAND HEIGHT

| 4,000 m 13,124 ft | 2,000 m 6,562 ft | 1,000 m 3,281 ft | 500 m 1,640 ft | 200 m 656 ft | Sea level |

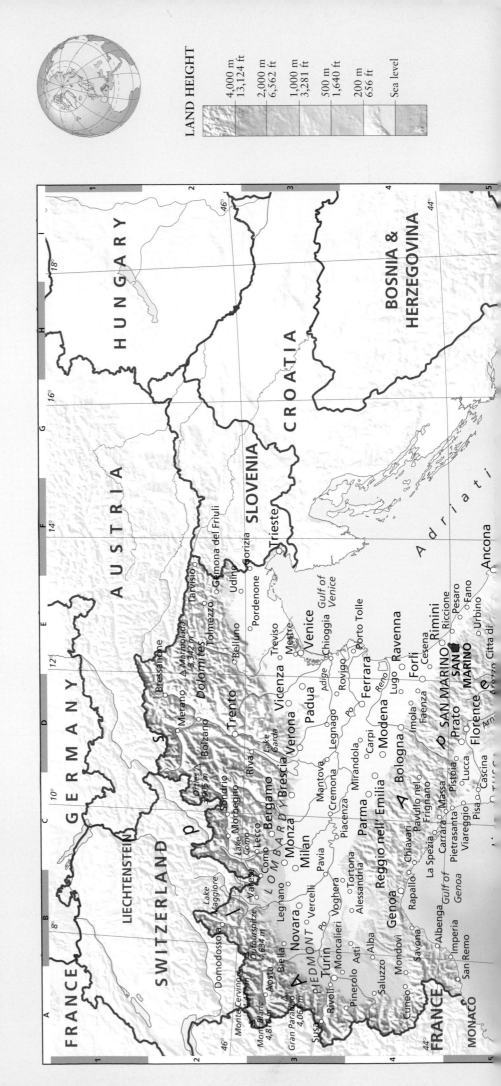

Italy
San Marino
Vatican City
Malta

Ligurian Sea

Corsica (to France)

Strait of Bonifacio

Sardinia

Punta La Marmora △1,834 m

Porto Torres
Sassari
Alghero
Ozieri
Macomer
Nuoro
Siniscola
Olbia
Terralba
Oristano
Tirso
Guspini
Iglesias
Carbonia
San Antioco
Guspini
Villaputzu
Quartu Sant'Elena
Cagliari
Capo Carbonara
Capo Spartivento
Tortolì

Piombino
Elba
Follonica
Grosseto
Orbetello
Civitavecchia
Lido di Ostia

Lake Trasimeno
Perugia
Assisi
Spoleto
Terni
Orvieto
Lake Bolsena
Viterbo
Tiber
ITALY
VATICAN CITY
ROME
Anzio
Terracina

Fermo
Ascoli Piceno
Teramo
San Benedetto del Tronto
Pescara
Chieti
L'Aquila
Rieti
Corno Grande △2,912 m
Avezzano
Tivoli
Sora
Latina
Gaeta
Gulf of Gaeta

Vasto
Lanciano
Sulmona
Termoli
Isernia
Cassino
Formia

San Severo
Campobasso
Manfredonia
Gargano Peninsula
Lake Varano
Lake Lesina
Gulf of Manfredonia

Foggia
Cerignola
Benevento
Caserta
Avellino
Naples
Capri
Ischia
Gulf of Salerno
Salerno
Battipaglia
Eboli
Agropoli
Vesuvius 1,279 m
Ponziane Islands

Andria
Barletta
Molfetta
Bitonto
Bari
Rionero in Vulture
Altamura
Potenza
Matera
Basento
Appennino Lucano
Lauria
Maratea

Gioia del Colle
Ostuni
Nardo
Gallipoli
Taranto
Gulf of Taranto
Castrovillari
Cetraro
Cetraro

Brindisi
Lecce
Otranto
Capo Santa Maria di Leuca

Corigliano Calabro
Rossano
Ciro Marina
Cosenza
Crotone
Capo Colonna
Catanzaro
Gulf of Squillace
Lamezia
CALABRIA
Vibo Valentia
Rosarno
Reggio di Calabria
Capo Spartivento

Stromboli
Aeolian Islands
Messina
Strait of Messina
Milazzo
Taormina
△Mount Etna 3,350 m
Adrano
Paternò
Catania
Siracusa
Avola
Pachino
Capo Passero

Ustica
Cefalù
Palermo
Bagheria
Capo San Vito
Partinico
Trapani
Marsala
Mazara del Vallo
Castelvetrano
Sciacca
Agrigento
Licata
Caltanissetta
Enna
Caltagirone
Gela
Vittoria
Modica
Ragusa
Sicily

Mediterranean Sea

Tyrrhenian Sea

Ionian Sea

Strait of Sicily

Pantelleria
Linosa
Pelagic Islands
Lampedusa

Malta Channel
Gozo
MALTA ■VALLETTA
Malta

TUNISIA

ALGERIA

200 km
100
50
0
100 miles
50
0

EASTERN EUROPE

The countries of eastern Europe have a varied landscape which extends from the cliffs and sandy beaches of the Baltic coast, through the vast Pripet Marshes in southern Belarus, to the great open steppes that cover almost three-quarters of the Ukraine.

Most of the countries in this region have spent long periods of their history under Russian rule. For much of the 20th century, they all formed part of the Soviet Union. The Soviets encouraged the growth of heavy industry and manufacturing, turning these

states into industrial nations. When the Soviet Union broke up in 1991, the countries of this area became independent and their old-fashioned factories had to compete with the modern, high-tech businesses of the rest of Europe. For a number of years there were price rises and food shortages. Recently, however, this region has developed new high-tech industries, and the countries have also formed trade links with western Europe.

Farming is the main source of employment for much of the population. The rich black soils of

the Ukraine are ideal for growing cereal crops and sugar beet. The smaller countries of the Baltic coast have many cattle and pig farms. The Baltic states have few natural resources, and they have to import goods and services from their larger, richer neighbours.

In 1986, the world's worst nuclear accident took place at the power station at Chernobyl, in the Ukraine near the border with Belarus. Thirty-one people were killed immediately, and radioactive particles spread over a huge area, contaminating farmland and making thousands of people ill.

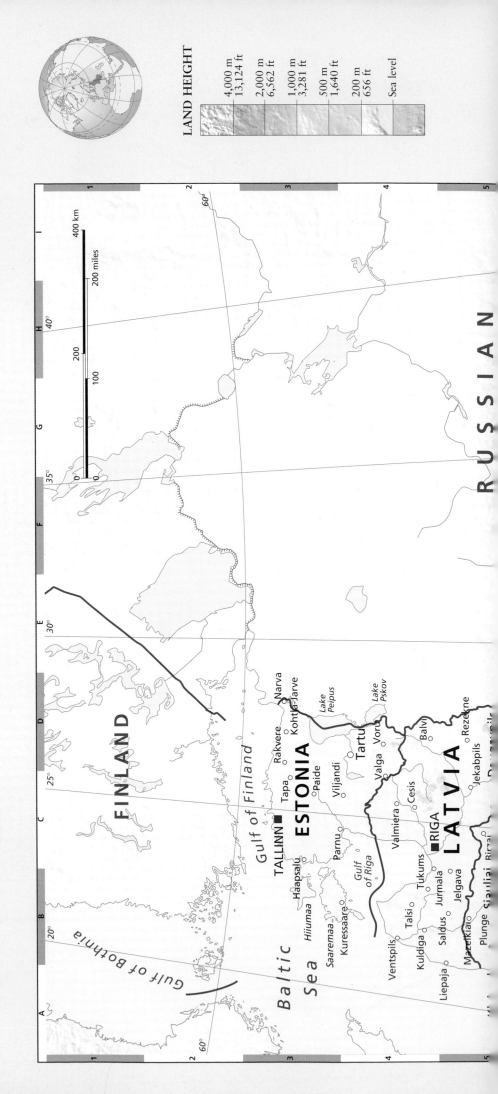

LAND HEIGHT

| 4,000 m 13,124 ft | 2,000 m 6,562 ft | 1,000 m 3,281 ft | 500 m 1,640 ft | 200 m 656 ft | Sea level |

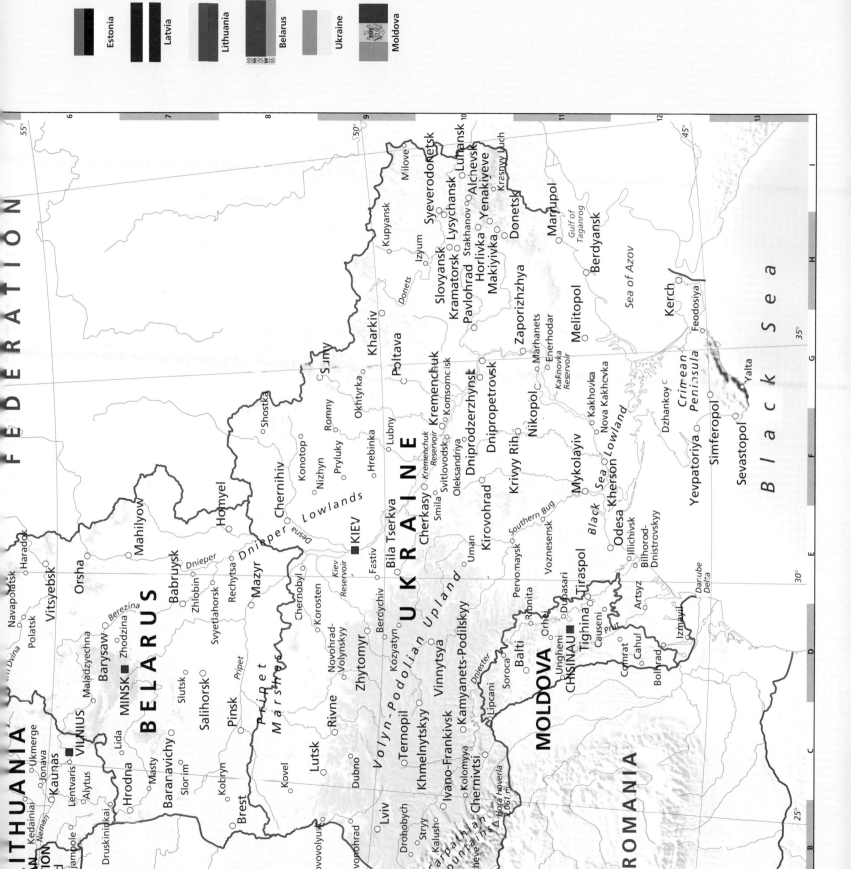

CENTRAL EUROPE

Central Europe is made up of two plains, which are divided by a chain of mountains. To the north, in Poland, is the North European Plain. The Great Hungarian Plain, with its farmlands and grasslands, lies in the south. Much of the land area of the Czech Republic and Slovakia falls in the mountainous region in the centre. For most of the 20th century, these countries were united as Czechoslovakia, but in 1993, they split into two separate nations.

Central Europe's farmers grow cereal crops such as barley, oats, wheat and rye, as well as large

quantities of potatoes and sugar beet. They also raise livestock, especially pigs. In Hungary, where the climate is warmer, farmers grow grapes for wine and sweet peppers for paprika, a hot spice that is used in Hungarian cooking. Much of Slovakia is covered with forest and the country has a large timber industry.

Poland has enormous reserves of a brown coal, called lignite, which is exported. A variety of minerals are mined in the mountains of the Czech Republic and Slovakia. Hungary has a wide range of industries, producing vehicles,

metals, chemicals, textiles and electrical goods, while the Czech Republic is famous for its breweries and fine glassware.

For much of the 20th century, the countries of central Europe were ruled by communist governments, which were dominated by the powerful, Russian-led Soviet Union. The old-fashioned heavy industries that were developed under communist rule have caused terrible pollution in some places. However, the countries of central Europe are now moving towards more modern, high-tech industries.

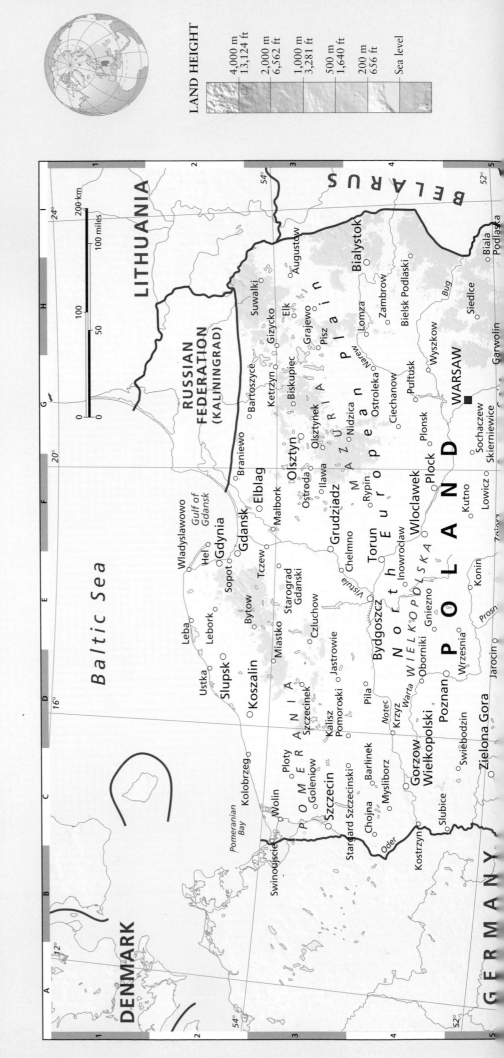

LAND HEIGHT

| 4,000 m 13,124 ft | 2,000 m 6,562 ft | 1,000 m 3,281 ft | 500 m 1,640 ft | 200 m 656 ft | Sea level |

Poland
Czech Republic
Slovakia
Hungary

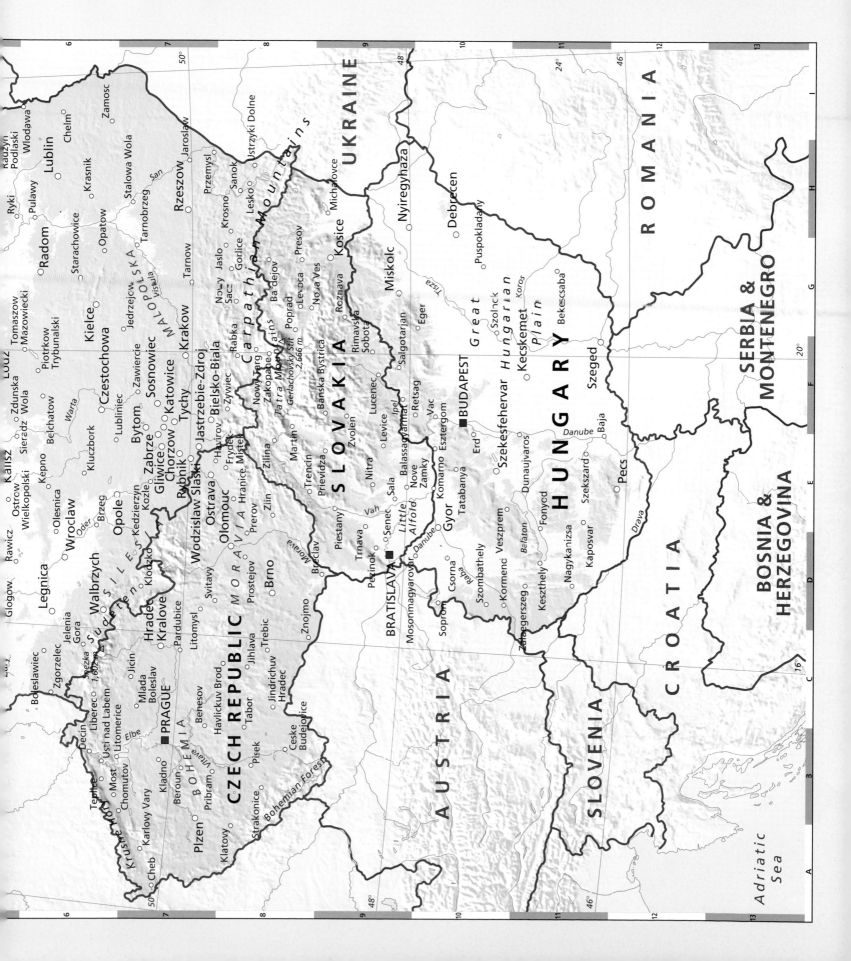

UKRAINE

ROMANIA

SERBIA & MONTENEGRO

BOSNIA & HERZEGOVINA

CROATIA

SLOVENIA

AUSTRIA

HUNGARY

SLOVAKIA

CZECH REPUBLIC

MORAVIA

BOHEMIA

MALOPOLSKA

SILESIA

Sudeten Mountains

Krusne Mory

Carpathian Mountains

Tatra Mountains

Great Hungarian Plain

Little Alföld

Bohemian Forest

Adriatic Sea

Ladzyn
Podlaski
Ryki
Pulawy
Wlodawa
Chelm
Lublin
Krasnik
Stalowa Wola
Zamosc
Radom
Starachowice
Opatow
Tarnobrzeg
Przemysl
Jaroslaw
Rzeszow
Sanok
Ustrzyki Dolne
Kielce
Jedrzejow
Tarnow
Krosno
Lesko
Michalovce
Kosice
Miskolc
Nyiregyhaza
Debrecen
Puspokladany
Piotrkow Trybunalski
Czestochowa
Zawiercie
Sosnowiec
Krakow
Nowy Sacz
Gorlice
Ba dejov
Presov
No va Ves
Roznava
Eger
Salgotarjan
Szolnok
Koros
Kecskemet
Bekescsaba
Szeged
Lodz
Tomaszow Mazowiecki
Sieradz
Belchatow
Kepno
Zdunska Wola
Lubliniec
Kluczbork
Bytom
Zabrze
Chorzow
Katowice
Tychy
Bielsko-Biala
Zywiec
Rabka
Nowy Targ
Zakopane
Gerlachovsky Stit
2,666 m
Poprad
Le vo ca
Rimavska Sobota
Banska Bystrica
Zvolen
Lucenec
Retsag
Vac
Szekesfehervar
Erd
Esztergom
Kalisz
Ostrow Wielkopolski
Rawicz
Olesnica
Wroclaw
Opole
Kedzierzyn Kozle
Gliwice
Rybnik
Wodzislaw Slaski
Ostrava
Havirov
Fryder
Hranice
Prerov
Martin
Zilina
Trencin
Prievidza
Nitra
Levice
Ipel
Balassagyarmat
Nove Zamky
Komarno
Gyor
Tatabanya
Veszprem
Dunaujvaros
Szekszard
Pecs
Glogow
Legnica
Jelenia Gora
Zgorzelec
Boleslawiec
Snezka
1,602 m
Walbrzych
Klodzko
Hradec Kralove
Pardubice
Svitavy
Prostejov
Olomouc
Zlin
Znojmo
Breclav
Piestany
Trnava
Senec
Sala
Pezinok
BRATISLAVA
Mosonmagyarovar
Csorna
Sopron
Szombathely
Zalaegerszeg
Keszthely
Balaton
Nagykanizsa
Kaposvar
Drava
Fonyod
Kormend
Raba
Danube
Baja
BUDAPEST
Tepli
Decin
Usti nad Labem
Liberec
Litomerice
Mlada Boleslav
Benesov
Havlickuv Brod
Jihlava
Trebic
Brno
Litomysl
Jicin
Most
Chomutov
Karlovy Vary
Cheb
Teplice
Kladno
PRAGUE
Beroun
Pribram
Tabor
Jindrichuv Hradec
Ceske Budejovice
Pisek
Klatovy
Plzen
Strakonice
Oder
Warta
Vistula
San
Elbe
Vltava
Morava
Vah
Danube
Tisza
50°
48°
46°
6°
16°
18°
20°
24°
46°

SOUTHEASTERN EUROPE

Southeastern Europe extends east from the Adriatic Sea to the Black Sea, south to the Mediterranean Sea and north to the Carpathian Mountains. The ancient country of Greece lies in the far south. It has been an independent nation since 1829. Albania, Romania and Bulgaria were ruled by communist governments for almost 50 years, until the 1990s. The rest of this region was part of a communist union of states called Yugoslavia. In 1991, a civil war led to the break-up of this union, and after the war, five separate countries were created.

Southeastern Europe is mainly mountainous, but the northern part of the region has good soils where cereals, vegetables and fruits are grown. The upland areas are used for grazing sheep and goats. Further south, and in the coastal areas, grapes and olives are the main crops. Southeastern Europe has some textile, engineering and manufacturing businesses, and these are concentrated around major cities, such as Zagreb and Bucharest. Fumes from motor vehicles and factories combine to pollute the atmosphere in the urban areas. The Greek government controls the number of vehicles that come into Athens, but despite this, the air quality here is still bad. Mainland Greece and the islands in the Aegean Sea are centres of a thriving tourist trade, while tourism on the Black Sea coast is growing steadily.

LAND HEIGHT

4,000 m
13,124 ft

2,000 m
6,562 ft

1,000 m
3,281 ft

500 m
1,640 ft

200 m
656 ft

Sea level

UKRAINE

Databani
Botosani
Satu Mare
Baia Mare
Suceava
Zalau
Bistrita
Iasi
MOLDOVA
Oradea
Piatra-Neamt
Roman
R O M A N I A
Cluj-Napoca
Miercurea
Turda
Ciuc
Bacau
Targu Mures
Sfantu
Vaslui
Alba Iulia
T R A N S Y L V A N I A
Medias
Gheorghe
Barlad
Arad
Deva
Fagaras
Timisoara
Hunedoara
Sibiu
Focsani
Caransebes
Brasov
Galati
Zrenjanin
Resita
Transylvanian Alps
Braila
Zemun
Ramnicu Valcea
Buzau
Tulcea
Danube
Delta
Pancevo
Danube
Targu Jiu
Pitesti
Ploiesti
BELGRADE
Drobeta-Turnu
Targoviste
SERBIA &
Severin
Slatina
BUCHAREST
Slobozia
Craiova
W A L A C H I A
Constanta
Cacak
Kragujevac
Vidin
Calarasi
Alexandria
Giurgiu
Zajecar
Calafat
Islaz
Ruse
Dobrich
Kraljevo
Krusevac
Montana
Danube
Razgrad
SERBIA
Aleksinac
Iskur
Pleven
Shumen
Nis
Vratsa
Lovech
Veliko Turnovo
Varna
MONTENEGRO
Leskovac
Balkan
Gabrovo
Kosovska
Mountains
Sliven
Mitrovica
SOFIA
Stara Zagora
Nesebur
Pristina
Pernik
Burgas
KOSOVO
Urosevac
Vranje
B U L G A R I A
Yambol
Prizren
Kumanovo
Musala
Pazardzhik
Plovdiv
Tsarevo
Tetovo
2,925 m
Blagoevgrad
SKOPJE
Khaskovo
Likes
Gostivar
Stip
Kocani
Rhodope
Gorab
Veles
Mountains
Kurdzhali
153 m
M A C E D O N I A
Marikostinovo
Kicevo
A x i o s
Strumica
Drama
Komotini
Evros
Ohrid
Prilep
M A C E D O N I A
Serres
Xanthi
T H R A C E
Bitola
Kilkis
Kavala
Alexandroupoli
Lake
Lake
Edessa
Sea of
Ohrid
Prespa
Thessaloniki
Thasos
Marmara
Korce
Veroia
Kozani
Chalkidiki
Samothrace
Kastoria
Katerini
Smolikas
Olympus
Singitic Gulf
Limnus
2,637 m
2,917 m
Gulf of Kassandra
Grevena
A e g e a n
Larisa
S e a
annina
Pineios
Volos
THESSALY
Lesbos
Pindus
Karditsa
Northern
Sporades
Mytilini
Arta
Lamia
Skyros
Preveza
Loutra Edipsou
Psara
Lefkada
Kifisos
Kymi
G R E E C E
Itea
Euboea
Chios
Mesolongi
Chalkida
Chios
Patra
Gulf of Corinth
Karystos
Samos
argoli
Corinth
Piraeus
ATHENS
Andros
Ikaria
Samos
Gastouni
Lavrio
Tinos
kynthos
Pyrgos
Nafplio
Mykonos
Kalymnos
akynthos
Tripoli
Ermoupoli
Kos
Kyparissiakos
Leonidi
C y c l a d e s
Serifos
Paros
Naxos
Kolpos
Sparta
Mirtoan
Sifnos
Naxos
Amorgos
Tilos
Rhodes
Kalamata
Gytheio
Sea
Milos
Ios
Dodecanese
Lindos
Pylos
Neapoli
Santorini
Rhodes
Megisti
Gulf of Messina
Kythira
Sea of
Karpathos
Crete
Chania
Crete
Iraklejo
Kasos
Rethymno
Agios
Nikolaos

UKRAINE

Black
Sea

TURKEY

AFRICA

Africa, the world's second-largest continent, is separated from Asia by the Red Sea and from Europe by the Mediterranean Sea. A major feature of this huge landmass is the Sahara, the planet's biggest desert. South of the Sahara, the landscape consists mainly of broad plateaux, broken by the basins of major rivers, such as the Congo and the Zambezi. The Great Rift Valley cuts through the uplands of east Africa. Some of the rivers have dramatic waterfalls, such as the Victoria Falls, where the Zambezi plunges into

a chasm more than 120 m deep. Africa also has high mountains, such as the Atlas range in the northwest and the Drakensberg in the south.

Most experts believe that the human race first evolved in Africa, but the continent's long history has been a troubled one. In the 19th century, European powers such as Britain, France and Belgium took over much of the continent. Most areas won independence from their foreign rulers in the 1960s, to create 53 separate African nations. These contain many different peoples, and have a rich variety

of languages. A number of countries, however, have struggled to develop as modern states.

Some African countries rely on income from a single 'cash crop', such as oranges, olives or sugar cane. This means that their economies suffer badly if prices for the crop decrease or the harvests fail. The continent's rapidly rising population is often hit hard by famine, and some countries have suffered war. Africa also has lots of advantages, from its plentiful natural resources to some of the planet's most spectacular scenery and fascinating wildlife.

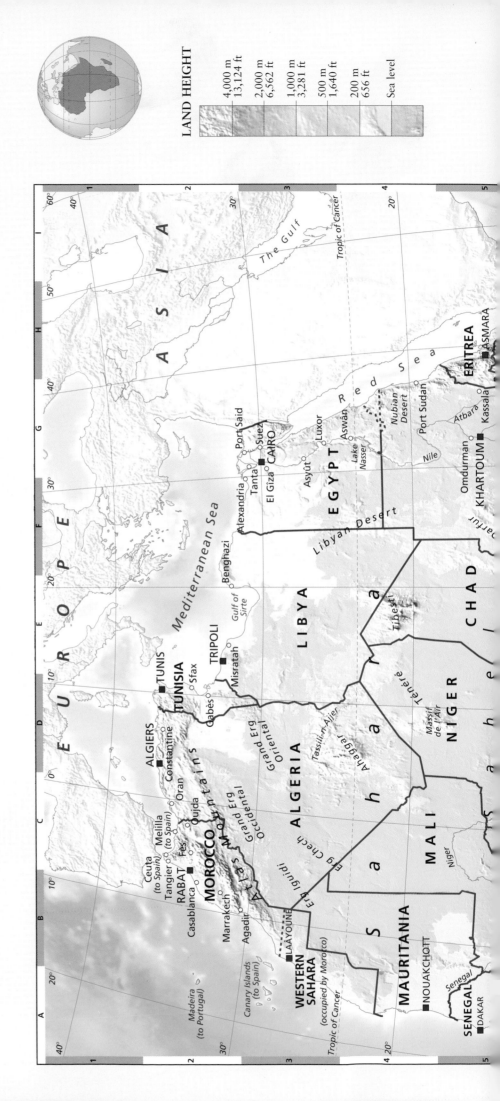

LAND HEIGHT

4,000 m	13,124 ft
2,000 m	6,562 ft
1,000 m	3,281 ft
500 m	1,640 ft
200 m	656 ft
Sea level	

SUDAN
ETHIOPIA
SOMALIA
DJIBOUTI
KENYA
UGANDA
RWANDA
BURUNDI
TANZANIA
CENTRAL AFRICAN REPUBLIC
DEMOCRATIC REPUBLIC OF CONGO
CONGO
GABON
CAMEROON
EQUATORIAL GUINEA
SÃO TOMÉ & PRÍNCIPE
NIGERIA
BENIN
TOGO
GHANA
IVORY COAST
LIBERIA
SIERRA LEONE
GUINEA
ANGOLA
ZAMBIA
MALAWI
MOZAMBIQUE
ZIMBABWE
BOTSWANA
NAMIBIA
SOUTH AFRICA
LESOTHO
SWAZILAND
MADAGASCAR
COMOROS
ATLANTIC OCEAN
INDIAN OCEAN
Gulf of Guinea
Gulf of Aden
Mozambique Channel
Equator
Tropic of Capricorn
Great Rift Valley
Congo Basin
Kalahari Desert
Namib Desert
Skeleton Coast
Ethiopian Highlands
Adamawa Highlands
Bié Plateau
Masai Steppe
Horn of Africa
Ogaden
Drakensberg
Cape of Good Hope
Cape Agulhas
Lake Victoria
Lake Tanganyika
Lake Nyasa
Lake Turkana
Lake Volta
Okavango Delta
Victoria Falls
Kilimanjaro 5,895 m
Kirinyaga 5,199 m
MOGADISHU
ADDIS ABABA
NAIROBI
KAMPALA
KIGALI
BUJUMBURA
DODOMA
KINSHASA
BRAZZAVILLE
BANGUI
NDJAMENA
YAOUNDÉ
LIBREVILLE
MALABO
SÃO TOMÉ
ABUJA
PORTO-NOVO
LOMÉ
ACCRA
YAMOUSSOUKRO
MONROVIA
FREETOWN
CONAKRY
BISSAU
BAMAKO
OUAGADOUGOU
LUANDA
LUSAKA
LILONGWE
HARARE
MAPUTO
MBABANE
PRETORIA
GABORONE
WINDHOEK
MASERU
BLOEMFONTEIN
CAPE TOWN
ANTANANARIVO
MORONI
DJIBOUTI
Mombasa
Dar es Salaam
Zanzibar
Tanga
Arusha
Kismaayo
Hargeysa
Dire Dawa
Juba
Kisumu
Mwanza
Kisangani
Mbandaka
Kananga
Mbuji-Mayi
Lubumbashi
Kolwezi
Kasama
Kitwe
Ndola
Livingstone
Bulawayo
Gweru
Mutare
Blantyre
Beira
Quelimane
Nampula
Inhambane
Francistown
Johannesburg
Durban
Pietermaritzburg
East London
Port Elizabeth
Walvis Bay
Benguela
Huambo
Namibe
Pointe-Noire
Port-Gentil
Douala
Port Harcourt
Aba
Benin City
Lagos
Ibadan
Ilorin
Kaduna
Zaria
Kano
Jos
Maiduguri
Abidjan
El Obeid
Toamasina
Mahajanga
Fianarantsoa
Congo
Lualaba
Kasai
Cuango
Cuando
Cubango
Zambezi
Limpopo
Orange River
Vaal
Niger
Benue
Uele
Shebeli
Sudd
White Nile
Blue Nile
Chad
Ascension Island (to St Helena)
St Helena (to UK)
Aldabra Group (to Seychelles)
Mayotte (to France)
ANGOLA (CABINDA)
0 500 1000 miles
0 1000 2000 km

NORTHWEST AFRICA

Morocco, Algeria, Tunisia and Libya occupy the coast of northwestern Africa and part of the northern Sahara Desert. The region's uplands, including the Atlas Mountains, stretch from the north of Tunisia to the Atlantic coast of Morocco. Most of the people live in towns and villages on a fertile strip of land along the north coast, although Western Sahara and the southern parts of Algeria and Libya are thinly populated by Tuareg nomads.

On the coast, farmers grow grapes and olives, or raise sheep and goats. The bark of the cork tree is harvested in Morocco and Algeria, and dates are grown at oases in the desert. This region has a thriving textile industry, producing colourful rugs and fabrics, and in the past few decades, oil and natural gas have brought wealth to Libya. Tourism is also a strong industry in the area, with ancient cities and hot weather attracting many overseas visitors.

The main environmental problem in northwest Africa is the northward spread of the Sahara Desert due to droughts and the cutting down of trees and plants for fuel and animal food. As a result, farmers are losing land, and they are forced to overgraze the existing pastures. This puts more stress on the land, and leads to the further expansion of the desert.

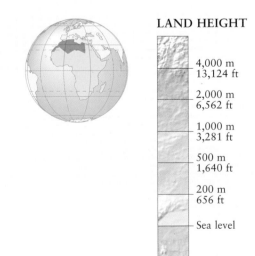

LAND HEIGHT

	4,000 m 13,124 ft
	2,000 m 6,562 ft
	1,000 m 3,281 ft
	500 m 1,640 ft
	200 m 656 ft
	Sea level

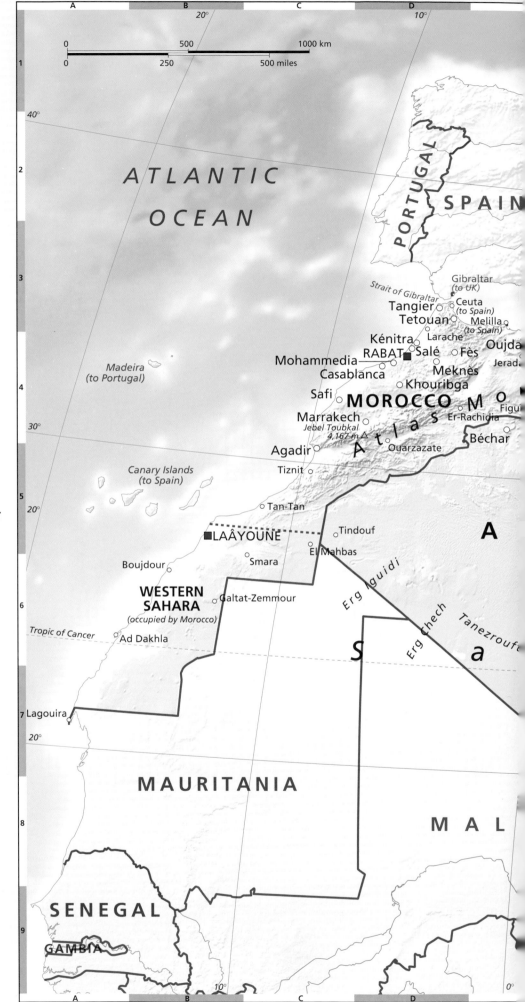

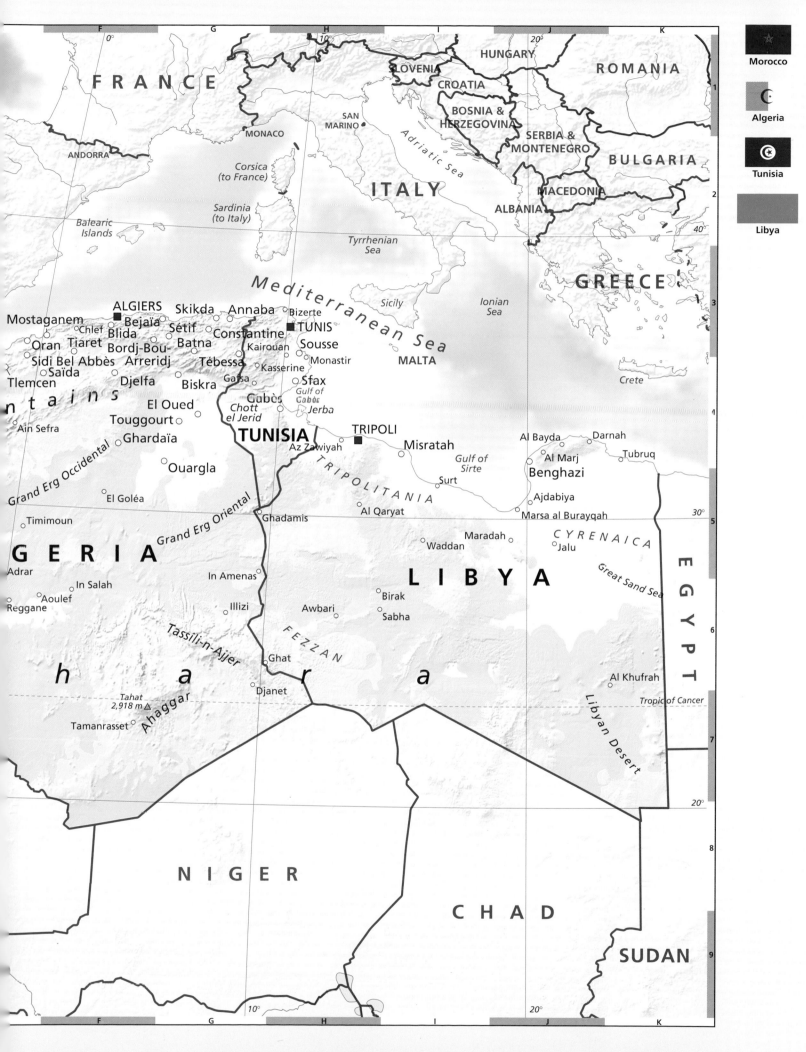

Morocco

Algeria

Tunisia

Libya

FRANCE

ANDORRA

MONACO

SAN MARINO

Corsica (to France)

Sardinia (to Italy)

Balearic Islands

ITALY

SLOVENIA

CROATIA

BOSNIA & HERZEGOVINA

SERBIA & MONTENEGRO

ALBANIA

MACEDONIA

HUNGARY

ROMANIA

BULGARIA

GREECE

Adriatic Sea

Tyrrhenian Sea

Sicily

MALTA

Ionian Sea

Crete

Mediterranean Sea

Mostaganem

ALGIERS

Chlef

Blida

Oran

Tiaret

Sidi Bel Abbès

Saïda

Tlemcen

Bejaïa

Sétif

Bordj-Bou-
Arreridj

Djelfa

Skikda

Annaba

Constantine

Batna

Tébessa

Biskra

Bizerte

TUNIS

Kairouan

Sousse

Monastir

Kasserine

Sfax

Gafsa

Gabès

Jerba

Gulf of Gabès

Chott el Jerid

TUNISIA

El Oued

Touggourt

Ain Sefra

Ghardaïa

Ouargla

El Goléa

Timimoun

Grand Erg Occidental

Grand Erg Oriental

Ghadamis

GERIA

Adrar

In Salah

Aoulef

Reggane

In Amenas

Illizi

Tassili-n-Ajjer

Ghat

FEZZAN

Djanet

Tahat 2,918 m △

Ahaggar

Tamanrasset

h   a   r   a

Az Zawiyah

TRIPOLI

Misratah

Surt

TRIPOLITANIA

Al Qaryat

Waddan

Maradah

Birak

Awbari

Sabha

LIBYA

Gulf of Sirte

Al Bayda

Al Marj

Benghazi

Ajdabiya

Marsa al Burayqah

Darnah

Tubruq

CYRENAICA

Jalu

Great Sand Sea

Libyan Desert

Al Khufrah

EGYPT

Tropic of Cancer

NIGER

CHAD

SUDAN

40°

30°

20°

0°

10°

20°

10°

20°

NORTHEAST AFRICA

The land in the northeastern part of Africa is mainly arid. To the north, Egypt and northern Sudan are desert areas. Only the Nile valley provides a narrow strip of fertile soil, where people can live and farm. Smaller deserts lie in Somalia, Ethiopia and Djibouti. There are some forests on Ethiopia's highlands, but much of the rest of this region is covered by dry scrubland and the occasional tree.

People settled in northeast Africa over 6,000 years ago, and by about 3000 BCE, one of the greatest early civilizations was established in

Egypt. For much of its history, this region was an important international centre of trade, with great cities and monuments. In 1867, the Suez Canal was opened to provide a shipping link between the Red and Mediterranean Seas.

Today, there are few big cities in northeast Africa, and most people live in the countryside and work the land. Farmers have to grow what crops they can in this hot, dry environment, where rainfall is rare and many rivers dry up for much of the year. Cotton and sugar cane are grown along the Nile river, dates grow well in

oases in the desert, and coffee is Ethiopia's main crop. Sheep, goats and cattle are raised on the grasslands, while the region's factories process food. There is also a local textile industry.

In the past few decades, life has been very hard for the people of this region. Rapid population growth has forced farmers to clear land to grow food and to cut down trees for fuel. The removal of trees and plants has allowed the wind to erode the soil, turning large areas into desert. A series of famines and wars have brought death and suffering to millions of people in this area.

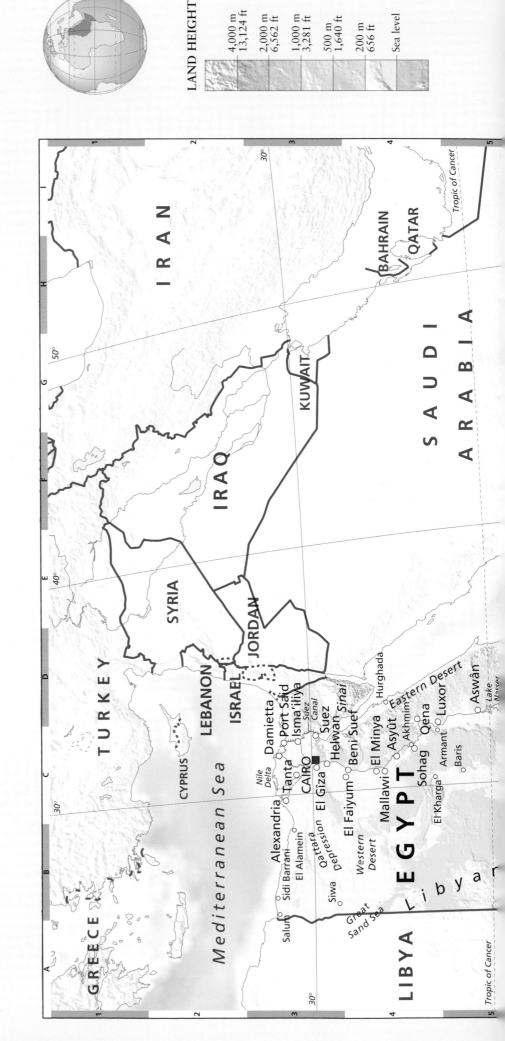

LAND HEIGHT

4,000 m / 13,124 ft
2,000 m / 6,562 ft
1,000 m / 3,281 ft
500 m / 1,640 ft
200 m / 656 ft
Sea level

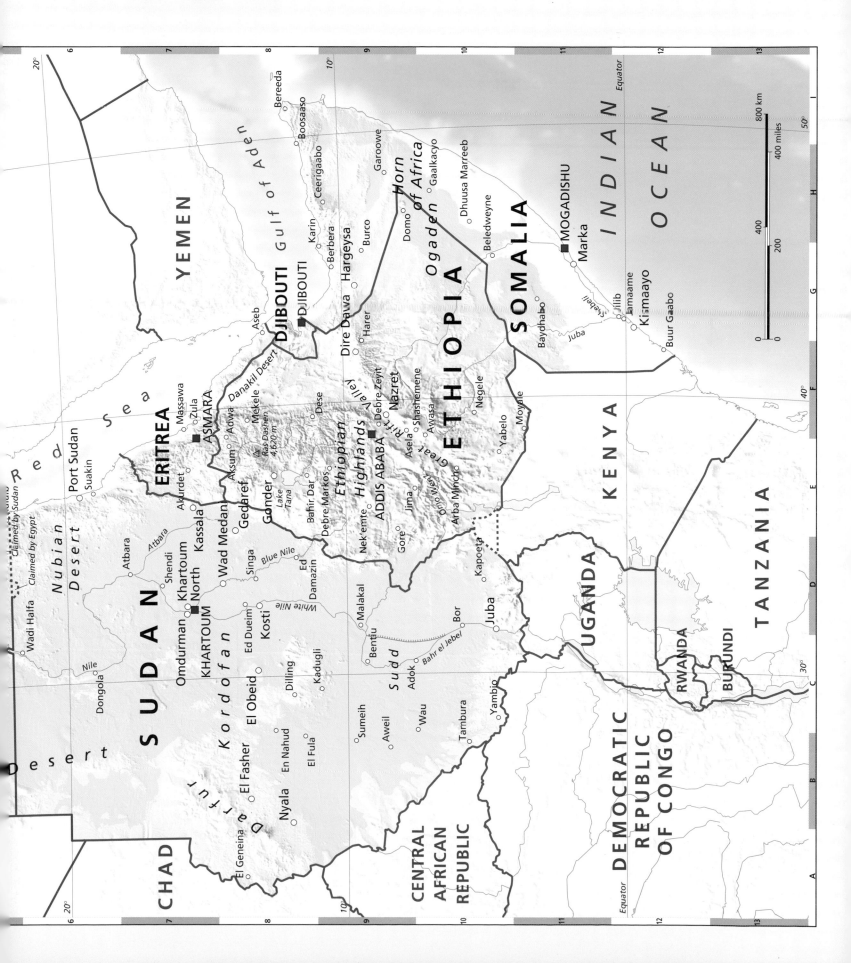

Egypt
Sudan
Eritrea
Ethiopia
Djibouti
Somalia

20°

I

6   7   8   9   10   11   12   13

10°

Equator

50°

800 km

400 miles

400

200

0

H

Bereeda

Boosaaso

G u l f   o f   A d e n

Garoowe

Ceerigaabo

Horn

of Africa

Gaalkacyo

I N D I A N

O C E A N

YEMEN

Karin

Bereda

Burco

Dhuusa Marreeb

MOGADISHU

G

Berbera

Hargeysa

Domo

Beledweyne

Marka

Aseb

DJIBOUTI

Dire Dawa

Harer

Ogaden

SOMALIA

Jilib

Lamaame

Kismaayo

Buur Gaabo

DJIBOUTI

G u l f   o f   A d e n

Shebeli

Bayrdhabo

Juba

F

Red
Sea

Massawa

Zula

Adwa

Mekele

Dese

Debre Zeyit

Nazret

Negele

40°

Port Sudan

Suakin

ASMARA

Aksum

Ras Dashen
4,620 m

Debre Zeyit

Shashemene

Moyale

E

ERITREA

Akurdet

Ethiopian

Highlands

ADDIS ABABA

Awasa

Yabelo

KENYA

Gonder

Asela

Arba Minch

Atbara

Atbara

Gedaref

Bahir Dar

Nek'emte

Jima

Omo Wenz

Kapoeta

Wadi Halfa

Nubian

Desert

Shendi

Kassala

Lake
Tana

Debre Markos

Gore

D

Dongola

Nile

Omdurman

Khartoum
North

Wad Medani

Singa

Blue Nile

Ed
Damazin

Malakal

UGANDA

TANZANIA

KHARTOUM

Ed Dueim

White Nile

Bentiu

Bor

Juba

RWANDA

Kosti

SUDAN

Kordofan

El Obeid

Dilling

Kadugli

Sudd

Bahr el Jebel

Adok

BURUNDI

C

Desert

El Fasher

En Nahud

Sumeih

Wau

Yambio

DEMOCRATIC

REPUBLIC

OF CONGO

30°

B

Nyala

El Geneina

El Fula

Aweil

Tambura

CENTRAL

AFRICAN

REPUBLIC

CHAD

Equator

A

20°

6   7   8   9   10   11   12   13

WEST AFRICA

In the northern part of this region, the edge of the Sahara meets a wide band of semi-desert scrubland called the Sahel, which stretches from Mauritania to Niger. South of the Sahel is a strip of grassland and further south, along the coast, is a region of land where higher rainfall feeds areas of tropical rainforest. Many rivers cross the southern half of this area. The longest of these is the Niger, which forms a vast, swampy delta at the coast.

Cash crops such as cotton, cocoa and peanuts are grown throughout the southern part of this region. Further north, farmers raise sheep and goats, and grow food crops such as yams and cassava. The biggest industries are connected with food – the processing of nuts to extract oil, for example. Many people in Nigeria also work in the chemical industry, or on wells that tap the region's rich supplies of gas and oil.

West Africa is an area with large deposits of minerals, ranging from iron ore to diamonds. In the past, it has been home to successful civilizations, such as the empires of Mali and Asante, which benefited from these resources. In spite of new wealth from oil and tourism, most west Africans remain poor. Their lives are made difficult by frequent droughts and the growth of the desert in the north of the region.

LAND HEIGHT

	4,000 m 13,124 ft
	2,000 m 6,562 ft
	1,000 m 3,281 ft
	500 m 1,640 ft
	200 m 656 ft
	Sea level

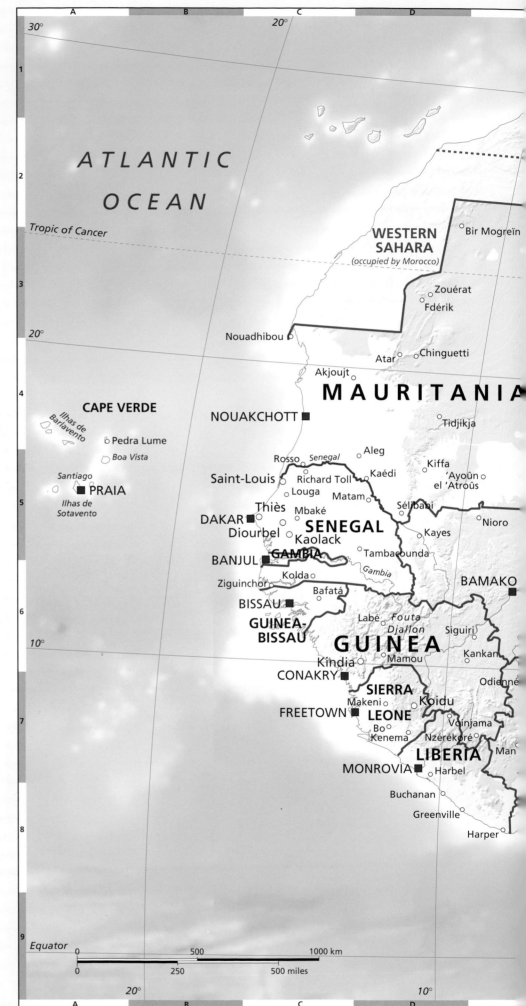

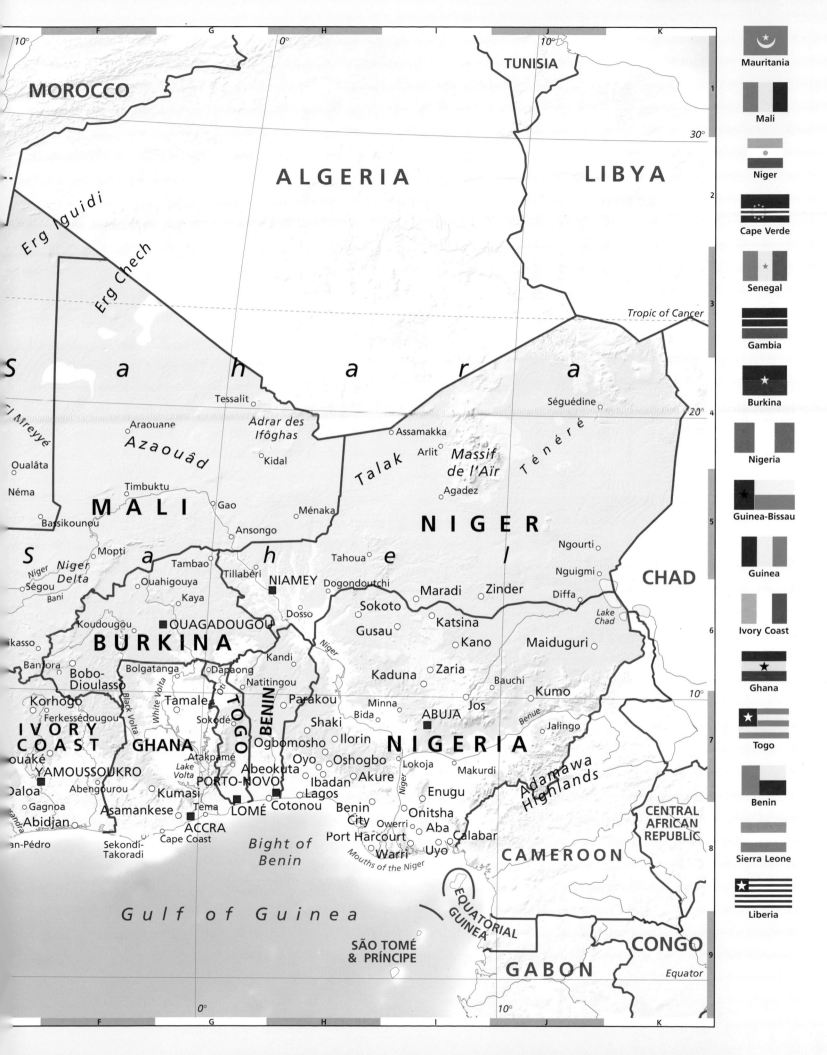

MOROCCO

TUNISIA

ALGERIA

LIBYA

Erg Iguidi

Erg Chech

Tropic of Cancer

S a h a r a

Tessalit

Séguédine

Araouane

Adrar des Ifôghas

Assamakka

El Mreyyé

Oualâta

Kidal

Arlit

Massif de l'Aïr

Ténéré

Azaouâd

Talak

Néma

Timbuktu

Agadez

Bassikounou

Gao

M A L I

Ansongo

N I G E R

CHAD

S a h e l

Mopti

Niger Delta

Tambao

Tahoua

Ngourti

Ségou

Tillabéri

NIAMEY

Dogondoutchi

Nguigmi

Bani

Ouahigouya

Maradi

Zinder

Diffa

Koudougou

Kaya

Dosso

Sokoto

Lake Chad

ikasso

OUAGADOUGOU

Gusau

Katsina

Maiduguri

BURKINA

Kandi

Niger

Kano

Banfora

Bolgatanga

Dapaong

Natitingou

Kaduna

Zaria

Bauchi

Bobo-Dioulasso

Parakou

Minna

Kumo

Korhogo

White Volta

Black Volta

Tamale

TOGO

BENIN

Shaki

Bida

ABUJA

Jos

Benue

Jalingo

Ferkessédougou

Sokodé

Ogbomosho

Ilorin

NIGERIA

IVORY COAST

GHANA

Atakpamé

Oyo

Oshogbo

Lokoja

Makurdi

Adamawa Highlands

ouaké

YAMOUSSOUKRO

Lake Volta

Abeokuta

Ibadan

Akure

Enugu

CENTRAL AFRICAN REPUBLIC

Daloa

Abengourou

Kumasi

PORTO-NOVO

Lagos

Niger

Gagnoa

Asamankese

Tema

LOMÉ

Cotonou

Benin City

Onitsha

Aba

Abidjan

ACCRA

Owerri

Calabar

an-Pédro

Sekondi-Takoradi

Cape Coast

Port Harcourt

Uyo

CAMEROON

Bight of Benin

Warri

Mouths of the Niger

EQUATORIAL GUINEA

CONGO

Gulf of Guinea

SÃO TOMÉ & PRÍNCIPE

GABON

Equator

Mauritania

Mali

Niger

Cape Verde

Senegal

Gambia

Burkina

Nigeria

Guinea-Bissau

Guinea

Ivory Coast

Ghana

Togo

Benin

Sierra Leone

Liberia

CENTRAL AND EAST AFRICA

This region extends from Africa's Atlantic coast to the Indian Ocean. In the west is the Congo, the continent's second-longest river. Its basin is covered by the Earth's largest tropical rainforest. So far, this area has survived well, but some parts of it are being cut away. In the east is the Great Rift Valley, which runs from the north to the south, and cuts through the uplands and grasslands of Uganda and Tanzania. The Nile river rises in the uplands, and flows north on its way to the Mediterranean Sea.

To the west, among the dense forests of the Democratic Republic of Congo, rubber and oil palm trees are grown in large plantations. The Congo river and its many tributaries provide a source of fish for the local people. Elsewhere, cattle and goats are herded. In the east, farmers grow crops for export, such as vegetables and coffee.

The Democratic Republic of Congo mines its rich supplies of copper, diamonds, silver and cobalt. Other countries, such as Kenya, have developed manufacturing industries. Tourism is growing steadily in Kenya and Tanzania, where each year, thousands of overseas visitors come to visit the countries' amazing wildlife. Although the tourist industry employs a great number of people here, most of the population still makes its living from the land.

LAND HEIGHT

4,000 m
13,124 ft

2,000 m
6,562 ft

1,000 m
3,281 ft

500 m
1,640 ft

200 m
656 ft

Sea level

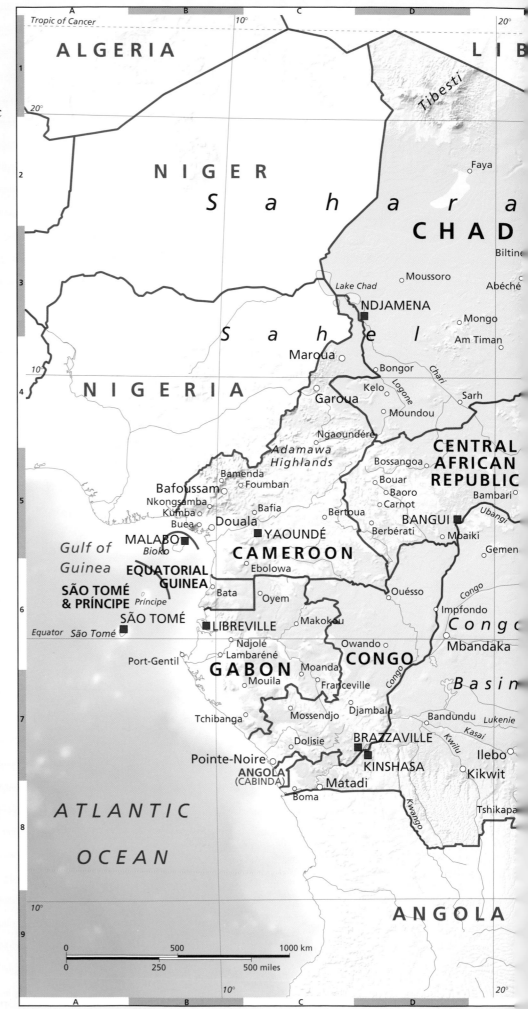

EGYPT

SAUDI
ARABIA

20°

SUDAN

ERITREA

YEMEN

DJIBOUTI

Birao

ETHIOPIA

10°

Massif des Bongo

Bria

Bangassou

Obo

SOMALIA

Bondo

Uele

Watsa

Lodwar

Lake Turkana

Moyale

Bumba

Buta

Isiro

Aruwimi

Mungbere

Lira

Gulu

Moroto

Marsabit

Yangambi

Kisangani

Lake Albert

Masindi

Mbale

Eldoret

Meru

Equator

DEMOCRATIC

Tshuapa

Ikoli

KAMPALA

Entebbe

Tororo

Jinja

Kakamega

△ *Kirinyaga 5,199 m*

Nyeri

Garissa

REPUBLIC

Lake Edward

Mbarara

Kisumu

Nakuru

Thika

OF CONGO

Kindu

Lake Kivu

Goma

Kabale

Lake Victoria

NAIROBI

Machakos

Malindi

Kasongo

Bukavu

KIGALI

Serengeti Plain

△ *Kilimanjaro 5,895 m*

Kananga

Kabinda

BUJUMBURA

Mwanza

Moshi

Kongolo

BURUNDI

Shinyanga

Arusha

Pemba

Mombasa

Mbuji-Mayi

Kigoma

Tabora

Singida

Masai Steppe

Tanga

Kalémié

Lake Tanganyika

Mwene-Ditu

Kabalo

Mpanda

DODOMA

Zanzibar

Zanzibar

Kamina

Morogoro

Dar es Salaam

Sumbawanga

Iringa

Rufiji

Mafia

Kamina

Lake Mweru

Mbeya

Makumbako

Mohoro

Aldabra Group (to Seychelles)

Dilolo

Kolwezi

Likasi

Lake Nyasa

Masasi

Lindi

Songea

Ruvuma

Mtwara

Lubumbashi

COMOROS

Mayotte (to France)

ZAMBIA

MALAWI

MOZAMBIQUE

Chad

Cameroon

Central African Republic

Democratic Republic of Congo

Kenya

Uganda

Equatorial Guinea

Congo

São Tomé & Príncipe

Gabon

Rwanda

Tanzania

Burundi

SOUTHERN AFRICA

This region has a huge variety of scenery, from the parched Namib and Kalahari deserts of the west to the eastern grasslands and the Drakensberg mountains in the southeast. Off the eastern coast of southern Africa is Madagascar, a large island that split from the mainland about 1,345 million years ago. Madagascar's wildlife, from lemurs to chameleons, includes many species of plants and animals that cannot be found anywhere else in the world.

Cattle are farmed on the grasslands, while much of the land in the south is used for growing fruit for the export market. With rich deposits of precious minerals and metals, such as diamonds and gold, South Africa is the wealthiest part of this region. The country also has many other industries, including food canning, steel production, manufacturing and textiles. These types of businesses are found in other countries in southern Africa, but on a smaller scale.

In many areas, trees have been cut down for fuel, and the soils have been blown away, leaving barren, infertile deserts. The region also has political problems. For much of the 20th century, the black South Africans were denied basic human rights by the South African government. This system, known as apartheid, was abolished in 1994, when black South Africans were allowed to vote for the first time, and the country became a truly democratic state.

LAND HEIGHT

4,000 m
13,124 ft

2,000 m
6,562 ft

1,000 m
3,281 ft

500 m
1,640 ft

200 m
656 ft

Sea level

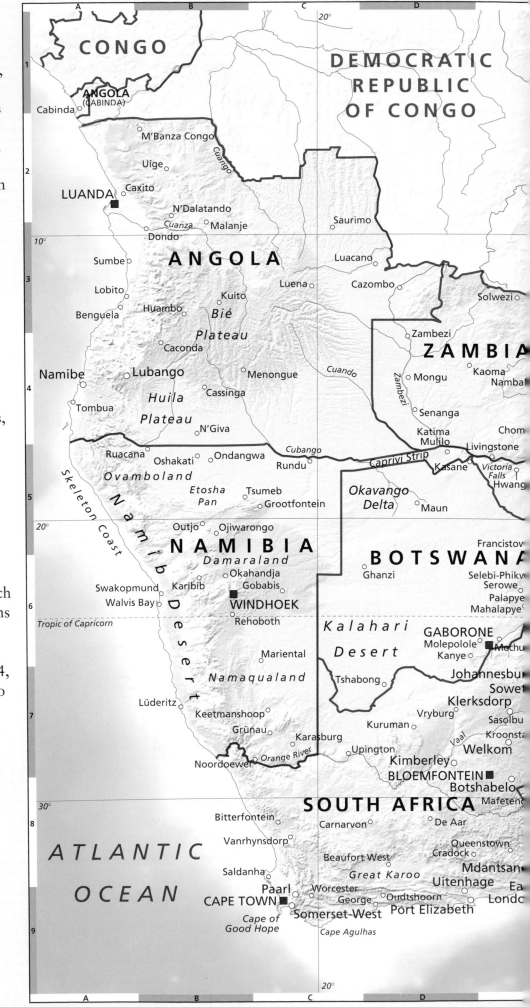

TANZANIA

INDIAN OCEAN

Great Rift Valley

Lake Mweru

Isoka

Lake Bangweulu

Kasama

Mansa   Samfya

Chingola

Mufulira   Mpika

Kitwe   Serenje

Ndola

Luanshya

Mzuzu

Chipata

MALAWI

Kabwe   LILONGWE

LUSAKA

Lake Cahora Bassa

Kafue

Mazabuka   Blantyre

Monze   Kariba

Lake Kariba

Chinhoyi   Bindura

Tete

Kadoma   HARARE   Chitungwiza

Kwekwe   Mutare

ZIMBABWE   Chimoio

Gweru   Dondo

Bulawayo   Masvingo   Beira

Gwanda

mpopo   Messina

MOZAMBIQUE

Pietersburg

Maxixe   Inhambane

Chokwe

RETORIA   Nelspruit   Macia   Xai-Xai

Benoni

Ermelo   MAPUTO

ereeniging   MBABANE   Maputo Bay

Manzini

SWAZILAND

Newcastle

Bethlehem   Ladysmith   Ulundi

ESOTHO

ASERU   Pietermaritzburg

akensberg   Durban

Umtata

Rovuma

Negomane

Mucojo

Pemba

Montepuez

Lichinga

Salima

Zomba

Cuamba

Mocambique

Nampula

Angoche

Mocuba

Gurué

Quelimane

Sofala Bay

Lake Nyasa

Zambezi

Lake

COMOROS

Grand Comore

MORONI

Mohéli   Anjouan

Mamoudzou

Mayotte (to France)

Aldabra Group (to Seychelles)

Antsiranana

Antalaha

Maroantsetra

Mahajanga

MADAGASCAR

Ambatosoratra   Fenoarivo

ANTANANARIVO   Toamasina

Betafo

Morondava   Antsirabe

Fianarantsoa   Mananjary

Ihosy

Toliara   Manakara

Vangaindrano

Tropic of Capricorn

Ambovombe

Tolanaro

Mozambique Channel

INDIAN OCEAN

30°

40°

10°

20°

30°

50°

1
2
3
4
5
6
7
8
9

F   G   H   I   J   K

SOUTH AFRICA'S THREE CAPITALS

PRETORIA – administrative capital

CAPE TOWN – legislative capital

BLOEMFONTEIN – judicial capital

0   300   600 km

0   150   300 miles

Angola

Zambia

Malawi

Mozambique

Comoros

Madagascar

Zimbabwe

Namibia

Botswana

South Africa

Swaziland

Lesotho

THE INDIAN OCEAN

From the coast of Africa in the west to Australia and the islands of southeast Asia in the east, the Indian Ocean measures almost 10,000 km across at its widest point. Under the water are three ridges that form an upside-down 'Y' shape. The ridges mark where three continental plates meet. Here, volcanic activity is common.

The climate of the Indian Ocean varies according to latitude. The regions in the north, near India, have a warm climate. In the south, freezing temperatures have created pack ice and icebergs. Monsoon winds bring heavy rainfall to many coastal countries. They also have an effect on the ocean's currents, which reverse direction completely between March and August.

For thousands of years, the Indian Ocean has provided important trade routes between the eastern and western parts of the world. Among the first traders to sail its waters were the ancient Egyptians, who travelled along the east African coast more than 4,000 years ago. In the 15th century, European explorers made pioneering journeys across the Indian Ocean to Asia. They were soon followed by merchants who brought back silks, spices and tea from India and China. Today, huge tankers carry oil from the Persian Gulf to many of the ocean's international ports. A large number of these boats travel along the Red Sea and through the Suez Canal to reach Europe.

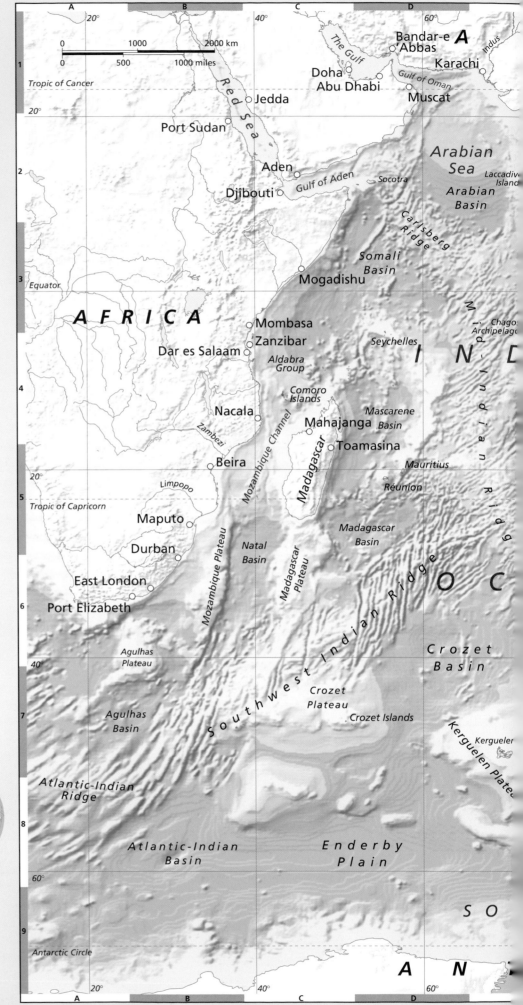

S I A

Ganges *Brahmaputra*

Chittagong

Sittwe

Irrawaddy

Salween

PACIFIC

Narmada

Tropic of Cancer

20°

Mumbai
(Bombay)

Godavari

Moulmein

OCEAN

Chennai
(Madras)

Bay of
Bengal

South
China
Sea

2

Cochin

*Andaman
Islands*

Trivandrum

*Andaman
Sea*

*Sri
Lanka*

*Nicobar
Islands*

Colombo

Maldives

Strait of Malacca

Lagos-Laccadive Plateau

Borneo

Equator

3

Padang

Sumatra

Ceylon
Plain

Ninetyeast Ridge

Investigator Ridge

Java Trench

Java

I A N

*Cocos
Islands*

*Christmas
Island*

4

Mid-Indian

North
Australian
Basin

Darwin

Basin

20°

Wharton
Basin

Tropic of Capricorn

5

E A N

AUSTRALIA

Perth
Basin

Broken Ridge

Perth

Great Australian
Bight

Adelaide

6

Amsterdam Island

South Australian
Basin

*St Paul
Island*

Southeast Indian Ridge

Melbourne

40°

Tasmania

Hobart

South Australian
Plain

Tasman
Plateau

7

*eard and
cDonald Islands*

8

South Indian
Basin

60°

H E R N   O C E A N

9

Antarctic Circle

A R C T I C A

ASIA

Stretching from the Black Sea in the west to Japan in the east, Asia is the world's largest continent. There are many types of landscapes, from the snowy Mount Everest, the world's highest mountain, to the Arabian Desert. Uplands stretch across much of the middle of Asia and there are great rivers, such as China's Yangtze and India's Ganges. The Earth's lowest place, the Dead Sea, is located on the border of Israel and Jordan.

Asia has a variety of peoples with many different beliefs, languages and lifestyles. The huge communist state of China is the most populous country in the world. India, with over 1 billion people, is the world's largest democratic nation. The break-up of the Soviet Union, which stretched from the eastern edge of the Russian Federation to Iran, created four countries in central Asia – Kazakhstan, Kyrgyzstan, Tajikistan and Turkmenistan. These, and the older states to the west, are mainly Muslim nations.

Few people live in the cold and windswept areas of central and northern Asia. Those who inhabit these regions are often poor, and live without many of the luxuries of modern life. Further south are some of the world's major cities, such as Mumbai, Beijing and Tokyo. The cities and countries of western Asia have grown rich from oil, while those of the Pacific coast have modern industries that have brought a high standard of living to many people.

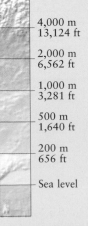

LAND HEIGHT

4,000 m
13,124 ft

2,000 m
6,562 ft

1,000 m
3,281 ft

500 m
1,640 ft

200 m
656 ft

Sea level

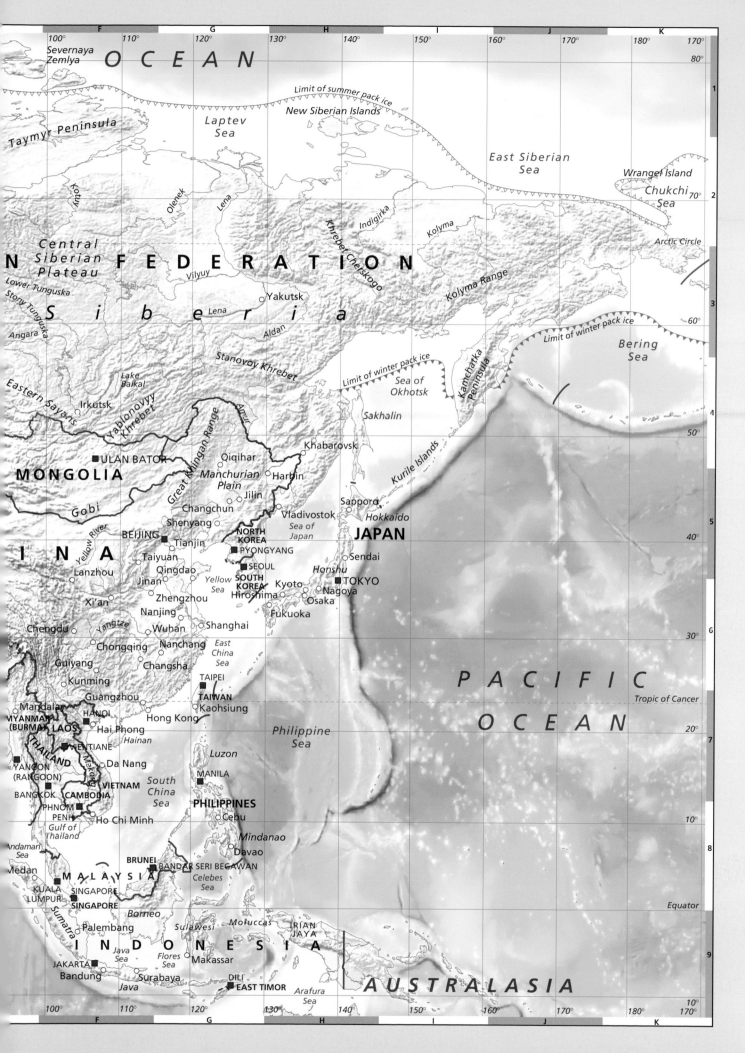

O C E A N

Severnaya
Zemlya

80°

Limit of summer pack ice

New Siberian Islands

1

Taymyr Peninsula

Laptev
Sea

East Siberian
Sea

Wrangel Island

Chukchi
Sea

70°

2

Central
N Siberian
Plateau

F E D E R A T I O N

Kotuy

Olenek

Lena

Vilyuy

Indigirka

Khrebet Cherskogo

Kolyma

Kolyma Range

Arctic Circle

Lower Tunguska

S i b e r i a

Yakutsk

3

Stony Tunguska

Lena

60°

Angara

Aldan

Limit of winter pack ice

Bering
Sea

Stanovoy Khrebet

Kamchatka Peninsula

Limit of winter pack ice

Eastern Sayans

Lake
Baikal

Yablonovyy
Khrebet

Amur

Sea of
Okhotsk

Sakhalin

4

Irkutsk

50°

ULAN BATOR

Qiqihar

Khabarovsk

Kurile Islands

Great Khingan Range

Manchurian
Plain

Harbin

MONGOLIA

Jilin

Sapporo

Hokkaido

Gobi

Changchun

Vladivostok

Sea of
Japan

JAPAN

5

Shenyang

Yellow River

BEIJING

Tianjin

NORTH
KOREA

40°

I N A

Taiyuan

PYONGYANG

Sendai

Lanzhou

Qingdao

SEOUL

Honshu

Jinan

Yellow
Sea

SOUTH
KOREA

Kyoto

TOKYO

Zhengzhou

Hiroshima

Nagoya

Xi'an

Osaka

Nanjing

Fukuoka

Chengdu

Yangtze

Wuhan

Shanghai

6

Chongqing

Nanchang

East
China
Sea

30°

Guiyang

Changsha

Kunming

TAIPEI

Guangzhou

TAIWAN

Tropic of Cancer

Mandalay

HANOI

Kaohsiung

MYANMAR
(BURMA)

LAOS

Hai Phong

Hong Kong

20°

7

THAILAND

VIENTIANE

Hainan

Philippine
Sea

YANGON
(RANGOON)

Da Nang

Luzon

BANGKOK

CAMBODIA

VIETNAM

South
China
Sea

MANILA

PHNOM
PENH

Ho Chi Minh

PHILIPPINES

10°

Gulf of
Thailand

Cebu

Andaman
Sea

Mindanao

8

Medan

BRUNEI

Davao

MALAYSIA

BANDAR SERI BEGAWAN

Celebes
Sea

KUALA
LUMPUR

SINGAPORE

Equator

SINGAPORE

Borneo

Sumatra

Palembang

Sulawesi

Moluccas

IRIAN
JAYA

9

I N D O N E S I A

Java
Sea

Flores
Sea

Makassar

JAKARTA

Bandung

Surabaya

DILI

10°

Java

EAST TIMOR

Arafura
Sea

A U S T R A L A S I A

P A C I F I C

O C E A N

THE RUSSIAN FEDERATION

The western part of the Russian Federation falls in Europe, while the area east of the Ural Mountains is in Asia. Just east of the mountains is a flat region of marshes and streams, called the West Siberian Plain. The plain gradually rises to the Central Siberian Plateau, and then again to highlands in the south and east. Great coniferous forests cover most of this land. Much of European Russia lies on the North European Plain. This region is covered in large forests of birch and pine trees, and is watered by several great rivers, including the Volga. In the far north is frozen tundra.

In the east, a cold climate and harsh living conditions keep the population low. Many of those who do live here herd reindeer or work in forestry. The majority of people live in the west, where farmers grow root crops and wheat. This part of the country is highly industrialized, producing goods such as chemicals, cars and textiles. The region is also one of Europe's main sources of oil.

The Russian Federation was created when the communist Soviet Union broke up in 1991. The communists controlled farming, and they developed heavy industries, many of which caused pollution. Today, the country is modernizing its industries, and tackling the environmental problems caused during the Soviet period.

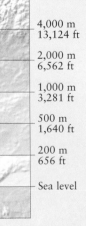

LAND HEIGHT

4,000 m
13,124 ft

2,000 m
6,562 ft

1,000 m
3,281 ft

500 m
1,640 ft

200 m
656 ft

Sea level

Russian Federation

ARCTIC OCEAN

UNITED STATES OF AMERICA
(ALASKA)

Bering Strait

Chukchi
Sea

Wrangel
Island

Bering
Sea

Arctic Circle

Franz Josef Land

Ostrov
Komsomolets
Ostrov
Oktyabrskoy
Revolyutsii
Ostrov
Bolshevik

Severnaya
Zemlya

New
Siberian
Islands

East Siberian
Sea

Pevek

Anadyr

Cherskiy

Laptev
Sea

Taymyr
Peninsula

Tiksi

Olenek

Kotuy

Indigirka

Kolyma

Khrebet Cherskogo

Gora
Pobeda
△ 3,003 m

Kolyma Range

Palana

Ust-Kamchatsk

Sopka Klyuchevskaya
4,750 m

Gydanskiy
Poluostrov

Dudinka

Norilsk

Siberia

Central

Verkhoyanskiy Khrebet

Lena

Magadan

Kamchatka
Peninsula

Urengoy
Turukhansk

Yenisey

Lower Tunguska

Siberian
Plateau

Tura

Vilyuy

Yakutsk

Aldan

Petropavlovsk
Kamchatskiy

Sea of
Okhotsk

Bor

Stony Tunguska

Mirnyy

Olekminsk

RUSSIAN FEDERATION

Kurile Islands

Angara

Ust-Ilimsk

Lena

Olekma

Aldan

Stanovoy Khrebet

Berkakit

Nogliki

Tomsk

Kansk

Bratsk

Severobaykalsk

Tynda

Komsomolsk-
na-Amure

Sakhalin

Kemerovo

Prokopyevsk

Krasnoyarsk

Eastern Sayans

Angarsk

Vitim

Svobodnyy

Belogorsk

Sovetskaya
Gavan

Yuzhno-
Sakhalinsk

Novokuznetsk

Blagoveshchensk

Khabarovsk

Biysk

Abakan

Lake Baikal

Chita

Karymskoye

Amur

Bikin

Gorno-Altaysk

Kyzyl

Gora Munku-
Sardyk
3,492 m

Irkutsk

Ulan-Ude

Khilok

Yablonovyy Khrebet

Aginskoye

Ussuriysk

A Gora Belukha
4,506 m

Mountains

MONGOLIA

Vladivostok

Nakhodka

Sea of
Japan

NORTH
KOREA

JAPAN

SOUTH
KOREA

CHINA

0   500   1000 km

0   250   500 miles

WEST ASIA

In the north of west Asia lie the Taurus Mountains and the plateau of Anatolia. The eastern part of this region is also dominated by uplands, including the Elburz and Zagros Mountains. In the south is the huge Arabian Peninsula, which is separated from the rest of Asia by the valleys of the Tigris and Euphrates rivers. Mountains run along the peninsula's Red Sea coast, and much of the rest of this region is covered in dry, barren deserts.

West Asia has a long history. Some of the world's first great civilizations developed in Iraq about 5,000 years ago, and the Arabian Peninsula was the home of the prophet Muhammad, and the first Muslims. This region is still mainly Muslim, although it also contains the Jewish state of Israel.

Oil and natural gas are important sources of income for many of the countries in west Asia. Other industries produce a range of goods, from industrial machinery in Georgia to carpets in Iran. Cattle and sheep are raised in the north, while goats are herded on the southern tip of the Arabian Peninsula. Hazelnuts are the main crop along the Black Sea coast, root crops are produced in Anatolia, and olives, figs, grapes and peaches are cultivated on Turkey's southern coast. Wheat is harvested in the fertile valleys of the Euphrates and Tigris rivers. Cotton, dates and fruits for the export market are also grown here.

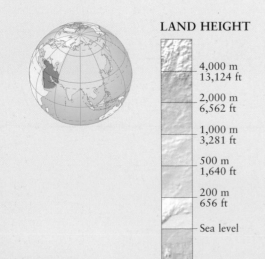

LAND HEIGHT

4,000 m	13,124 ft
2,000 m	6,562 ft
1,000 m	3,281 ft
500 m	1,640 ft
200 m	656 ft
Sea level	

RUSSIAN FEDERATION
Sokhumi
40
GEORGIA
Kutaisi
Batumi
Hopa
Trabzon
Erzurum
Bitlis
Diyarbakir
Batman
Al Qamishli
Summel
Mosul
Al Jazirah
Dayr az Zawr
Abu Kamal
Tikrit
Samarra'
Ba'qubah
IRAQ
Karbala
An Najaf
Ar Ramadi
'Ar 'ar
Rafhah

Caucasus
Kazbek
5,047 m
Rustavi
TBILISI
Vanadzor
Gyumri
ARMENIA
YEREVAN
AZERBAIJAN
Naxçivan
Lake
Van
Van
Khvoy
Orumiyeh
Lake
Urmia
Al Hasakah
Arbil
Kirkuk
BAGHDAD
Al Kut
Al Hillah
Tigris
An
Nasiriyah
Euphrates

KAZAKHSTAN
50
Sumqayit
BAKU
AZERBAIJAN
Tabriz
Ardabil
Zanjan
Maragheh
Saray
Ilam
Bukan
As Sulaymaniyah
Sanandaj
Hamadan
Bakhtaran
Arak
Saveh
Borujerd
Khorramabad
Dezful
Al Amarah
Najafabad
Ahvaz
Basra
Abadan
Khorramshahr
Al Qurnah
Kazerun

55
UZBEKISTAN
60
65
70
40
1
Rasht
Qazvin
Qolleh ye Damavand
5,881 m
Elburz
KARAJ
TEHRAN
Qom
Kashan
Esfahan
Qomisheh
Shiraz

TURKMENISTAN
Bojnurd
Gonbad-e Kavus
Babol
Gorgan
Neyshabur
Mashhad
Sari
Amol
Emamshahr
Sabzevar
Semnan
Garmsar
Mountains
Dasht-e Kavir
Gonabad
IRAN
Iranian
Plateau
Yazd
Kerman
Tabas
Birjand
35
2
AFGHANISTAN
3
Zabol
30
Zahedan
PAKISTAN
Bam
Sirjan
Iranshahr
Jask
Chabahar
25

Zagros Mountains

Nafud
Ha'il
Arabian
Buraydah
'Unayzah
Shaqra'
Peninsula
Al Kharj
Halaban
RIYADH
Zalim
Layla
SAUDI ARABIA
As Sulayyil
t Ta'if
Ar Rub' al Khali
(Empty Quarter)
Al Bahah
Tathlith
nfidhah
Abha
Najran
Jizan
YEMEN
SANA
Hodeida
Dhamar
Ibb
Ta'izz
Mocha
Zinjibar
Aden
Bab el Mandeb
DJIBOUTI
Gulf of Aden
45

Hafar al Batin
Al Wari'ah
Ad Dahna
Ad Dammam
Al Majma'ah
Dhahran
Ad Dahna
Al Hufuf
BAHRAIN
MANAMA
DOHA
QATAR
KUWAIT
KUWAIT
Al Ahmadi
The Gulf
Bandar-e Bushehr
Kangan
Bandar-e Lengeh
Bandar-e 'Abbas
Qeshm
Strait of Hormuz
Al Khasab
Ajman
Sharjah
Dubai
ABU DHABI
UNITED ARAB
EMIRATES
Fujairah
OMAN
Suhar
'Ayn
Ar Rustaq
'Ibri
Nizwa
MUSCAT
Gulf of
Oman
Tropic of Cancer
4
5
6
OMAN
20
Masirah
Gulf of
Masirah
Hayma'
Mughshin
Zufar
Raysut
Salalah
Al Mahrah
Nishtun
Sayhut
Hawra'
Shibam
Al Mukalla
Lawdar
Hadramawt
Arabian
Sea
Socotra
(to Yemen)
'Abd Al Kuri
50
'Abd Al Kuri
55
INDIAN
OCEAN
7
8
15
9
60

CENTRAL ASIA

A wall of mountains cuts through central Asia in a diagonal line from the Tien Shan in the northeast, through the Pamirs in the centre, to the Hindu Kush in the southwest. In the northwest are the sandy deserts of Uzbekistan and Turkmenistan. There are rolling grasslands in Kazakhstan, in the north. Central Asia receives very little rain and the region experiences extremes of temperature – winters are cold and summers are very hot.

With very few large cities, the peoples of central Asia live mainly in rural areas and make their living from the land. Farming is difficult in the desert and mountain regions, so agriculture is concentrated around the river valleys in the east. Here, a variety of cereals and fruits, including peaches, melons and apricots, are grown. Cotton, which is central Asia's main export, is grown on land irrigated by the Amu Darya river. Herds of cattle, sheep and goats are raised in the south and east, and on the grasslands of Kazakhstan in the north.

Fossil fuels, including oil, gas and coal, are extracted and processed throughout the region.

There are a number of traditional industries, which make products such as carpets and leather goods. The main industrial area is located in the east, in the Fergana Valley, where old-fashioned factories cause air pollution.

Once the fourth largest lake in the world, the Aral Sea has shrunk by almost half its size since 1960. This is because the rivers feeding the lake have been diverted to irrigate fields of cotton. The dry climate, combined with poor vegetation cover, means that desertification is another environmental problem in central Asia.

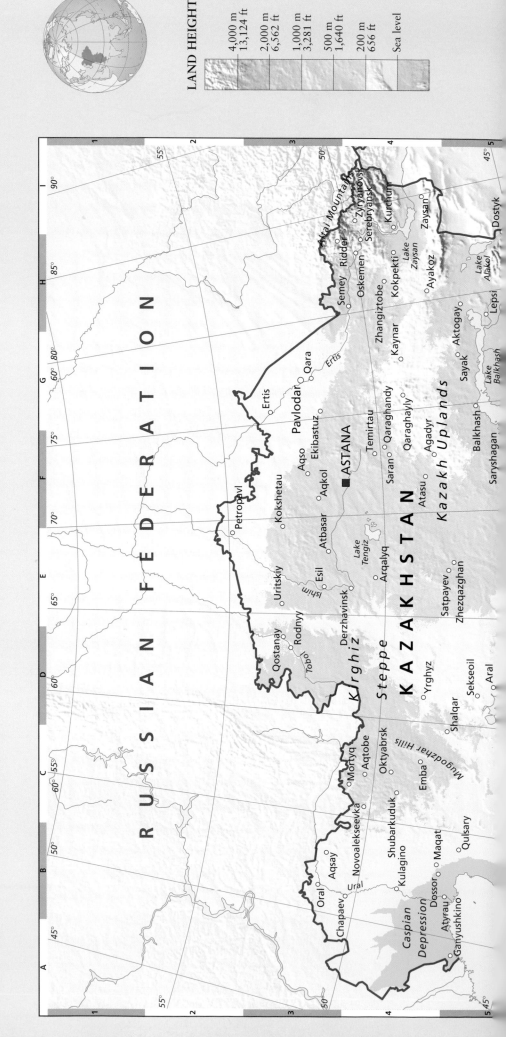

LAND HEIGHT

| 4,000 m 13,124 ft | 2,000 m 6,562 ft | 1,000 m 3,281 ft | 500 m 1,640 ft | 200 m 656 ft | Sea level |

Kazakhstan Uzbekistan Kyrgyzstan Turkmenistan Tajikistan Afghanistan Pakistan

SOUTH ASIA

South Asia is separated from the rest of Asia by the Thar Desert in the northwest and a wall of mountains, including the towering Himalayas, in the north and east. The great floodplains of the Ganges, Brahmaputra and Indus rivers lie at the foothills of the mountains. Further south are rolling plateaux, which are fringed by a line of coastal hills, called the Eastern and Western Ghats. To the southeast are the mountainous islands of Sri Lanka.

More than half of south Asia's population makes its living from agriculture. Farmers grow rice in the wet areas of the east and west, while corn and millet are the main crops on the Deccan plateau. Elsewhere, groundnuts are grown for cooking oil, and tea for the export market is harvested on huge plantations. Livestock are raised throughout the region, and fishing is common along the entire coast. There is serious

Large-scale industries, from car manufacturing to chemicals, have expanded in the region's cities in recent years. Service industries are also growing steadily. In the countryside, a number of people work in traditional trades, providing goods to the local people. Products such as clothing, leather and jewellery are among south Asia's leading exports.

This part of Asia's huge population is growing rapidly. The majority of the people live in rural areas, but increasing numbers are moving to the cities in search of work. There is serious overcrowding in both rural and urban regions, and slums have developed in the larger cities. Deforestation is also a major problem, with trees being cut down in the southern and Himalayan regions for fuel.

LAND HEIGHT

| 4,000 m 13,124 ft | 2,000 m 6,562 ft | 1,000 m 3,281 ft | 500 m 1,640 ft | 200 m 656 ft | Sea level |

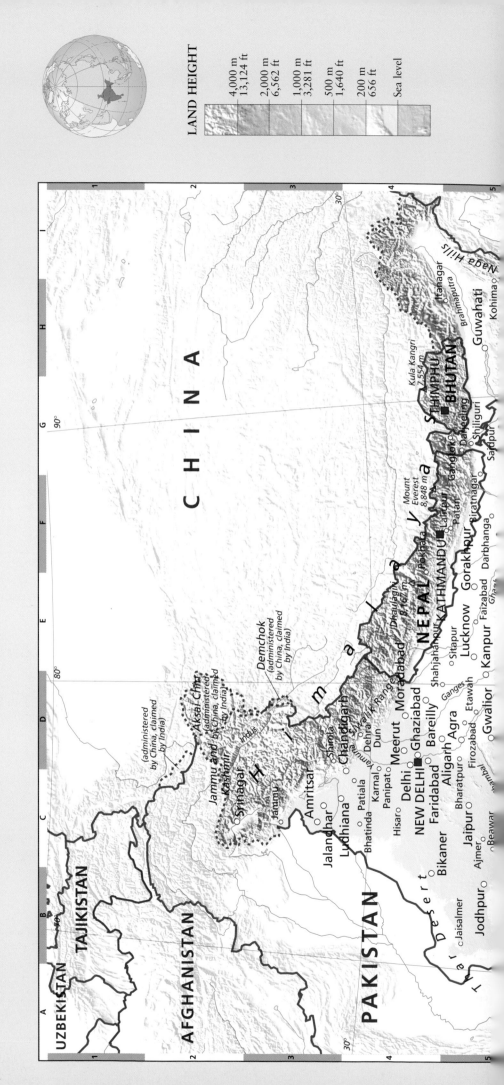

India
Nepal
Bhutan
Bangladesh
Sri Lanka
Maldives

SRI LANKA'S TWO CAPITALS
COLOMBO – capital
SRI JAYEWARDENEPURA KOTTE –
legislative capital

800 km
400 miles
400
200

MYANMAR (BURMA)

Tropic of Cancer

Silchar
Aizawl
Agartala
Comilla
Chittagong

BANGLADESH
DHAKA
Pabna
Rajshahi
Durgapur
Jessore
Khulna
Barisal
Kolkata (Calcutta)
Hao'a
Ganges
Mouths of the Ganges
Baleshwar
Bhubaneshwar
Puri

Bhagalpur
Ganges
Varanasi
Gaya
Dhanbad
Bokaro
Ranchi
Jamshedpur
Kharagpur
Raurkela
Bilaspur
Sambalpur
Hirakud Reservoir
Mahanadi
Cuttack
Brahmapur

Murwara
Chota Nagpur Range
Jabalpur
Kobra
Raipur
Bhilai
Durg

Bay of Bengal

North Andaman
Middle Andaman
South Andaman
Port Blair
Little Andaman
Ten Degree Channel
Car Nicobar
Sombrero Channel
Nicobar Islands (to India)
Great Nicobar
Great Channel

Andaman Islands (to India)

Equator

INDIA

Sagar
Ujjain
Vindhya Range
Indore
Bhopal
Narmada
Satpura Range
Nagpur
Amravati
Akola
Chandrapur
Jagdalpur
Godavari
Rajahmundry
Kakinada
Machilipatnam

Deccan

Visakhapatnam

Gandhinagar
Ahmadabad
Vadodara
Bharuch
Surat
Dhole
Khandwa
Jalgaon
Malegaon
Nashik
Kalyan
Thana
Mumbai (Bombay)
Bhiwandi
Pune
Solapur
Aurangabad
Parbhani
Nanded
Latur
Bhima
Nizamabad
Warangal
Secunderabad
Hyderabad
Vijayawada
Guntur
Krishna
Ongole
Nellore

Coromandel Coast

Chennai (Madras)

Bhavnagar
Rajkot
Surendranagar
Jamnagar
Junagadh
Porbandar
Veraval
Gulf of Kambhat
Daman

Aravalli Range
Gandhi Sagar
Udaipur

Rann of Kachchh
Gulf of Kachchh
Tropic of Cancer

Arabian Sea

Panaji
Goa
Hubli
Gadag
Belgaum
Kolhapur
Sangli
Bijapur
Gulbarga
Raichur
Kurnool
Bellary
Anantapur
Cuddapah
Nandyal
Tirupati
Vellore
Pondicherry

Western Ghats

Bangalore
Mysore
Davangere
Bhadravati
Shimoga
Mangalore
Malabar Coast
Cannanore
Calicut
Trichur
Coimbatore
Tiruppur
Erode
Salem
Madurai

Eastern Ghats

Tiruchchirappalli
Rajapalaiyam
Tuticorin
Tirunelveli
Nagercoil
Trivandrum
Quilon
Alleppey
Cochin
Ernakulam

Jaffna
Gulf of Mannar
Anuradhapura
Kandy
Batticaloa
SRI LANKA
SRI JAYEWARDENEPURA KOTTE
Negombo
COLOMBO
Galle

INDIAN OCEAN

Laccadive Islands (to India)

Nine Degree Channel
Minicoy Island
Eight Degree Channel

MALE
MALDIVES

SOUTHEAST ASIA

Southeast Asia is made up of many thousands of tropical islands and a mainland area. The landscape of the mainland is dominated by a string of mountain ranges, which are covered in dense forests and crossed by wide river valleys. The many islands to the southeast of the mainland are also forested. Most of these islands were formed by volcanoes, many of which are still active. In the centre of the region is the island of Borneo. The third-largest island in the world, it is divided between the countries of Malaysia, Indonesia and Brunei.

Rice is the main food crop in this region, while bananas, pineapples and sugar cane are grown as cash crops. Large quantities of fish are caught in the surrounding waters. Over the last few decades, the types of industries in southeast Asia have changed dramatically. There are still a number of traditional companies, which process the area's raw materials, including timber and metals, but many parts of the region now have large high-tech industries.

The forests of southeast Asia are home to thousands of unique species of plants and animals. This wildlife is now under threat, however, because vast numbers of trees are being cut away for use in the region's timber industry. In Indonesia, trees are burned to clear land for crops. The smoke from the fires creates terrible smog.

LAND HEIGHT

	4,000 m / 13,124 ft
	2,000 m / 6,562 ft
	1,000 m / 3,281 ft
	500 m / 1,640 ft
	200 m / 656 ft
	Sea level

TAIWAN

Batan Islands

Luzon Strait

Babuyan Islands

Laoag
Aparri
Luzon
Ilagan
San Fernando
Baguio
Dagupan
Cabanatuan
Angeles
San Fernando
■ MANILA
Batangas
Naga
Catanduanes
Mindoro
Legaspi
Calbayog
Samar
Roxas City
Masbate
Calamian Group
Panay
Leyte Tacloban
Cadiz
Ormoc
PHILIPPINES
Iloilo
Bacolod City
San Carlos
Cebu Cebu
Puerto Princesa
Dumaguete
Bohol
Surigao
Negros
Butuan
Cagayan de Oro
Iligan
Mindanao
Zamboanga
Mount Apo △
2,954 m
Davao
Basilan
Jolo
General Santos

South China Sea

Spratly Islands

Palawan

Sulu Sea

Balabac Strait
Kudat
Gunung Kinabalu
△ 4,094 m
Kota Kinabalu
Sandakan
Ranau
SABAH
Tawitawi
Sulu Archipelago

Talaud Islands

Celebes Sea

Sangir Islands

Morotai

P A C I F I C

O C E A N

Tropic of Cancer

MICRONESIA

PALAU

Equator

IA
EGAWAN
BRUNEI
Miri
ARAWAK
Tarakan
Pegunungan Range
Rajang
Kayan
n e o
Kapuas Mountains
Tanjungredeb

Manado

Gorontalo

Halmahera

Ternate

Gulf of Tomini

Molucca Sea

Halmahera Sea
Sorong
Waigeo
Manokwari
Biak

Samarinda
Mahakan
ALIMANTAN
Balikpapan
Palu
Poso
Peleng
Bacan
Obi
Jazirah Doberai
Yapen
IRIAN JAYA
Mamberamo
Jayapura

anjarmasin
Martapura
Barito
Sulawesi
Malunda
Parepare
Kendari
Sula Islands
Moluccas
Ceram Sea
Seram
Misool
Puncak Jaya
5,030 m
Pegunungan Maoke

Buru
Ambon

D O N E S I A
Muna
Kai Islands
Aru Islands

Yos Sudarso

PAPUA NEW GUINEA

Makassar
Buton
Selayar
Banda Sea

Madura
Surabaya
Jember
Bali
Lombok
Sumbawa
Flores Sea
Wetar
Tanimbar Islands

Malang
Denpasar
Mataram
Flores
Lomblen
Alor
Lombok
■ DILI
EAST TIMOR
Arafura Sea
Sumba
Lesser Sunda Islands
Timor
Kupang
Timor Sea
AUSTRALIA

sea
ea

Legend (right margin)

Myanmar

Laos

Vietnam

Thailand

Philippines

Cambodia

Malaysia

Brunei

Singapore

Indonesia

East Timor

EAST ASIA

East Asia's landscape may be divided into four main areas. In the southwest is the Plateau of Tibet. Here, high mountain peaks surround small areas of pasture and arid deserts. There are dry highlands in the northwest, and in the north there are cold deserts. Great plains lie to the east. These plains were formed from soils that were carried to the region by China's rivers.

Although most of China's land is either too poor or too mountainous for cultivation, almost three-quarters of this country's enormous population of almost 1.3 billion people make their living from farming. The majority of the people live in the east, where the land is flatter and more fertile. Wheat, corn, soya beans and cotton are grown on the plains, and further south, rice is the main crop. Pigs are raised here in large numbers. In Mongolia, in the north, farmers mainly herd sheep.

China became a communist country in 1949, and since then, it has become a major industrial nation. The country's industries, including iron and steel production, chemicals, engineering and textiles, are concentrated in the cities on the east coast, such as Qingdao and Shanghai. Hong Kong and Beijing are also major financial centres. Taiwan exports electronic goods, shoes and textiles throughout the world, while Mongolia's economy is mainly based on agriculture.

LAND HEIGHT

4,000 m
13,124 ft

2,000 m
6,562 ft

1,000 m
3,281 ft

500 m
1,640 ft

200 m
656 ft

Sea level

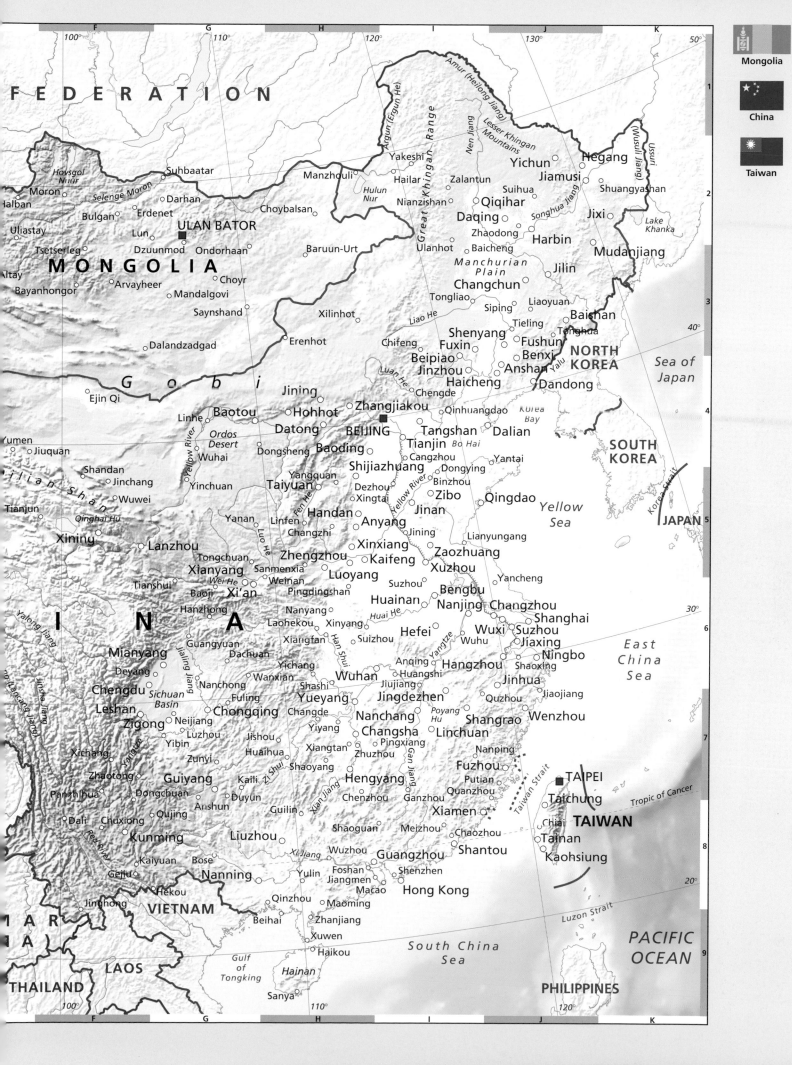

Mongolia

China

Taiwan

FEDERATION

50°

Amur (Heilong Jiang)

Argun (Ergun He)

Great Khingan Range

Nen Jiang

Lesser Khingan Mountains

(Wusuli Jiang) Ussuri

Yakeshi

Hegang

Yichun

Jiamusi

1

Manzhouli

Hailar

Zalantun

Shuangyashan

Hulun Nur

Nianzishan

Suihua

Qiqihar

Jixi

Hovsgol Nuur

Suhbaatar

Darhan

Daqing

Zhaodong

Lake Khanka

Moron

Selenge Moron

Zhaodong

Halban

Bulgan

Erdenet

Choybalsan

Harbin

Mudanjiang

2

Uliastay

Lun

ULAN BATOR

Baruun-Urt

Ulanhot

Baicheng

Jilin

Tsetserleg

Dzuunmod

Ondorhaan

Changchun

Altay

Arvayheer

Choyr

Tongliao

Liaoyuan

Baishan

Bayanhongor

Mandalgovi

Siping

Tieling

Tonghua

MONGOLIA

Saynshand

Xilinhot

Liao He

Shenyang

Fushun

40°

Dalandzadgad

Erenhot

Chifeng

Fuxin

Benxi

NORTH KOREA

Sea of Japan

3

Gobi

Jining

Beipiao

Jinzhou

Anshan

Yalu

Dandong

Ejin Qi

Luan He

Chengde

Haicheng

Linhe

Baotou

Hohhot

Zhangjiakou

Qinhuangdao

Korea Bay

Yumen

Datong

BEIJING

Tangshan

Dalian

4

Jiuquan

Ordos Desert

Baoding

Tianjin

Bo Hai

SOUTH KOREA

Shandan

Wuhai

Dongsheng

Cangzhou

Yantai

Jinchang

Yinchuan

Shijiazhuang

Dongying

Yellow River

Wuwei

Taiyuan

Dezhou

Binzhou

Qingdao

Korea Strait

Tianjun

Qinghai Hu

Yangquan

Xingtai

Zibo

Jinan

Yellow Sea

JAPAN

5

Xining

Lanzhou

Yanan

Linfen

Handan

Anyang

Jining

Lianyungang

Tongchuan

Changzhi

Xinxiang

Kaifeng

Zaozhuang

Xianyang

Sanmenxia

Zhengzhou

Luoyang

Xuzhou

Yancheng

Tianshui

Baoji

Wei He

Weinan

Pingdingshan

Suzhou

Bengbu

Xi'an

Pingdingshan

Nanyang

Huainan

Nanjing

Changzhou

30°

Hanzhong

Laohekou

Xinyang

Huai He

Hefei

Shanghai

6

Mianyang

Guangyuan

Xiangfan

Suizhou

Wuhu

Wuxi

Suzhou

Deyang

Dachuan

Yichang

Han Shui

Wuhan

Anqing

Hangzhou

Jiaxing

Nanchong

Wanxian

Shashi

Huangshi

Shaoxing

Ningbo

East China Sea

Chengdu

Sichuan Basin

Jialing Jiang

Fuling

Yueyang

Jiujiang

Jingdezhen

Jinhua

Leshan

Chongqing

Changde

Nanchang

Quzhou

Jiaojiang

Zigong

Neijiang

Yiyang

Poyang Hu

Shangrao

Wenzhou

7

Xichang

Luzhou

Jishou

Changsha

Linchuan

Zhaotong

Yibin

Huaihua

Xiangtan

Zhuzhou

Pingxiang

Nanping

Zunyi

Shaoyang

Gan Jiang

Fuzhou

Panzhihua

Guiyang

Kaili

Hengyang

Putian

Quanzhou

TAIPEI

Dongchuan

Duyun

Chenzhou

Ganzhou

Taichung

Tropic of Cancer

Dali

Chuxiong

Anshun

Guilin

Xiamen

Chiai

TAIWAN

Kunming

Liuzhou

Shaoguan

Meizhou

Chaozhou

Tainan

8

Kaiyuan

Bose

Wuzhou

Guangzhou

Shantou

Kaohsiung

Gejiu

Nanning

Yulin

Foshan

Shenzhen

20°

Hekou

Jiangmen

Macao

Hong Kong

Jinghong

VIETNAM

Qinzhou

Maoming

Luzon Strait

Beihai

Zhanjiang

PACIFIC OCEAN

MAR

Xuwen

South China Sea

9

IA

Haikou

PHILIPPINES

THAILAND

LAOS

Gulf of Tongking

Hainan

Sanya

100°

110°

120°

JAPAN AND THE KOREAS

South and North Korea lie on a peninsula that juts out from the northeast coast of China. To the east is Japan, a long chain of more than 4,000 islands in the Pacific Ocean. Mountains and hills dominate the landscape of these three countries, so most of this region's cities and towns are located on lower-lying land near the coasts.

Rice is grown throughout this region, and large quantities of fish are caught off the coasts. North Korea's communist government controls its industries and farms, and this country does very little trade with other nations. South Korea and Japan, however, export goods all over the globe. These two countries have few natural resources, so they have specialized in the production of high-value goods. South Korea makes cars, ships and textiles, while Japan is a world leader in the production of high-tech goods, such as cameras, computers and electronics, as well as cars.

Japan's environment suffers from acid rain caused by pollution from the factories of North Korea and the Russian Federation. Nuclear waste is dumped in the Sea of Japan. This country is also located in a major earthquake zone. Although buildings are constructed to withstand tremors, major quakes, such as the one that destroyed Kobe in 1995, are still a big threat in Japan.

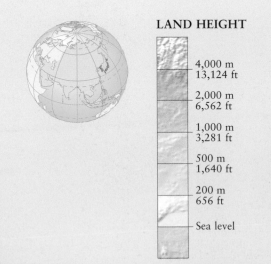

LAND HEIGHT

	4,000 m 13,124 ft
	2,000 m 6,562 ft
	1,000 m 3,281 ft
	500 m 1,640 ft
	200 m 656 ft
	Sea level

135°
140°
145°

RUSSIAN FEDERATION

Sea of Okhotsk

La Perouse Strait
Soya-misaki
Rebun-to
Rishiri-to

Wakkanai

Kurile Islands
(administered by Russian Federation)

Japan

North Korea

South Korea

Nayoro
Monbetsu
Shiretoko-misaki
Abashiri
Rumoi
Kitami
Shibetsu
Asahikawa
Takikawa
△ Asahi-dake
2,290 m
Kussharo-ko
Nemuro
Otaru
Ebetsu
Hokkaido
Iwanai
Sapporo
Chitose
Obihiro
Kushiro
Tomakomai
Muroran

Uchiura-wan

Okushiri-to

Hakodate
Erimo-misaki

Tsugaru-kaikyo

Shimokita-hanto

Mutsu-wan

Aomori

Sea of Japan

Hirosaki
Hachinohe

Noshiro

Oga
Morioka
40°
Akita
Miyako
Yokote

Sakata
Kesennuma

Sado-shima
Furukawa
Ishinomaki
Yamagata
Ryotsu
Sendai
Niigata
Sendai-wan
Fukushima

Nagaoka
Honshū
Koriyama

Noto-hanto
Joetsu
Iwaki

JAPAN
Toyama-wan
Nikko
Hitachi
Takaoka
Toyama
Nagano
Kuroiso
Kanazawa
Utsunomiya
Matto
Ueda
Maebashi
Mito
Komatsu
Matsumoto
Takasaki
Oyama
Tsuchiura
Fukui
Takayama
Chino
Urawa
Funabashi
i-shoto
Tsuruga
Kofu
TOKYO
Choshi
Wakasa-wan
Kawasaki
Chiba
Tottori
Ogaki
Gifu
Ichihara
Maizuru
Fujinomiya
△ Mount
35°
Otsu
Yokkaichi
Nagoya
Fuji
Yokohama
Biwa-ko
Toyota
Fuji
3,776 m
kayama
Himeji
Okazaki
Fujieda
Shizuoka
Kyoto
Nara
Toyohashi
Yaizu
Kurashiki
Tsu
Ise-wan
Nojima-zaki
Kobe
Osaka
Hamamatsu
Sakai
Ise
Takamatsu
Wakayama
hama
Tokushima
Kiisuido
Sagami-nada
chi
Tanabe
Izu-shoto
sa-n
Muroto-zaki
Shiono-misaki

PACIFIC OCEAN

0   200   400 km
0   100   200 miles

East China Sea

Amami-o-shima
Naze

Tokuno-shima

Ryukyu Islands
Okinawa
Kume-jima
Okinawa
Naha

Philippine Sea

Iriomote-jima
Miyako-jima
Ishigaki-jima

PACIFIC OCEAN

0   200   400 km
0   100   200 miles

135°
140°
145°
30°

AUSTRALASIA AND OCEANIA

Australasia and Oceania is made up of 14 countries. They include the vast landmass of Australia, the islands of New Zealand and Papua New Guinea, and the many thousands of coral atolls and islands that extend into the Pacific Ocean.

Before European explorers started to visit this part of the globe during the 16th century, the region was occupied by native peoples who lived by traditional means, such as hunting and gathering. Eventually, the Europeans began to settle and take over these lands. Some of the islands became overseas territories of the United Kingdom, France and the USA. In the past 20 years, a number of these dependencies, such as Palau, have become independent nations.

Natural resources are of major economic importance throughout Australasia and Oceania. Australia exports raw materials, such as coal, iron ore and bauxite. Sheep are raised for their wool and meat in New Zealand and Australia, and fishing is important throughout the Pacific islands. Manufacturing companies are found only in the large coastal cities of Australia and New Zealand. Until recently, both of these countries relied on Europe for trade. However, they have now begun to form trade links with the neighbouring countries of east and southeast Asia.

LAND HEIGHT

	4,000 m 13,124 ft
	2,000 m 6,562 ft
	1,000 m 3,281 ft
	500 m 1,640 ft
	200 m 656 ft
	Sea level

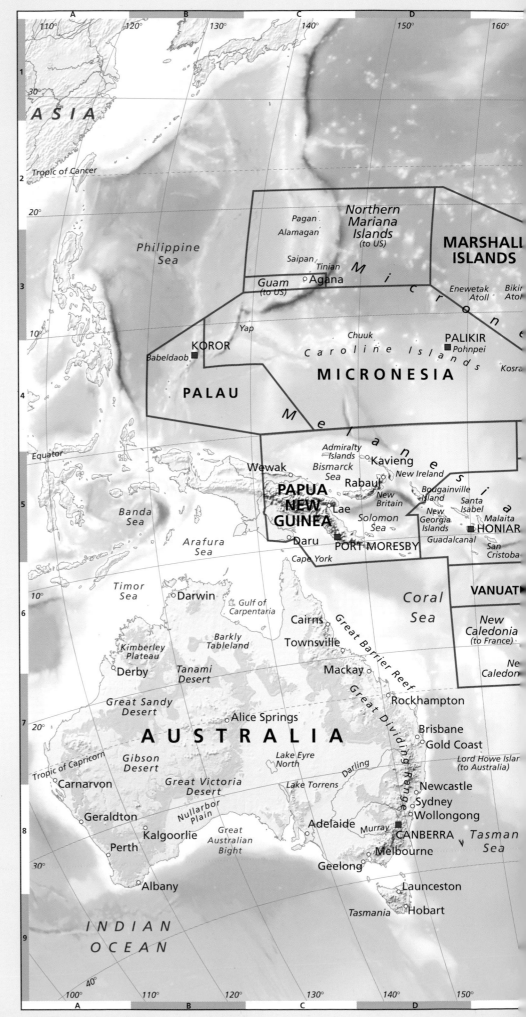

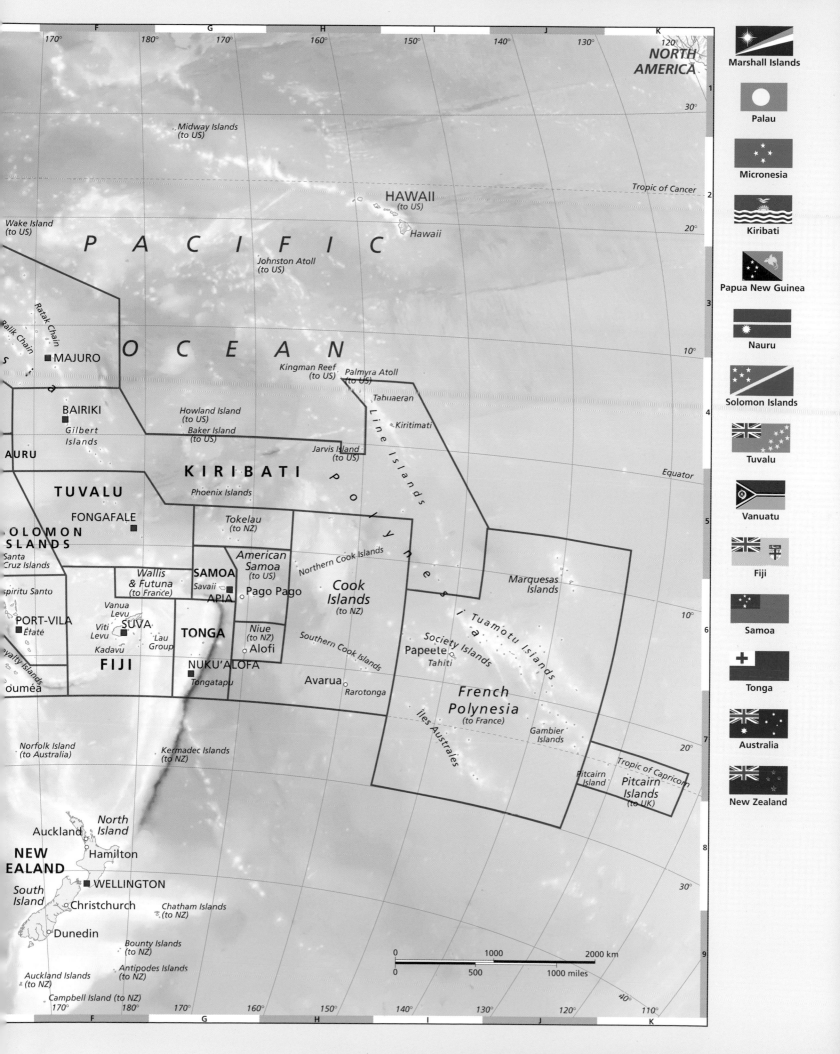

NORTH
AMERICA

170° 180° 170° 160° 150° 140° 130° 120°

30°

*Midway Islands
(to US)*

Tropic of Cancer

20°

*Wake Island
(to US)*

HAWAII
(to US)

Hawaii

P A C I F I C

*Johnston Atoll
(to US)*

Ratak Chain

Ralik Chain

■ MAJURO

O C E A N

10°

*Kingman Reef
(to US)* *Palmyra Atoll
(to US)*

■ BAIRIKI

Tahuaeran

*Gilbert
Islands*

*Howland Island
(to US)*

Kiritimati

AURU

*Baker Island
(to US)*

Line Islands

Equator

*Jarvis Island
(to US)*

K I R I B A T I

P   o   l   y   n   e   s   i   a

TUVALU

Phoenix Islands

■ FONGAFALE

*Tokelau
(to NZ)*

*Marquesas
Islands*

10°

OLOMON
SLANDS

*Santa
Cruz Islands*

*American
Samoa
(to US)*

Northern Cook Islands

*Wallis
& Futuna
(to France)*

SAMOA

Savaii

■ APIA

Pago Pago

Cook
Islands
(to NZ)

Tuamotu Islands

spiritu Santo

*Vanua
Levu*

*Niue
(to NZ)*

Society Islands

PORT-VILA

Éfaté

*Viti
Levu*

■ SUVA

TONGA

Papeete

Southern Cook Islands

Tahiti

Kadavu

*Lau
Group*

● Alofi

valty Islands

FIJI

■ NUKU'ALOFA

Tongatapu

Avarua

Rarotonga

ouméa

French
Polynesia
(to France)

Îles Australes

*Gambier
Islands*

20°

*Norfolk Island
(to Australia)*

*Kermadec Islands
(to NZ)*

Tropic of Capricorn

*Pitcairn
Island*

Pitcairn
Islands
(to UK)

North
Island

Auckland ●

NEW
EALAND

Hamilton

■ WELLINGTON

30°

South
Island

● Christchurch

*Chatham Islands
(to NZ)*

● Dunedin

*Bounty Islands
(to NZ)*

0 1000 2000 km

*Auckland Islands
(to NZ)*

*Antipodes Islands
(to NZ)*

0 500 1000 miles

40°

Campbell Island (to NZ)

170° 180° 170° 160° 150° 140° 130° 120° 110°

Marshall Islands

Palau

Micronesia

Kiribati

Papua New Guinea

Nauru

Solomon Islands

Tuvalu

Vanuatu

Fiji

Samoa

Tonga

Australia

New Zealand

AUSTRALIA

One of the world's largest countries, Australia is located in the southern Pacific Ocean. Despite its huge size, this nation has a relatively small population of almost 19.5 million people, because much of the land is dry. In the west are semi-arid plains of scrub and grassland, while in the east the land rises to the peaks of the Great Dividing Range. In the north, there are tropical rainforests and mangrove swamps.

Sugar cane is harvested near the east coast. In the south and west, grapes for Australia's successful wine industry are produced, along with wheat. Large numbers of sheep and cattle are raised in the southwest and on the Great Artesian Basin in the east. These provide meat and wool for export.

The first inhabitants of Australia were the Aboriginal peoples. Today, they are a tiny minority, and the majority of Australians are of European origin. Most people work and live in cities in the south and east, and around Perth in the west. In these urban areas are engineering and manufacturing businesses, and thriving service industries.

Australia has one of the world's biggest mining industries, which exploits the rich resources of gold, copper, coal and iron ore. Tourism is another important source of income, especially along the northeast coast, where people come to visit the sunny beaches and the Great Barrier Reef.

LAND HEIGHT

4,000 m 13,124 ft	
2,000 m 6,562 ft	
1,000 m 3,281 ft	
500 m 1,640 ft	
200 m 656 ft	
Sea level	

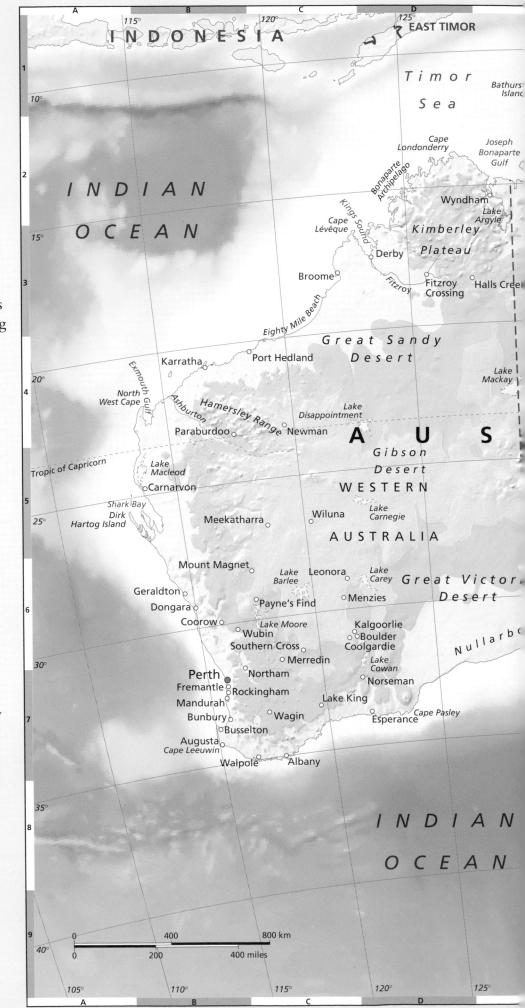

Australia

PAPUA NEW GUINEA

Arafura Sea

Torres Strait

Melville
Island

Van
Diemen
Gulf

•Darwin

*Arnhem
Land*

Wessel
Islands

Cape
Arnhem

Prince of
Wales Island

Cape York

*Coral
Sea*

Daly

Katherine

Mataranka

Victoria

Victoria River Roadhouse

Daly Waters

*Tanami
Desert*

Lake
Woods

•Tennant Creek

N O R T H E R N

T E R R I T O R Y

Macdonnell Ranges

△ •Alice Springs

Lake
Amadeus

△ *Uluru*
(Ayers Rock)
867 m

Gulf of
Carpentaria

Sir Edward
Pellew Group

Groote
Eylandt

Wellesley
Islands

Mitchell

Normanton

Croydon

Forsayth

Flinders

Camooweal

Cloncurry

Mount Isa

Duchess

Georgina

Boulia

Cape
York

Cape
York
Peninsula

Princess
Charlotte
Bay

Cooktown

Cairns

Georgetown

Richmond

Hughenden

Winton

Charters Towers

Torrens Creek

Townsville

Great Barrier Reef

Great Dividing Range

Proserpine

Mackay

Cape
Townshend

Q U E E N S L A N D

Longreach

Jericho

Clermont

Emerald

Rockhampton

Gladstone

Tropic of Capricorn

*Simpson
Desert*

Diamantina

Birdsville

Blackall

*Great Artesian
Basin*

Thomson

*Buckland
Tableland*

Theodore

Bundaberg

Hervey Bay

T R A L I A

South Australia

Oodnadatta

Coober Pedy

Lake
Eyre North

Cooper Creek

Lake
Eyre South

Marree

*Sturt
Desert*

Quilpie

Durham
Downs

Charleville

Warrego

Mitchell

Cunnamulla

Injune

Maryborough

Roma

Miles

Saint George

Dirranbandi

Warwick

Talwood

Goondiwindi

Fraser Island

Gympie

Maroochydore-Mooloolaba

Caloundra

Toowoomba

Ipswich •**Brisbane**

Gold Coast

Ballina

Tarcoola

Lake Torrens

Lake
Blanche

Bourke

Moree

Lismore

Grafton

Lake Everard

Lake
Frome

Wilcannia

Darling

Walgett

Coonamble

Armidale

Coffs Harbour

Penong

Ceduna

Lake
Gairdner

Broken Hill

N E W S O U T H

W A L E S

Tamworth

Dividing Range

Port Macquarie

Streaky Bay

Whyalla

Port Augusta

Elliston

Kyancutta

Port Pirie

*Great
Australian
Bight*

Port Lincoln

Gawler

York Peninsula

Spencer Gulf

Gulf St Vincent

Waikerie

Mildura

Murray Bridge

Keith

Kangaroo Island

Naracoorte

Mount Gambier

Portland

Balranald

Murray

VICTORIA

Horsham

Ballarat

Hamilton

Ivanhoe

Lachlan

Hay

Wagga
Wagga

Albury

Wodonga

Bendigo

•**Melbourne**

Geelong

Sale

Cape Otway

Bass Strait

King Island

South East Point

Flinders Island

Cape Howe

Dubbo

Orange

Bathurst

Forster-Tuncurry

Newcastle

Gosford

Sydney

Goulburn

Wollongong

CANBERRA

AUSTRALIAN CAPITAL TERRITORY

Cooma

Mount Kosciuszko
2,230 m

*Tasman
Sea*

Stanley

Burnie

Devonport

Launceston

△ *Mount Ossa 1,617 m*

Furneaux
Group

TASMANIA

•**Hobart**

New Zealand

New Zealand lies in the southern Pacific Ocean, 1,600 km southeast of Australia. This country consists of two large islands – North Island and South Island – and many smaller ones. In the far north of North Island are coastal inlets, which are fringed by mangrove swamps. Further south are geysers, boiling mud pools and fertile plains that rise to volcanic peaks, such as Mount Egmont and Mount Ruapehu. There are also volcanoes in South Island, where the landscape is dominated by the Southern Alps. This towering mountain range stretches more than 480 km along the western side of the island. Many rivers flow down from these uplands to the east coast.

The first inhabitants of New Zealand were the Maori, a Polynesian people. In the 19th century, Europeans began to settle here, and they now make up more than 90 per cent of the whole population. The people are mainly concentrated in the country's coastal towns and cities, especially in Auckland, on North Island.

New Zealand has rich and fertile land that provides good pasture for millions of sheep and cattle. Fruits, such as apples, peaches, oranges and kiwi fruit, are grown and exported to many countries throughout the world.

New Zealand has a strong timber industry, and in the cities, high-tech businesses that produce electronic goods and computers are expanding. Agricultural products, however, such as lamb, wool and milk, remain the country's major exports. Tourism is also an important source of income. New Zealand's environment is generally unpolluted due to its low population and lack of heavy industries.

LAND HEIGHT

| 4,000 m 13,124 ft | 2,000 m 6,562 ft | 1,000 m 3,281 ft | 500 m 1,640 ft | 200 m 656 ft | Sea level |

New Zealand

NEW ZEALAND

SOUTH ISLAND

Tasman Sea

PACIFIC OCEAN

Cook Strait

Southern Alps

Fiordland

Stewart Island

Mahia Peninsula
Wairoa
Wairoa
△ Mount Ngauruhoe 2,291 m
△ Mount Ruapehu 2,797 m
Hawke Bay
Napier
Hastings
Waipukurau
Turangi
Waiouru
Mangaweka
Herbertville
Wanganui
Feilding
Palmerston North
Masterton
New Plymouth ○ Mount Egmont
(Taranaki)
△ 2,518 m
Cape Egmont
Stratford
Hawera
Opunake
Waverley
Wanganui
Levin
Porirua
Lower Hutt
WELLINGTON
Cape Palliser
South Taranaki Bight

Cape Farewell
Golden Bay
D'Urville Island
Cloudy Bay
Clarence
Collingwood
Motueka
Nelson
Tasman Bay
Picton
Blenheim
Kaikoura
Karamea Bight
Waimangaroa
Westport
Owen River
Parnassus
Cape Foulwind
Reefton
Rotherham
Pegasus Bay
Greymouth
Waipara
Banks Peninsula
Hokitika
Rangiora
Christchurch
Sheffield
Dunsandel
Lake Ellesmere
Fox Glacier
△ Mount Cook
3,754 m
Canterbury Plains
Ashburton
Lake Tekapo
Canterbury Bight
Haast
△ Mount Aspiring
3,030 m
Omarama
Lake Havea
Timaru
Cascade Point
Wanaka
Lake Wanaka
Lake Wakatipu
Cromwell
Kurow
Oamaru
Alexandra
Palmerston
Roxburgh
Dunedin
Otago Peninsula
Milford Sound
Queenstown
Beaumont
Milton
Lake Te Anau
Kingston
Lumsden
Clutha
Balclutha
Te Anau
Mossburn
Gore
Resolution Island
Waiau
Ohai
Mataura
West Cape
Tuatapere
Invercargill
Foveaux Strait
Halfmoon Bay
South West Cape

0 50 100 200 km
0 100 miles

THE PACIFIC OCEAN

Stretching over about one-third of the Earth's surface, the Pacific is the planet's largest ocean. It extends east from Japan to the Americas, and south from the Arctic Ocean to Antarctica. The ocean's floor is generally deeper in the west than in the east, and at its deepest point, the Mariana Trench, the Pacific plunges to –11,034 m.

The many thousands of islands scattered across the Pacific Ocean were created by volcanic eruptions. Some of these islands became fringed with coral, and the islands eventually dropped back into the sea, leaving circles of coral, or atolls. A string of active volcanoes, known as the 'Ring of Fire', surrounds the ocean. The Pacific region is plagued by tropical storms, called typhoons. The area is also prone to tidal waves, which are caused by volcanic eruptions or underwater earthquakes.

The peoples of the Pacific mainly grow food for their own consumption, although a few islands grow crops, such as coconuts and oil palms, for export. Many of the small islands rely heavily on fishing for much-needed foreign income. These fish industries tend to be small and are forced to compete with the large fishing fleets of Japan and the Russian Federation. With palm-fringed beaches, spectacular coral reefs and a warm, sunny climate, the islands of the Pacific Ocean have become popular tourist destinations.

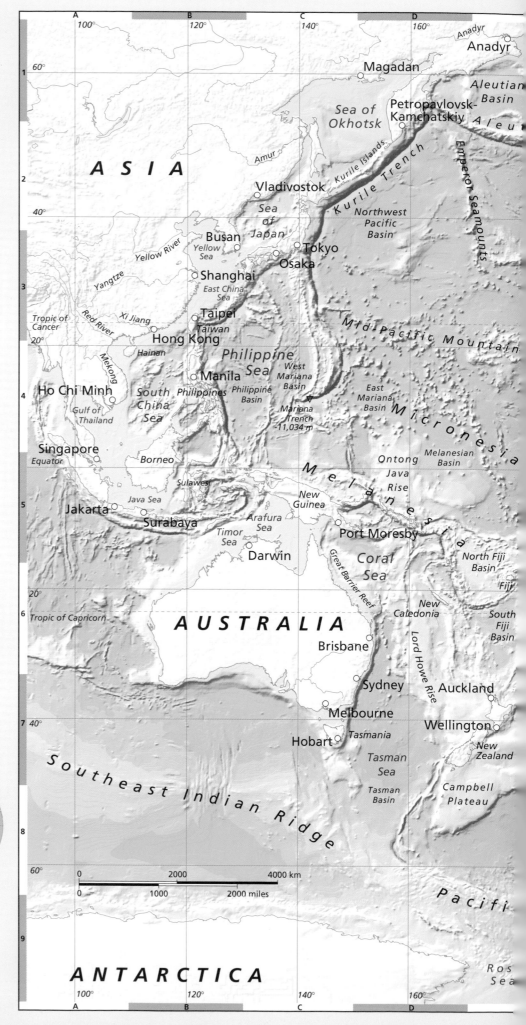

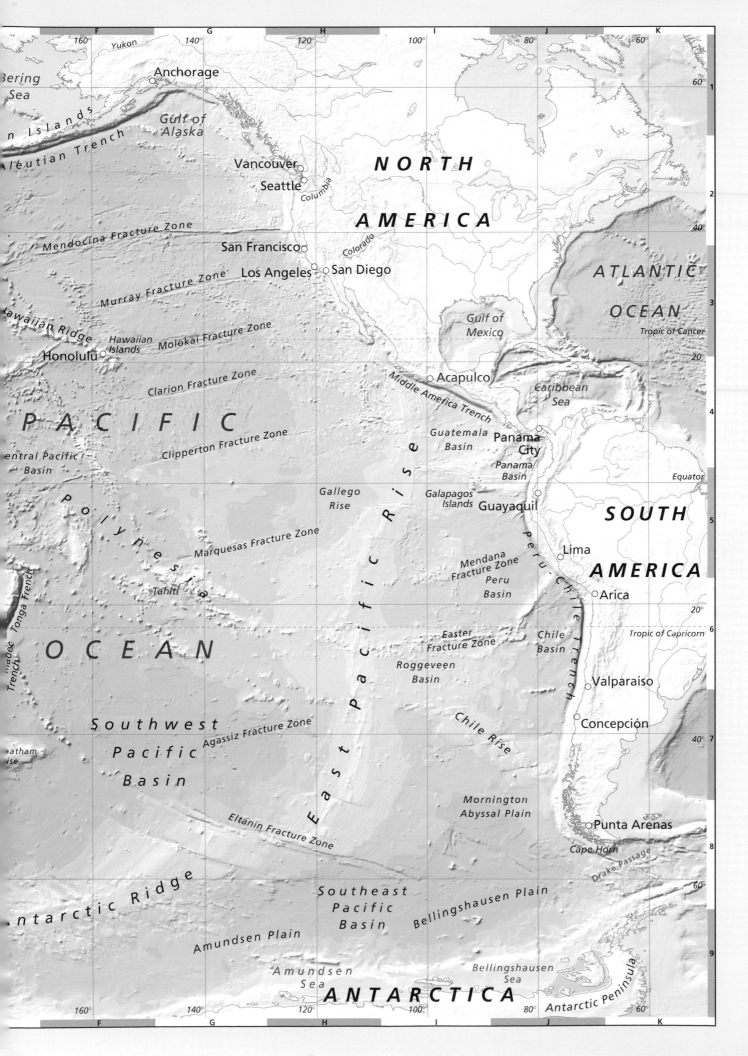

F 160° Yukon 140° 120° H 100° 80° J 60° K

Bering
Sea

Anchorage

n Islands *Gulf of
Alaska*

Aleutian Trench

NORTH

60° 1

Vancouver

Seattle *Columbia*

AMERICA

2

40°

Mendocina Fracture Zone

San Francisco *Colorado*

ATLANTIC

Murray Fracture Zone Los Angeles San Diego

OCEAN

3

awaiian Ridge

*Hawaiian
Islands* *Molokai Fracture Zone*

*Gulf of
Mexico*

Tropic of Cancer

20°

Honolulu

Clarion Fracture Zone

Acapulco

Middle America Trench

*Caribbean
Sea*

P A C I F I C

4

*entral Pacific
Basin*

Clipperton Fracture Zone

*Guatemala
Basin* Panama
City

East Pacific Rise

*Panama
Basin*

*Gallego
Rise* *Galapagos
Islands* Guayaquil

Equator

SOUTH

5

P o l y n e s i a

Marquesas Fracture Zone

*Mendana
Fracture Zone* Lima

Peru-Chile Trench

*Peru
Basin*

AMERICA

Tahiti

Arica

20°

Tonga Trench

*Easter
Fracture Zone* *Chile
Basin*

Tropic of Capricorn

6

O C E A N

*Roggeveen
Basin*

Valparaiso

Southwest *Agassiz Fracture Zone*

*atham
se*

Pacific

Chile Rise

Concepción

40° 7

Basin

East Pacific Rise

Eltanin Fracture Zone

*Mornington
Abyssal Plain*

Punta Arenas

Cape Horn *Drake Passage*

8

ntarctic Ridge

**Southeast
Pacific
Basin** *Bellingshausen Plain*

60°

Amundsen Plain

9

*Amundsen
Sea* *Bellingshausen
Sea* *Antarctic Peninsula*

A N T A R C T I C A

160° 140° 120° 100° 80° 60°

F G H I J K

GLOSSARY

The following glossary explains certain geographical and technical terms used in this atlas.

Acid rain

Rain and snow that has absorbed gases released by power stations and vehicle exhausts. Acid rain can cause severe environmental damage.

Arctic Circle

An imaginary line (latitude) that runs east-west around the Earth. The Arctic Circle lies at a latitude of 66° 32'N.

Biodiversity

The quantity of different plant or animal species in a given area.

Cash crops

Crops grown for sale, often for the export market, rather than for consumption in the area in which they are grown.

Climate

The average weather conditions in a given region.

Deforestation

The cutting down of large areas of forest for timber, farmland or urban development. It can lead to soil erosion, flooding and landslides.

Delta

A low-lying, fan-shaped area at a river mouth. It is formed when the river drops layers of sediment as it slows down when entering the sea.

Desertification

The gradual spread of desert conditions in arid or semi-arid regions. Desertification may be caused by changes in the climate or by human activities, such as overgrazing and **deforestation**.

Equator

The imaginary line (latitude) which circles the middle of the Earth. Lying at 0°, it is equidistant from the North and South Poles.

European Union (EU)

A group of European countries that have joined together to promote trade, industry and agriculture. The EU was formed in 1965, and was formerly known as the European Economic Community (EEC), then the European Community (EC).

Flood plain

The broad, flat part of a river valley, bordering the river. Flood plains are formed by sediment deposited during flooding.

Heavy industry

A type of industry that uses vast amounts of energy and raw materials to make heavy goods such as machinery and ships.

High-tech industry

A type of industry that produces high-value, technologically advanced goods, such as computers and other electronic equipment.

Ice shelf

Floating ice attached to the edge of a coast. The edge facing the sea is usually a steep cliff up to 30 m high.

Irrigation

The artificial supply of water to land. It usually involves the construction of canals and the diversion of natural watercourses.

Manufacturing

A type of industry that makes vast quantities of finished goods, from clothes to cars, which are sold to large numbers of people.

Natural resources

Fuel and raw materials, such as oil, ores and timber, which occur naturally and are found in large quantities in a given area.

Peninsula

A thin strip of land that juts out into the sea, and is surrounded by water on three of its sides. Large examples include Florida and the Koreas.

Plain

A flat, level region of land. It is often relatively low-lying.

Service industry

A type of industry that does not produce goods, but provides services such as banking and tourism.

Shanty town

An area in or around a city where people live in makeshift shacks, usually without basic facilities such as running water.

Tropics

The area between the **Tropic of Cancer** and the **Tropic of Capricorn** where the **climate** is hot.

Tropic of Cancer

An imaginary circle around the Earth, north of the Equator. It lies at a latitude of 23° 28'N.

Tropic of Capricorn

An imaginary circle around the Earth, south of the Equator. It lies at a latitude of 23° 28'S.

United Nations (UN)

An association of countries that was established in 1945. It seeks to maintain international peace and security, and promote co-operation over economic, social, cultural and humanitarian problems.

INDEX

The following index lists all the placenames and features on the regional and continental maps in this atlas. The entry names are settlements unless otherwise indicated by the use of italicized definitions. Each name is located within a region, country, sea or ocean. Physical feature names that are made up of a proper name and a description, such as Mount Etna, are positioned alphabetically by the proper name. The description appears after the proper name. For example, Mount Etna appears as 'Etna, Mount' in the index.

The first number at the end of each entry is the page number of the map on which the feature or place may be found. The letter and figure after the page number give the grid square in which the name is located.

COLORADO PLATEAU–DUNHUANG . 113

Colorado Plateau *plateau* W USA 23 C8, 27 G8
Colorado Springs Colorado, USA 28 E7
Columbia *river* Canada/USA 23 C7, 26 D1
Columbia Missouri, USA 29 J7
Columbia *state capital* South Carolina, USA 23 G9, 31 J4
Columbia Basin *physical region* Washington, USA 26 D2
Columbia Plateau *plateau* Idaho/Oregon, USA 26 E5
Columbus Georgia, USA 31 H5
Columbus Mississippi, USA 31 G4
Columbus Nebraska, USA 29 H6
Columbus *state capital* Ohio, USA 23 F9, 32 E7
Comilla Bangladesh 93 H6
Como Italy 62 B3
Comodoro Rivadavia Argentina 43 D10
Como, Lake *lake* Italy 62 C2
Comoro Islands *island group* Comoros 82 C4
Comoros *country* W Indian Ocean 71 H9, 81 J3
Compiègne France 55 F2
Comrat Moldova 65 D11
Conakry *country capital* Guinea 71 A6, 76 C7
Concepción Chile 43 B7
Concepción Paraguay 42 G2
Conception, Point *headland* California, USA 27 B10
Conchos *river* Mexico 34 C3
Concord California, USA 27 B8
Concord *state capital* New Hampshire, USA 33 I5
Concordia Argentina 43 G5
Congo *country* C Africa 71 E8, 78 D6
Congo *river* Congo/Democratic Republic of Congo 71 E8, 78 D7
Congo Basin *physical region* C Africa 71 E7, 78 E6
Congo, Democratic Republic of *country* C Africa 71 F8, 79 F6
Connaught *cultural region* Republic of Ireland 51 B8
Connecticut *state* USA 33 I5
Constance Germany 59 D12
Constance, Lake *lake* Germany/Switzerland 59 D12, 60 D4
Constanta Romania 47 G7, 69 I3
Constantine Algeria 70 D2, 73 G3
Constitución Chile 43 B7
Coober Pedy South Australia, Australia 103 F6
Cook Islands *NZ dependent territory* C Pacific Ocean 101 H6
Cook, Mount *mountain* New Zealand 105 C10
Cook Strait *strait* New Zealand 105 F7
Cooktown Queensland, Australia 103 I2
Coolgardie Western Australia, Australia 102 C6
Cooma New South Wales, Australia 103 I8
Coonamble New South Wales, Australia 103 I6
Cooper Creek *seasonal river* Queensland/South Australia, 103 G5
Coorow Western Australia, Australia 102 B6
Coos Bay Oregon, USA 26 A4
Copenhagen *country capital* Denmark 46 E4, 49 C12
Copiapó Chile 42 C4
Coppermine Nunavut, Canada 24 D4
Coquimbo Chile 42 C5
Coral Sea *sea* SW Pacific Ocean 100 D6, 103 J2, 106 D5
Corcovado, Gulf of *gulf* Chile 43 C9
Córdoba Argentina 39 D9, 43 E5
Córdoba Spain 46 A7, 56 D7
Corfu *island* Greece 68 E6
Corigliano Calabro Italy 63 H9
Corinth Greece 69 F7
Corinth, Gulf of *gulf* Aegean Sea/Ionian Sea 69 F7
Cork Republic of Ireland 51 B10
Corner Brook Newfoundland & Labrador, Canada 25 J7
Corno Grande *mountain* Italy 63 F6
Coro Venezuela 40 D1
Coromandel New Zealand 104 G3
Coromandel Coast *coastal region* India 93 D10
Coromandel Peninsula *peninsula* New Zealand 104 G3
Coronel Oviedo Paraguay 42 G3
Coronel Pringles Argentina 43 F7
Coropuna, Nevado *mountain* Peru 40 D6
Corpus Christi Texas, USA 30 D7
Corrib, Lough *lake* Republic of Ireland 51 B9
Corrientes Argentina 42 F4
Corrientes, Cabo *headland* Mexico 34 C5
Corse, Cap *headland* Corsica, France 55 K8
Corsica *island* France 46 D7, 55 K9
Cortona Italy 63 D5
Coruche Portugal 56 B6
Corum Turkey 88 D1
Corumba Brazil 41 F7
Corvallis Oregon, USA 26 B4
Cosenza Italy 63 H9
Costa Rica *country* Central America 23 F13, 35 I8
Cotonou Benin 77 H7
Cotopaxi *volcano* Ecuador 40 B3
Cotswold Hills *hill range* England, United Kingdom 51 G11
Cottbus Germany 59 I6
Council Bluffs Iowa, USA 29 H6
Courland Lagoon *lagoon* Lithuania/Russian Federation 65 A6
Coventry England, United Kingdom 51 G10
Covilha Portugal 56 B5
Cowan, Lake *seasonal lake* Western Australia, Australia 102 D6
Cozumel, Isla *island* Mexico 35 H5
Cradock South Africa 80 D8
Craiova Romania 69 G3
Crawley England, United Kingdom 51 H11
Creil France 55 F2
Cremona Italy 62 C3
Cres *island* Croatia 68 B3
Crescent City California, USA 27 A5
Crete *island* Greece 47 F9, 69 G9
Créteil France 55 F3
Crete, Sea of *sea* NE Mediterranean Sea 69 H9
Creuse *river* France 55 E5
Crimean Peninsula *peninsula* Ukraine 47 H6, 65 G12
Croatia *country* SE Europe 47 E7, 68 C2
Cromwell New Zealand 105 C11
Crotone Italy 63 H10
Croydon Queensland, Australia 103 H3
Crozet Basin *undersea feature* S Indian Ocean 82 D6
Crozet Islands *island group* SW Indian Ocean 82 C7
Crozet Plateau *undersea feature* SW Indian Ocean 82 C7
Csorna Hungary 67 D10
Cuamba Mozambique 81 H4
Cuando *river* S Africa 71 E10, 80 C4
Cuango *river* Angola/Democratic Republic of Congo 71 E9, 80 B2
Cuanza *river* Angola 80 B3
Cuautla Mexico 34 E6
Cuba *country* W West Indies 23 F11, 36 C3
Cubango *river* S Africa 71 E10, 80 C5
Cúcuta Colombia 38 B2, 40 C2
Cuddapah India 93 D9
Cuenca Ecuador 40 B4
Cuenca Spain 57 F5
Cuernavaca Mexico 34 E6
Cuiabá Brazil 41 G6
Culiacán Mexico 34 C4
Cumaná Venezuela 40 E1
Cuneo Italy 62 A4
Cunnamulla Queensland, Australia 103 H5
Curaçao *island* Netherlands Antilles 37 G8
Curitiba Brazil 39 G8, 41 H8
Cusco Peru 40 D6
Cuttack India 93 F7
Cuxhaven Germany 58 D3
Cyclades *island group* Greece 69 G8
Cyprus *country* W Asia 84 A6, 88 C3
Cyrenaica *cultural region* Libya 73 I5
Czech Republic *country* C Europe 46 E6, 67 B8
Czestochowa Poland 67 F6
Czluchow Poland 66 E3

D

Dachau Germany 59 D11
Dachuan China 97 G6
Daegu South Korea 98 C6
Daejon South Korea 98 B6
Dagupan Philippines 95 G3
Dakar *country capital* Senegal 70 A5, 76 C5
Dalälven *river* Norway/Sweden 49 D9
Dalandzadgad Mongolia 97 F3
Da Lat Vietnam 94 D4
Dali China 97 F8
Dalian China 97 J4
Dallas Texas, USA 23 E9, 30 E5
Dalmatia *cultural region* Croatia 68 D4
Daloa Ivory Coast 77 E7
Daly *river* Northern Territory, Australia 103 E2
Daly Waters Northern Territory, Australia 103 F2
Daman India 93 B7
Damaraland *physical region* Namibia 80 B6
Damascus *country capital* Syria 84 A6, 88 D3
Damavand, Qolleh ye *mountain* Iran 89 H3
Damietta Egypt 74 C3
Danakil Desert *desert* Ethiopia 75 F8
Da Nang Vietnam 85 F7, 94 D4
Dandong China 97 J4
Dannenberg Germany 59 G11
Danube *river* C Europe 47 F7, 59 C9, 61 J3, 67 E11, 69 F3
Danube Delta *delta* Romania/Ukraine 65 E12, 69 I3
Danville Virginia, USA 33 F9
Dapaong Togo 77 G6
Daqing China 97 J2
Darabani Romania 69 H1
Darbhanga India 92 F5
Dar es Salaam Tanzania 71 H8, 79 J8
Darfur *cultural region* Ethiopia/Sudan 70 F5, 75 C8
Darganata Turkmenistan 91 D7
Dargaville New Zealand 104 F2
Darhan China 97 G2
Darien, Gulf of *gulf* S Caribbean Sea 35 K8, 40 C2
Darjeeling Bhutan 92 G5
Darling *river* SW Australia 100 C7, 103 H6
Darmstadt Germany 59 C9
Darnah Libya 73 J4
Darnley, Cape *headland* Antarctica 21 E2
Daroca Spain 57 G4
Dart *river* England, United Kingdom 51 E12
Dartmoor *moorland* England, United Kingdom 51 E12
Daru Papua New Guinea 100 C5
Darvishan Afghanistan 91 D10
Darwin *state capital* Northern Territory, Australia 100 B6, 103 E1
Dashhowuz Turkmenistan 91 C6
Datong Mongolia 97 H4
Daugavpils Latvia 64 D5
Davangere India 93 C9
Davao Philippines 85 G8, 95 H5
Davenport Iowa, USA 29 J6
David Panama 35 J9
Davis Strait *strait* Baffin Bay/Labrador Sea 22 H4, 25 H3, 44 C2
Davos Switzerland 60 D5
Dawson Yukon Territory, Canada 24 B3
Dax France 54 D7
Dayr az Zawr Syria 89 E3
Dayton Ohio, USA 32 D7
Daytona Beach Florida, USA 31 J6
De Aar South Africa 80 D8
Deán Funes Argentina 42 E5
Death Valley *valley* California, USA 23 C8, 27 D9
Debrecen Hungary 67 H10
Debre Markos Ethiopia 75 E9
Debre Zeyit Ethiopia 75 F9
Decatur Alabama, USA 31 H4
Decatur Illinois, USA 32 B7
Deccan *plateau* India 84 D7, 93 C7
Decin Czech Republic 67 B6
Dee *river* Scotland, United Kingdom 50 F5
Deggendorf Germany 59 G10
Dehra Dun India 92 D4
Deh Shu Afghanistan 91 D10
Delano California, USA 27 C9
Delaware *state* USA 33 H7
Delaware Bay *inlet* NE USA 33 H7
Delémont Switzerland 60 B4
Delft Netherlands 53 D6
Delfzijl Netherlands 52 I2
Delhi India 92 D4
Delicias Mexico 34 C3
Delmenhorst Germany 58 D4
Del Rio Texas, USA 30 C6
Deltona Florida, USA 31 J6
Demchok *disputed region* China/India 92 D3, 97 B6
Demerara Plain *undersea feature* W Atlantic Ocean 45 D7
Den Helder Netherlands 52 E3
Denia Spain 57 H6
Denizli Turkey 88 C2
Denmark *country* N Europe 46 D4, 49 B12
Denmark Strait *strait* Greenland/Iceland 20 B5, 25 J1, 44 E2
Denov Uzbekistan 91 E8
Denpasar Indonesia 95 F9
Denver *state capital* Colorado, USA 23 D8, 28 E7
Dera Ghazi Khan Pakistan 91 F10
Dera Ismail Khan Pakistan 91 F10
Derbent Uzbekistan 91 E8
Derby England, United Kingdom 51 G9
Derby Western Australia, Australia 100 A6, 102 D3
Derry *see* Londonderry
Derzhavinsk Kazakhstan 90 E4
Dese Somalia 75 F8
Deseado *river* Argentina 43 D10
Des Moines *river* C USA 29 I5
Des Moines *state capital* Iowa, USA 29 I6
Desna *river* Russian Federation/Ukraine 65 E8
Dessau Germany 59 G6
Desventurados, Islas de los *island group* Chile 39 A8
Detmold Germany 59 D6
Detroit Michigan, USA 23 F8, 32 F5
Deva Romania 69 F2
Deventer Netherlands 52 G5
Devon Island *island* Nunavut, Canada 25 F2
Devonport Tasmania, Australia 103 H9
Deyang China 97 G6
Dezful Iran 89 G4
Dezhou China 97 I5
Dhahran Saudi Arabia 89 G6
Dhaka *country capital* Bangladesh 84 E7, 93 H6
Dhamar Yemen 89 F9
Dhanbad India 93 F6
Dhaulagiri *mountain* Nepal 92 E4
Dhole India 93 C7
Dhuusa Marreeb Somalia 75 H10
Diamantina *seasonal river* Queensland/South Australia, Australia 103 G5
Dickinson North Dakota, USA 29 F3
Diekirch Luxembourg 53 G12
Diepholz Germany 58 C5
Dieppe France 55 E2
Diest Belgium 53 E9
Diffa Niger 77 J6
Digne France 55 I7
Dijon France 55 H4
Dili *country capital* East Timor 85 G9, 95 H9
Dilling Sudan 75 C8
Dillon Montana, USA 29 B3
Dilolo Democratic Republic of Congo 79 E9
Dinajpur Bangladesh 92 G5
Dinant Belgium 53 E11
Dinaric Alps *mountain range* Bosnia & Herzegovina 68 D4
Dingle Bay *bay* Republic of Ireland 51 A10
Diourbel Senegal 76 C5
Dire Dawa Ethiopia 71 H6, 75 F9
Dirk Hartog Island *island* Western Australia, Australia 102 A5
Dirranbandi Queensland, Australia 103 I6
Disappointment, Lake *seasonal lake* Western Australia, Australia 102 C4
Divinópolis Brazil 41 H7
Diyarbakir Turkey 89 E2
Djambala Congo 78 C7
Djanet Algeria 73 G6
Djelfa Algeria 73 F4
Djibouti *country* E Africa 71 H5, 75 G8
Djibouti *country capital* Djibouti 71 H6, 75 G8
Dnieper *river* E Europe 47 G6, 65 E7
Dnieper Lowlands *physical region* Ukraine Belarus 65 E8
Dniester *river* Moldova/Ukraine 47 F6, 65 D10
Dniprodzerzhynsk Ukraine 65 G10
Dnipropetrovsk Ukraine 47 H6, 65 G10
Doberai, Jazirah *peninsula* Indonesia 95 I7
Doboj Bosnia & Herzegovina 68 D3
Dobrich Bulgaria 69 I4
Dodecanese *island group* Greece 69 H8
Dodge City Kansas, USA 29 G8
Dodoma *country capital* Tanzania 71 G8, 79 I8
Dogo *island* Japan 98 E6
Dogondoutchi Niger 77 H6
Doha *country capital* Qatar 84 B6, 89 H6
Dolisie Congo 78 C7
Dolomites *mountain range* Italy 62 D2
Dombås Norway 49 B7
Dominica *country* E West Indies 23 I12, 37 J6
Dominican Republic *country* C West Indies 23 H11, 37 G4
Domo Ethiopia 75 H9
Domodossola Italy 62 B2
Don *river* Russian Federation 47 H5, 86 A5
Don *river* Scotland, United Kingdom 50 F5
Donaueschingen Germany 59 C12
Donauwörth Germany 59 D10
Don Benito Spain 56 D6
Doncaster England, United Kingdom 51 G9
Dondo Angola 80 B3
Dondo Mozambique 81 G5
Donegal Republic of Ireland 51 C7
Donegal Bay *bay* NE Atlantic Ocean 51 B8
Donets *river* Russian Federation/Ukraine 65 H9
Donetsk Ukraine 47 H6, 65 H10
Dongara Western Australia, Australia 102 B6
Dongchuan China 97 F8
Donghae South Korea 98 C5
Dong Hoi Vietnam 94 D3
Dongola Sudan 75 C6
Dongsheng China 97 G4
Dongying China 97 I5
Donostia-San Sebastián Spain 57 F2
Dordogne *river* France 55 F6
Dordrecht Netherlands 53 E6
Dorfen Germany 59 G11
Dornbirn Switzerland 60 D4
Dorotea Sweden 49 E6
Dortmund Germany 59 B6
Dortmund-Ems-Canal *canal* Germany 59 B6
Dos Hermanas Spain 56 D8
Dosso Niger 77 H6
Dossor Kazakhstan 90 B4
Dostyk Kazakhstan 90 I5
Dothan Alabama, USA 31 H5
Douala Cameroon 71 D7, 78 B5
Douglas Isle of Man 51 E8
Dourados Brazil 41 G7
Douro *river* Portugal/Spain 46 A7, 56 B4 *see also* Duero
Dover England, United Kingdom 51 I11
Dover *state capital* Delaware, USA 33 H7
Dover, Strait of *strait* France/United Kingdom 51 I11, 55 E1
Dovrefjell *plateau* Norway 49 B7
Dozen *island* Japan 98 E6
Drachten Netherlands 52 G2
Drakensberg *mountain range* Lesotho/South Africa 71 F12, 81 E8
Drake Passage *strait* E Atlantic Ocean 45 C12
Drama Greece 69 G5
Drammen Norway 49 C9
Drau *river* Austria 61 H5
Drava *river* C Europe 61 J6, 67 E12, 68 D2
Dresden Germany 59 H7
Drina *river* Bosnia & Herzegovina/Serbia & Montenegro 68 E3
Drobeta-Turnu Severin Romania 69 F3
Drogheda Republic of Ireland 51 D8
Drohobych Ukraine 65 B9
Dronning Maud Land *physical region* Antarctica 21 C1
Drummond Montana, USA 28 B3
Drummondville Québec, Canada 25 I8
Druskininkai Lithuania 65 B6
Duba Saudi Arabia 88 D5
Dubai United Arab Emirates 89 I6
Dubasari Moldova 65 D11
Dubawnt Lake *lake* Nunavut, Canada 24 E5
Dubbo New South Wales, Australia 103 I7
Dublin *country capital* Republic of Ireland 46 B4, 51 D9
Dubno Ukraine 65 C9
Dubrovnik Croatia 68 D4
Dubuque Iowa, USA 29 J5
Duchess Queensland, Australia 103 G4
Dudinka Russian Federation 87 F4
Duero *river* Portugal/Spain 57 F3 *see also* Douro
Dufourspitze *mountain* Italy/Switzerland 60 C6, 62 B3
Duisburg Germany 59 B6
Duluth Minnesota, USA 29 I3
Dumaguete Philippines 95 G5
Dumfries Scotland, United Kingdom 51 E7
Dumont d'Urville Sea *sea* S Pacific Ocean 21 D5
Dunaujvaros Hungary 67 E11
Dundalk Republic of Ireland 51 D8
Dundee Scotland, United Kingdom 51 F5
Dunedin New Zealand 101 F9, 105 D12
Dunfermline Scotland, United Kingdom 51 F6
Dungeness *headland* England, United Kingdom 51 I12
Dungun Malaysia 94 C6
Dunhuang China 96 E4

FUKUSHIMA–HALLET, CAPE . 115

Fukushima Japan 99 H5
Fukuyama Japan 98 E7
Fulda Germany 59 D8
Fulda *river* Germany 59 D7
Fuling China 97 G7
Funabashi Japan 99 H6
Fundy, Bay of *bay* New Brunswick/Nova Scotia, Canada 25 J8
Furneaux Group *island group* Tasmania, Australia 103 I8
Fürth Germany 59 E9
Furukawa Japan 99 H5
Fushun China 97 J3
Fuxin China 97 I3
Fuzhou China 97 J7
Fyn *island* Denmark 49 B12

G

Gaalkacyo Somalia 75 H10
Gabès Tunisia 70 D2, 73 H4
Gabès, Gulf of S Mediterranean Sea 73 H4
Gabon *country* C Africa 71 D8, 78 B6
Gaborone *country capital* Botswana 71 F11, 80 E6
Gabrovo Bulgaria 69 G4
Gadag India 93 C8
Gaeta Italy 63 F7
Gaeta, Gulf of *gulf* N Tyrrhenian Sea 63 E8
Gafsa Tunisia 73 G4
Gagnoa Ivory Coast 77 E8
Gainesville Florida, USA 31 I6
Gairdner, Lake *seasonal lake* South Australia, Australia 103 F6
Galapagos Islands *island group* Ecuador 40 A8
Galati Romania 69 I2
Galdhopiggen *mountain* Norway 49 B8
Galicia *cultural region* Spain 56 B2
Galle Sri Lanka 93 D12
Gallego Rise *undersea feature* E Pacific Ocean 107 H5
Gallipoli Italy 63 I8
Gallipoli Turkey 88 B1
Gällivare Sweden 48 F4
Gallup New Mexico, USA 30 A3
Galtat-Zemmour Western Sahara 72 B6
Galveston Texas, USA 31 E6
Galway Republic of Ireland 51 B9
Galway Bay *bay* Republic of Ireland 51 B9
Gambia *country* W Africa 70 A5, 76 C5
Gambia *river* Gambia 76 D6
Gambier Islands *island group* French Polynesia 101 J7
Ganca Azerbaijan 89 G1
Gander Newfoundland & Labrador, Canada 25 K6
Gandhinagar India 93 B6
Gandhi Sagar *lake* India 93 C5
Gandia Spain 57 H6
Ganges *river* Bangladesh/India 84 D6, 92 D5
Ganges, Mouths of the *delta* Bangladesh/India 93 G7
Gangneung South Korea 98 C5
Gangtok Bhutan 92 G5
Gan Jiang *river* China 97 I7
Ganyushkino Kazakhstan 90 A5
Ganzhou China 97 I7
Gao Mali 77 G5
Gap France 55 I7
Gar China 96 B6
Garabogaz Aylagy *bay* Turkmenistan 91 B6
Garagum *desert* Turkmenistan 91 C7
Garagum Canal *canal* Turkmenistan 91 B7
Garda, Lake *lake* Italy 62 D3
Gardelegen Germany 58 F5
Garden City Kansas, USA 29 F8
Gardez Afghanistan 91 F9
Gargano Peninsula *peninsula* Italy 63 G7
Garissa Kenya 79 J6
Garland Texas, USA 30 E5
Garmisch-Partenkirchen Germany 59 F12
Garmsar Iran 89 H3
Garonne *river* France 46 C6, 55 E7
Garoowe Somalia 75 H9
Garoua Cameroon 78 C4
Garut Indonesia 94 D9
Garwolin Poland 66 G5
Gary Indiana, USA 32 C6
Gascony *cultural region* France 54 D7
Gascony, Gulf of *gulf* France/Spain 57 F1, 54 C7
Gastonia North Carolina, USA 31 I3
Gastouni Greece 69 F7
Gata, Cabo de *headland* Spain 57 F8
Gävle Sweden 49 E9
Gawler South Australia, Australia 103 G7
Gaya India 93 F5
Gaza Israel 88 D4
Gazanjyk Turkmenistan 91 B7
Gaziantep Turkey 88 E2
Gazojak Turkmenistan 91 D7
Gdansk Poland 47 E5, 66 E2
Gdansk, Gulf of *gulf* S Baltic Sea 66 F2
Gdynia Poland 66 E2
Gebze Turkey 88 C1
Gedaref Sudan 75 E8
Geel Belgium 53 E8
Geelong Victoria, Australia 100 D8, 103 H8
Geilo Norway 49 B8
Gejiu China 97 F8
Gela Italy 63 F12
Gelsenkirchen Germany 59 B6
Gembloux Belgium 53 E10
Gemena Democratic Republic of Congo 78 E5
Gemona del Friuli Italy 62 E2
General Roca Argentina 43 D8
General Santos Philippines 95 H6
Geneva Switzerland 60 A6
Geneva, Lake *lake* France/Switzerland 55 I5, 60 B5
Genk Belgium 53 F9
Genoa Italy 46 D7, 62 B4
Genoa, Gulf of *gulf* N Ligurian Sea 62 B5
Geok-Tepe Turkmenistan 91 C8
George South Africa 80 D9
Georgetown Queensland, Australia 103 H3
Georgetown *country capital* Guyana 38 E2, 41 F2
George Town Malaysia 94 B6
George V Land *physical region* Antarctica 21 D5
Georgia *country* SW Asia 84 B5, 89 E1
Georgia *state* USA 31 I5
Georgian Bay *lake bay* Ontario, Canada 25 H9, 33 E3
Georgievka Kazakhstan 91 G6
Georgina *seasonal river* C Australia 103 G4
Gera Germany 59 G7
Geraldton Western Australia, Australia 100 A8, 102 B6
Gereshk Afghanistan 91 D10
Gerlachovsky Stit *mountain* Slovakia 67 F8
German Bight *bay* SE North Sea 58 C2
Germany *country* W Europe 46 D5, 58–59
Getafe Spain 57 E5
Ghadamis Libya 73 G5
Ghaghara *river* S Asia 92 E5
Ghana *country* W Africa 71 C6, 77 G7
Ghanzi Botswana 80 D6
Ghardaïa Algeria 73 F4
Ghat Libya 73 G6
Ghazal, Bahr El *river* Sudan 75 C9
Ghaziabad India 92 D4
Ghazni Afghanistan 91 E9
Ghent Belgium 53 C8
Gibraltar *UK dependent territory* SW Europe 46 A8, 56 D9
Gibraltar, Strait of *strait* Atlantic Ocean/ Mediterranean Sea 46 A8, 56 C9, 72 D3
Gibson Desert *desert* Western Australia, Australia 100 A7, 102 D5
Giessen Germany 59 C8
Gifhorn Germany 58 E5
Gifu Japan 99 G7
Gijón Spain 56 D1
Gila *river* Arizona, USA 27 F12
Gilbert Islands *island group* Kiribati 101 F4
Gilgit Pakistan 91 G8
Gillette Wyoming, USA 28 E4
Gioia del Colle Italy 63 H8
Girona Spain 57 J3
Gironde *estuary* France 54 D6
Gisborne New Zealand 104 I5
Giurgiu Romania 69 H3
Gizycko Poland 66 H3
Gjøvik Norway 49 C8
Gladstone Queensland, Australia 103 J5
Glarner Alpen *mountain range* Switzerland 60 D5
Glasgow Scotland, United Kingdom 46 C4, 51 E6
Glen Canyon *canyon* Arizona/Utah, USA 27 G9
Glendale Arizona, USA 27 G11
Glendale California, USA 27 D11
Glendive Montana, USA 28 E3
Glens Falls New York, USA 33 I5
Glittertind *mountain* Norway 49 B8
Gliwice Poland 67 E7
Glogow Poland 67 D5
Glomma *river* Norway 49 C8
Gloucester England, United Kingdom 51 F10
Gmünd Austria 61 I2
Gmunden Austria 61 H3
Gniezno Poland 66 E4
Gobabis Namibia 80 C6
Gobernador Gregores Argentina 43 D11
Gobi *desert* China/Mongolia 85 F5, 97 F4
Godavari *river* India 84 D7, 93 D7
Godoy Cruz Argentina 43 C6
Goes Netherlands 53 C7
Goiânia Brazil 39 G6, 41 H6
Gol Norway 49 B8
Gold Coast Queensland, Australia 100 D7, 103 J6
Golden Bay *bay* New Zealand 105 E7
Goleniow Poland 66 C3
Golmud China 96 E5
Goma Democratic Republic of Congo 79 G6
Gonabad Iran 89 I3
Gonaïves Haiti 37 F4
Gonbad-e Kavus Iran 89 H2
Gonder Ethiopia 75 E8
Gondia India 93 D7
Good Hope, Cape of *headland* South Africa 45 H10, 71 E13, 80 C9
Goondiwindi Queensland, Australia 103 J6
Göppingen Germany 59 D10
Gorakhpur India 92 E5
Gore Ethiopia 75 E9
Gore New Zealand 105 C12
Gorgan Iran 89 H2
Gorizia Italy 62 F3
Gorlice Poland 67 G8
Görlitz Germany 59 I7
Gorno-Altaysk Russian Federation 87 E6
Gorontalo Indonesia 95 G7
Gorzow Wielkopolski Poland 66 C4
Gosford New South Wales, Australia 103 J7
Goslar Germany 59 E6
Gosselies Belgium 53 D10
Gostivar Macedonia 69 E5
Gotha Germany 59 E7
Gothenburg Sweden 46 E4, 49 C11
Gotland *island* Sweden 47 E4, 49 E11
Goto-retto *island group* Japan 98 C8
Göttingen Germany 59 E6
Gouda Netherlands 53 E6
Goulburn New South Wales, Australia 103 I7
Goya Argentina 42 F4
Gozo *island* Malta 63 F13
Grafton New South Wales, Australia 103 J6
Grajewo Poland 66 H3
Grampian Mountains *mountain range* Scotland, United Kingdom 50 E5
Granada Nicaragua 35 I8
Granada Spain 57 E8
Gran Chaco *physical region* C South America 39 D8, 42 E3
Grand Bahama Island *island* Bahamas 36 C1
Grand Canyon *canyon* Arizona, USA 23 C8, 27 F9
Grand Cayman *island* Cayman Islands 36 B4
Grand Comore *island* Comoros 81 J3
Grande, Bahia *bay* Argentina 39 D12, 43 D12
Grande Prairie Alberta, Canada 24 C6
Grand Erg Occidental *desert* Algeria 70 C3, 73 F3
Grande, Rio *river* Brazil 23 D9, 39 F7, 41 H7
Grande, Rio *river* Mexico/USA 30 B5, 34 D2 *see also* Bravo del Norte, Río
Grande Terre *island* Guadeloupe 37 J6
Grand Forks North Dakota, USA 29 H2
Grand Island Nebraska, USA 29 G6
Grand Junction Colorado, USA 28 C7
Grand Rapids Michigan, USA 32 D5
Grand River *river* South Dakota, USA 29 E3
Gran Paradiso *mountain* Italy 62 A3
Gransee Germany 58 H4
Grants Pass Oregon, USA 26 B5
Granville Lake *lake* Manitoba, Canada 25 E6
Graz Austria 61 J5
Great Abaco *island* Bahamas 36 D1
Great Artesian Basin *physical region* Queensland, Australia 103 H5
Great Australian Bight *bay* South Australia, Australia 83 I6, 100 B8, 103 E7
Great Barrier Island *island* New Zealand 104 G3
Great Barrier Reef *reef* Queensland, Australia 100 C6, 103 I1
Great Basin *physical region* W USA 23 C8, 27 E7
Great Bear Lake *lake* Northwest Territories, Canada 22 E5, 24 D4
Great Bend Kansas, USA 29 G7
Great Channel *channel* Andaman Sea/Indian Ocean 93 I12
Great Divide Basin *physical region* Wyoming, USA 28 C5
Great Dividing Range *mountain range* E Australia 100 C7, 103 H3
Greater Antarctica *plateau* Antarctica 21 D3
Greater Antilles *island group* West Indies 23 F11, 36 B4
Great Exhibition Bay *bay* New Zealand 104 E1
Great Falls Montana, USA 28 C2
Great Hungarian Plain *physical region* Hungary 67 F10
Great Inagua *island* Bahamas 37 E4
Great Karoo *plateau* South Africa 80 D8
Great Khingan Range *mountain range* China 85 G5, 97 I2
Great Lakes *lakes* Canada/USA 23 F7, 32 C2
Great Nicobar *island* Nicobar Islands, India 93 I11
Great Ouse *river* England, United Kingdom 51 H10
Great Plains *physical region* Canada/USA 23 E7, 24 D7, 29 E3, 30 C2
Great Rift Valley *valley* E Africa 71 E8, 75 F9, 79 G7, 81 F2
Great Salt Lake *salt lake* Utah, USA 23 D8, 27 G6
Great Salt Lake Desert *physical region* Utah, USA 27 F6
Great Sand Sea *desert* Ethiopia/Libya 73 K5, 74 A4
Great Sandy Desert *desert* Australia 100 A7, 102 C4
Great Slave Lake *lake* Northwest Territories, Canada 23 E5, 24 D5
Great Victoria Desert *desert* South Australia/Western Australia, Australia 100 B7, 102 D6
Greece *country* SE Europe 47 F8, 69 F7
Greeley Colorado, USA 28 E6
Green Bay Wisconsin, USA 32 C4
Greenland *Danish dependent territory* NE North America 20 B4, 22 H3
Greenland *island* NE North America Ocean 44 D1
Greenland Sea *sea* Arctic Ocean 20 C5, 44 F2
Greenock Scotland, United Kingdom 51 E6
Greensboro North Carolina, USA 31 J3
Greenville Liberia 76 D8
Greenville Mississippi, USA 31 F5
Greenville South Carolina, USA 31 I4
Greifswald Germany 58 H3
Grenada *country* SE West Indies 23 I12, 37 J8
Grenadines, The *island group* St Vincent & the Grenadines 37 J7
Grenoble France 55 H6
Grevena Greece 69 F6
Grevenmacher Luxembourg 53 H12
Greymouth New Zealand 105 D9
Grimsby England, United Kingdom 51 H9
Grímsstadhir Iceland 48 C2
Grojec Poland 66 G5
Groningen Netherlands 52 H2
Groote Eylandt *island* Northern Territory, Australia 103 G2
Grootfontein Namibia 80 C5
Grosseto Italy 63 D6
Grossglockner *mountain* Austria 61 G5
Groznyy Russian Federation 47 J7, 86 A6
Grudziadz Poland 66 F3
Grums Sweden 49 D9
Grünau Namibia 80 C7
Guadalajara Mexico 23 D11, 34 D5
Guadalajara Spain 57 F4
Guadalcanal *island* Solomon Islands 100 D5
Guadalquivir *river* Spain 46 A7, 56 D7
Guadeloupe *French dependent territory* E West Indies 37 K6
Guadeloupe Passage *channel* Antigua & Barbuda/Guadeloupe 37 J6
Guadiana *river* Portugal/Spain 56 B7
Gualeguaychu Argentina 43 F6
Guam *US dependent territory* W Pacific Ocean 100 C3
Guangyuan China 97 G6
Guangzhou China 85 F7, 97 I8
Guantánamo Cuba 36 E4
Guaporé *river* Bolivia/Brazil 39 D6, 41 E5
Guarda Portugal 56 C4
Guarulhos Brazil 39 G8, 41 H7
Guatemala *country* Central America 23 E12, 35 G7
Guatemala Basin *undersea feature* E Pacific Ocean 107 I4
Guatemala City *country capital* Guatemala 23 E12, 35 G7
Guaviare *river* Colombia/Venezuela 38 C3, 40 D2
Guayaquil Ecuador 38 A4, 40 B4
Guayaquil, Gulf of *gulf* Ecuador/Peru 40 B4
Guaymas Mexico 34 B3
Gubbio Italy 63 E5
Guernsey *island* Channel Islands 51 F13
Guiana Highlands *physical region* N South America 38 D2, 40 E2
Guilin China 97 H8
Guimarães Portugal 56 B3
Guinea *country* W Africa 71 A6, 76 D6
Guinea Basin *undersea feature* E Atlantic Ocean 45 F9
Guinea-Bissau *country* W Africa 71 A5, 76 C6
Guinea, Gulf of *gulf* E Atlantic Ocean 45 G7, 71 C7, 77 G9, 78 A5
Guiyang China 85 F6, 97 G7
Gujranwala Pakistan 91 G9
Gulbarga India 93 D8
Gulf Coastal Plain *physical region* S USA 30 E6
Gulfport Mississippi, USA 31 G6
Gulf, The *gulf* SW Asia 82 C1, 84 B6, 89 G5
Guliston Uzbekistan 91 E7
Gulu Uganda 79 H6
Gumdag Turkmenistan 91 B7
Gunnbjørn Fjeld *mountain* Greenland 20 B5
Gunsan South Korea 98 B6
Guntur India 93 E8
Gunzenhausen Germany 59 E10
Guri, Embalse de *reservoir* Venezuela 41 E2
Gurué Mozambique 81 G4
Gusau Nigeria 77 I6
Gushgy Turkmenistan 91 D9
Guspini Italy 63 B9
Gütersloh Germany 59 C6
Guwahati India 92 H5
Guyana *country* N South America 38 E2, 41 F2
Gwadar Pakistan 91 D12
Gwalior India 92 D5
Gwanda Zimbabwe 81 F5
Gwangju South Korea 98 B6
Gweru Zimbabwe 71 G10, 81 F5
Gyangze China 96 D7
Gydanskiy Poluostrov *peninsula* Russian Federation 87 E3
Gyeongju South Korea 98 C6
Gympie Queensland, Australia 103 J5
Gyor Hungary 67 E10
Gytheio Greece 69 F8
Gyumri Armenia 89 F1
Gyzylarbat Turkmenistan 91 B7

H

Haapsalu Estonia 64 C3
Haarlem Netherlands 52 E5
Haast New Zealand 105 B10
Hachinohe Japan 99 I4
Hadramawt *mountain range* Yemen 89 G9
Haeju North Korea 98 B5
Hafar al Batin Saudi Arabia 89 F5
Hagen Germany 59 B6
Hagi Japan 98 D7
Ha Giang Vietnam 94 D2
Hague, Cap de la *headland* France 54 D2
Haguenau France 55 I3
Haicheng China 97 J4
Haifa Israel 88 D4
Haikou Hainan, China 97 H9
Ha'il Saudi Arabia 89 E5
Hailar China 97 I2
Hainan *island* China 85 F7, 97 H9
Hai Phong Vietnam 85 F7, 94 D2
Haiti *country* C West Indies 23 G11, 37 E5
Hakodate Japan 99 H3
Halaban Saudi Arabia 89 F6
Halaib Egypt 75 E6
Halban Mongolia 97 E2
Halberstadt Germany 59 F6
Halden Norway 49 C10
Halfmoon Bay New Zealand 105 B13
Halifax Nova Scotia, Canada 23 H8, 25 J8
Halla-san *mountain* South Korea 98 B7
Halle Belgium 53 D9
Halle Germany 59 F7
Hallein Austria 61 G4
Halle-Neustadt Germany 59 F7
Hallett, Cape *headland* Antarctica 21 C5

LONGYEARBYEN–MELVILLE PENINSULA . 119

Longyearbyen Svalbard 20 C4
Löningen Germany 58 C4
Lop Nur *seasonal lake* China 96 D4
Lorca Spain 57 G7
Lord Howe Island *island* Australia 100 D7
Lord Howe Rise *undersea feature* SW Pacific Ocean 106 D6
Lorient France 54 C4
Los Alamos New Mexico, USA 30 B3
Los Andes Chile 43 C6
Los Angeles Chile 43 C7
Los Angeles California, USA 23 B8, 27 D11
Los Mochis Mexico 34 B4
Lot *river* France 55 F6
Louangphabang Laos 94 C3
Louga Senegal 76 C5
Louisiana *state* USA 31 F6
Louisville Kentucky, USA 32 C8
Lourdes France 54 E8
Loutra Edipsou Greece 69 F7
Lovech Bulgaria 69 G4
Lowell Massachusetts, USA 33 J5
Lower California *peninsula* Mexico 23 C9, 34 A2
Lower Hutt New Zealand 105 F7
Lower Lough Erne *lake* Republic of Ireland 51 C8
Lower Tunguska *river* Russian Federation 85 E3, 87 F4
Lowicz Poland 66 F5
Loyalty Islands *island group* New Caledonia 101 E6
Loznica Serbia & Montenegro 68 E3
Luacano Angola 80 D3
Lualaba *river* Democratic Republic of Congo 71 F8, 79 F7
Luanda *country capital* Angola 71 E9, 80 A2
Luan He *river* China 97 I4
Luanshya Zambia 81 E3
Lubango Angola 80 A4
Lübben Germany 59 H6
Lübbenau Germany 59 H6
Lubbock Texas, USA 30 C4
Lübeck Germany 58 E3
Lublin Poland 67 H6
Lubliniec Poland 67 E6
Lubny Ukraine 65 F9
Lubumbashi Democratic Republic of Congo 71 F9, 79 G9
Lucca Italy 62 C5
Lucenec Slovakia 67 F9
Lucerne Switzerland 60 C5
Lucknow India 92 E5
Lüderitz Namibia 80 B7
Ludhiana India 92 C3
Ludington Michigan, USA 32 C4
Ludvika Sweden 49 D9
Ludwigsburg Germany 59 D10
Ludwigshafen am Rhein Germany 59 C9
Ludwigslust Germany 58 F4
Luena Angola 80 C3
Lugano Switzerland 60 D6
Lugo Italy 62 D4
Lugo Spain 56 C2
Lugovoy Kazakhstan 91 F6
Luhansk Ukraine 65 I10
Lukenie *river* Democratic Republic of Congo 78 E7
Luleå Sweden 49 F5
Luleälven *river* Sweden 48 E4
Lumsden New Zealand 105 B12
Lun Mongolia 97 F2
Lund Sweden 49 C12
Lundy *island* England, United Kingdom 51 E11
Lüneburg Germany 58 E4
Lüneburg Heath *physical region* Germany 58 D4
Luo He *river* China 97 G5
Luoyang China 97 H5
Lusaka *country capital* Zambia 71 F10, 81 E4
Lut, Dasht-e *desert* Syria 89 I4
Luton England, United Kingdom 51 H10
Lutsk Ukraine 65 C9
Luxembourg *country* W Europe 46 D5, 53 G12
Luxembourg *country capital* Luxembourg 46 D5, 53 G12
Luxor Egypt 70 G3, 74 D4
Luz, Costa de la *coastal region* Spain 56 C8
Luzhou China 97 G7
Luzon *island* Philippines 85 G7, 95 G3
Luzon Strait *strait* Philippines/Taiwan 95 G3, 97 J9
Lviv Ukraine 47 F6, 65 B9
Lycksele Sweden 49 E6
Lyme Bay *bay* England, United Kingdom 51 F12
Lynchburg Virginia, USA 33 F8
Lyon France 46 C6, 55 H5
Lysychansk Ukraine 65 H10

M

Ma'an Jordan 88 D4
Maarianhamina *see* Mariehamn
Maas *river* W Europe 53 G7 *see also* Meuse
Maastricht Netherlands 53 F9
McAllen Texas, USA 30 D7
Macao China 97 I8
Macapá Brazil 41 G3
McClintock Channel *channel* Nunavut, Canada 24 E3
McDermitt Nevada, USA 27 D6
Macdonnell Ranges *mountain range* Northern Territory, Australia 103 F4
Macedonia *country* SE Europe 47 F7, 69 F5
Macedonia *cultural region* Greece 69 F5
Maceió Brazil 39 I5, 41 J5
Machakos Kenya 79 I7
Machala Ecuador 40 B4
Machilipatnam India 93 E8
Macia Mozambique 81 F6
Mackay Queensland, Australia 100 D6, 103 I4
Mackay, Lake *seasonal lake* Northern Territory/Western Australia, Australia 102 E4
Mackenzie *river* Northwest Territories, Canada 22 D5, 24 C4
Mackenzie Mountains *mountain range* Yukon Territory/ Northwest Territories, Canada 22 D4, 24 B4
McKinley, Mount *mountain* Alaska, USA 22 C4, 26 H2
Macleod, Lake *lake* Western Australia, Australia 102 B5
Macomer Italy 63 B8
Mâcon France 55 H5
Macon Georgia, USA 31 I4
Madagascar *country* SE Africa 71 H11, 81 J4
Madagascar *island* SE Africa 82 C5
Madagascar Basin *undersea feature* W Indian Ocean 82 C5
Madagascar Plateau *undersea feature* W Indian Ocean 82 C6
Madeira *Portuguese dependent territory* NW Atlantic Ocean 70 A2, 72 B4
Madeira *river* Bolivia/Brazil 38 D4, 41 E4
Mädelegabel *mountain* Germany 59 F13
Madison *state capital* Wisconsin, USA 32 B5
Madras *see* Chennai
Madre de Dios *river* Bolivia/Peru 39 C6, 40 D5
Madre, Laguna *lagoon* Mexico 35 E4
Madrid *country capital* Spain 46 B7, 57 E4
Madura *island* Indonesia 95 E9
Madurai India 93 D10
Maebashi Japan 99 H6
Mafeteng South Africa 80 E8
Mafia *island* Tanzania 79 J8
Magadan Russian Federation 87 J4
Magdalena *river* Colombia 40 C2
Magdeburg Germany 59 F6
Magellan, Strait of *strait* Argentina/Chile 39 D13, 43 D12
Magerøya *island* Norway 48 G1
Maggiore, Lake *lake* Italy/Switzerland 60 C6, 62 B2
Magnitogorsk Russian Federation 86 C5
Mahajanga Madagascar 71 I10, 81 J4
Mahakan *river* Indonesia 95 F7
Mahalapye Botswana 80 E6
Mahanadi *river* India 93 F7
Mahia Peninsula *peninsula* New Zealand 105 I6
Mahilyow Ukraine 65 E7
Mahón Balearic Islands, Spain 57 K5
Maiduguri Nigeria 71 E6, 77 J6
Main *river* Germany 59 E9
Main-Donau-Canal *canal* Germany 59 F10
Maine *state* USA 33 J3
Maine, Gulf of *gulf* NE USA 33 J4
Mainland *island* Orkney Islands, Scotland, United Kingdom 50 F3
Mainland *island* Shetland Islands, Scotland, United Kingdom 50 G1
Mainz Germany 59 C9
Maizuru Japan 99 F7
Majorca *see* Mallorca
Majuro *country capital* Marshall Islands 101 F4
Makassar Indonesia 85 G9, 95 G8
Makassar Strait *strait* Indonesia 95 F8
Makeni Sierra Leone 76 D7
Makhachkala Russian Federation 86 A6
Makiyivka Ukraine 65 H10
Makokou Gabon 78 C6
Makumbako Tanzania 79 H8
Makurdi Nigeria 77 I7
Malabar Coast *coastal region* India 93 C9
Malabo *country capital* Equatorial Guinea 71 D7, 78 B5
Malacca, Strait of *strait* Indonesia/Malaysia 83 G3, 94 B6
Maladzyechna Belarus 65 D6
Málaga Spain 46 A8, 56 E8
Malaita *island* Solomon Islands 100 E5
Malakal Sudan 75 D9
Malang Indonesia 95 E9
Malanje Angola 80 B2
Mälaren *lake* Sweden 49 E9
Malargüe Argentina 43 C7
Malatya Turkey 88 E2
Malawi *country* S Africa 71 G9, 81 G3
Malay Peninsula *peninsula* Malaysia/Thailand 94 B5
Malaysia *country* SE Asia 85 F8, 94 C6
Malbork Poland 66 F3
Maldives *country* N Indian Ocean 84 D8, 93 B12
Maldives *island group* N Indian Ocean 83 E3
Male *country capital* Maldives 84 D8, 93 B12
Malegaon India 93 C7
Malheur Lake *lake* Oregon, USA 26 D4
Mali *country* W Africa 70 C4, 77 F5
Malindi Kenya 79 J7
Mallaig Scotland, United Kingdom 50 D5
Mallawi Egypt 74 C4
Mallorca *island* Balearic Islands, Spain 46 C7, 57 J5
Malmberget Sweden 48 F4
Malmédy Belgium 53 G10
Malmö Sweden 46 E5, 49 C12
Malopolska *cultural region* Poland 67 G7
Malta *country* C Mediterranean Sea 46 E9, 63 F13
Malta *island* C Mediterranean Sea 63 F13
Malta Channel *channel* S Mediterranean Sea 63 F13
Malunda Indonesia 95 F8
Malung Sweden 49 D9
Mamberamo *river* Indonesia 95 K7
Mamoré *river* Bolivia/Brazil 40 E6
Mamou Guinea 76 D6
Mamoudzou Mayotte 81 J3
Man Ivory Coast 76 E7
Manacor Balearic Islands, Spain 57 J5
Manado Indonesia 95 H7
Managua *country capital* Nicaragua 23 F12, 35 I8
Manakara Madagascar 81 J6
Manama *country capital* Bahrain 84 B6, 89 H6
Mananjary Madagascar 81 J6
Manaus Brazil 38 E4, 41 F4
Manchester England, United Kingdom 46 C4, 51 F9
Manchester New Hampshire, USA 33 J5
Manchurian Plain *physical region* China 85 G5, 97 I3
Mandalay Myanmar 85 E7, 94 B2
Mandalgovi Mongolia 97 G3
Mandurah Western Australia, Australia 102 B7
Manfredonia Italy 63 G7
Manfredonia, Gulf of *gulf* SW Adriatic Sea 63 G7
Mangalore India 93 C9
Mangaweka New Zealand 105 G6
Manhattan Kansas, USA 29 H7
Manicouagan Reservoir *reservoir* Québec, Canada 25 I7
Maniitsoq Greenland 20 A4
Manila *country capital* Philippines 85 G7, 95 G4
Manisa Turkey 88 B2
Man, Isle of *island* United Kingdom 46 C4, 51 E8
Manitoba *province* Canada 25 E7
Manitoba, Lake *lake* Manitoba, Canada 24 E8
Manizales Colombia 40 C2
Mannar, Gulf of *gulf* India/Sri Lanka 93 D11
Mannheim Germany 59 C9
Manokwari Indonesia 95 J7
Manpo North Korea 98 B3
Manresa Spain 57 I3
Mansa Zambia 81 F3
Mansfield England, United Kingdom 51 G9
Mansfield Ohio, USA 32 E6
Manta Ecuador 40 B3
Mantova Italy 62 D3
Manukau Harbour *harbour* New Zealand 104 F4
Manurewa New Zealand 104 G3
Manzanares Spain 57 E6
Manzanillo Cuba 36 D4
Manzhouli China 97 H2
Manzini Swaziland 81 F7
Maoke, Pegunungan *mountain range* Indonesia 95 K8
Maoming China 97 H8
Maputo *country capital* Mozambique 71 G11, 81 F7
Maputo Bay *bay* W Indian Ocean 81 G7
Maqat Kazakhstan 90 B4
Maracaibo Venezuela 40 D1
Maracaibo, Lake *lake* Venezuela 38 C2, 40 C1
Maracay Venezuela 38 C2, 40 D1
Maradah Libya 73 J5
Maradi Niger 77 I6
Maragheh Iran 89 F2
Marajó, Baía de *bay* Brazil 41 H3
Marajó, Ilha de *island* Brazil 38 G3, 41 H3
Marañón *river* Peru 38 B4, 40 C4
Maratea Italy 63 G9
Marbella Spain 56 D8
Marburg Germany 59 C7
Marche-en-Famenne Belgium 53 F11
Marchena, Isla *island* Galapagos Islands 40 B8
Mar Chiquito, Laguna *lake* Argentina 39 D9
Mar del Plata Argentina 39 E10, 43 G7
Margarita, Isla de *island* Venezuela 41 E1
Margow, Dasht-e *desert* Afghanistan 91 D10
Marhanets Ukraine 65 G11
Mariana Trench *undersea feature* W Pacific Ocean 106 C4
Maribor Slovenia 61 J5
Marie Byrd Land *physical region* Antarctica 21 B4
Mariehamn Finland 49 F9
Mariental Namibia 80 C6
Mariestad Sweden 49 D10
Marijampole Lithuania 65 B6
Marikostinovo Bulgaria 69 F5
Marília Brazil 41 G7
Maringá Brazil 41 G7
Maritime Alps *mountain range* France/Italy 55 I7
Maritsa *river* SW Europe 69 H5
Mariupol Ukraine 65 H11
Marka Somalia 75 G11
Markermeer *lake* Netherlands 52 E4
Marktoberdorf Germany 59 E12
Marktredwitz Germany 59 G9
Marmara, Sea of *sea* Aegean Sea/Black Sea 69 I5
Marmaris Turkey 88 C2
Marmolada *mountain* Italy 62 E2
Marne *river* France 55 H3
Maroantsetra Madagascar 81 K4
Maroochydore-Mooloolaba Queensland, Australia 103 J5
Maroua Cameroon 78 C4
Marquesas Fracture Zone *undersea feature* C Pacific Ocean 107 G5
Marquesas Islands *island group* French Polynesia 101 J5
Marrakech Morocco 70 B2, 72 D4
Marree South Australia, Australia 103 G6
Marsa Al Burayqah Libya 73 J5
Marsabit Kenya 79 I6
Marsala Italy 63 E11
Marseille France 46 C7, 55 H8
Marshall Islands *country* W Pacific Ocean 100 D3
Martaban, Gulf of *gulf* Myanmar 94 B3
Martapura Indonesia 95 F8
Martha's Vineyard *island* Massachusetts, USA 33 J6
Martigny Switzerland 60 B6
Martin Slovakia 67 F8
Martinique *French dependent territory* E West Indies 37 J6
Martinique Passage *channel* Dominica/Martinique 37 J6
Mary Turkmenistan 91 D8
Maryborough Queensland, Australia 103 J5
Maryland *state* USA 33 G7
Maryville Missouri, USA 29 I6
Masai Steppe *physical region* Tanzania 71 H8, 79 I7
Masan South Korea 98 C6
Masasi Tanzania 79 I9
Masbate *island* Philippines 95 G4
Mascarene Basin *undersea feature* W Indian Ocean 82 D4
Maseru *country capital* Lesotho 71 F12, 80 E8
Mashhad Iran 84 C5, 89 I2
Masindi Uganda 79 H6
Masirah *island* Oman 89 J7
Masirah, Gulf of *gulf* NW Arabian Sea 89 J7
Mason City Iowa, USA 29 I5
Massa Italy 62 C5
Massachusetts *state* USA 33 I5
Massawa Eritrea 75 F7
Massena New York, USA 33 H4
Massif Central *plateau* France 46 C6, 55 F6
Masterton New Zealand 105 G7
Masty Belarus 65 C7
Masuda Japan 98 D7
Masvingo Zimbabwe 81 F5
Matadi Democratic Republic of Congo 78 C8
Matagalpa Nicaragua 35 I7
Matam Senegal 76 D5
Matamoros Mexico 35 E4
Matanzas Cuba 36 B3
Mataram Indonesia 95 F9
Mataranka Northern Territory, Australia 103 F2
Mataró Spain 57 J3
Mataura *river* New Zealand 105 B12
Matera Italy 63 H8
Mato Grosso, Planalto de *plateau* Brazil 39 E6, 41 G6
Matosinhos Portugal 56 B4
Matsue Japan 98 E6
Matsumoto Japan 99 G6
Matsuyama Japan 98 E7
Matterhorn *mountain* Italy/Switzerland 60 B6
Matto Japan 99 F6
Maturín Venezuela 41 E1
Maui *island* Hawaii, USA 27 B12
Maun Botswana 80 D5
Mauritania *country* W Africa 70 A4, 76 D4
Mauritius *island* W Indian Ocean 82 D5
Maxixe Mozambique 81 G6
Mayagüez Puerto Rico 37 H5
Maydan Shahr Afghanistan 91 F9
Maykop Russian Federation 86 A5
Mayotte *French dependent territory* S Africa 71 I9, 81 J3
May Pen Jamaica 36 D5
Mazabuka Zambia 81 E4
Mazara del Vallo Italy 63 E11
Mazar-e Sharif Afghanistan 91 E8
Mazatlán Mexico 34 C4
Mazeikiai Lithuania 64 B5
Mazuria *cultural region* Poland 66 F4
Mazyr Belarus 65 D8
Mbabane *country capital* Swaziland 71 G11, 81 F7
Mbaiki Central African Republic 78 D5
Mbaké Senegal 76 C5
Mbale Uganda 79 H6
Mbandaka Democratic Republic of Congo 71 E7, 78 D6
M'banza Congo Angola 80 B2
Mbarara Uganda 79 G6
Mbeya Tanzania 79 H8
Mbuji-Mayi Democratic Republic of Congo 71 F8, 79 F8
Mdantsane South Africa 80 E8
Mead, Lake *lake* Arizona/Nevada, USA 27 F9
Mecca Saudi Arabia 84 B7, 88 E7
Mechelen Belgium 53 D8
Meckenheim Germany 59 B8
Mecklenburg Bay *bay* S Baltic Sea 58 F2
Medan Indonesia 85 E8, 94 B6
Medellín Colombia 38 B2, 40 C2
Medford Oregon, USA 26 B5
Medias Romania 69 G2
Medicine Hat Alberta, Canada 24 C8
Medina Saudi Arabia 88 E6
Medina del Campo Spain 56 D4
Mediterranean Sea *sea* E Atlantic Ocean 63 C11, 68 D9
Meekatharra Western Australia, Australia 102 C5
Meerut India 92 D4
Megisti Greece 69 J8
Meiningen Germany 59 E8
Meizhou China 97 I8
Mekele Ethiopia 75 F8
Meknès Morocco 72 D4
Mekong *river* SE Asia 85 F7, 94 C2, 97 E6
Mekong, Mouths of the *delta* Vietnam 94 D5
Melaka Malaysia 94 C7
Melanesia *island group* W Pacific Ocean 100 C4, 106 C5
Melanesian Basin *undersea feature* W Pacific Ocean 106 D4
Melbourne *state capital* Victoria, Australia 100 D8, 103 H8
Melbourne Florida, USA 31 J6
Melilla *Spanish dependent territory* NW Africa 57 F9, 70 C2, 72 E3
Melitopol Ukraine 65 G11
Mellerud Sweden 49 C10
Melo Uruguay 43 H6
Melun France 55 F3
Melville Island *island* Northern Territory, Australia 103 E1
Melville Island *island* Northwest Territories/Nunavut, Canada 22 F4, 24 D2
Melville Peninsula *peninsula* Nunavut, Canada 25 F4

UNGAVA PENINSULA–WINSCHOTEN . 127

Ungava Peninsula *peninsula* Québec, Canada 23 G6, 25 G5
Ungheni Moldova 65 D11
Uniontown Pennsylvania, USA 33 F7
United Arab Emirates *country* SW Asia 84 C7, 89 H6
United Kingdom *country* NW Europe 46 C4, 51 E7
United States of America *country* N North America 26–33
Upington South Africa 80 C7
Upper Lough Erne *lake* Republic of Ireland/United Kingdom 51 C8
Uppsala Sweden 49 E9
Upua New Zealand 104 F2
Ural *river* Kazakhstan/Russian Federation 47 J4, 84 B4, 86 C5, 90 B4
Ural Mountains *mountain range* Asia/Europe 47 I1, 84 C3, 86 D4
Urawa Japan 99 H6
Urbino Italy 62 E5
Urengoy Russian Federation 87 E4
Urganch Uzbekistan 91 D7
Uritskiy Kazakhstan 90 E3
Urmia, Lake *lake* Iran 89 F2
Urosevac Serbia & Montenegro 69 E5
Uroteppa Tajikistan 91 F7
Uruguay *country* S South America 39 E9, 43 G6
Uruguay *river* S South America 39 E9, 41 C8, 42 G1
Urumqi China 84 E5, 96 D3
Usak Turkey 88 C2
Usedom *island* Germany 58 H3
Ushuaia Argentina 43 D13
Ussuri *river* China/Russian Federation 97 K2
Ussuriysk Russian Federation 87 J7
Ustica *island* Italy 63 E10
Ust-Ilimsk Russian Federation 87 G5
Usti nad Labem Czech Republic 67 B6
Ustka Poland 66 D2
Ust-Kamchatsk Russian Federation 87 K3
Ustrzyki Dolne Poland 67 H8
Ustyurt Plateau *plateau* Kazakhstan/Uzbekistan 91 B6
Usumacinta *river* Guatemala/Mexico 35 G6
Utah *state* USA 27 G8
Utica New York, USA 33 H5
Utiel Spain 57 G5
Utrecht Netherlands 53 E5
Utsjoki Finland 48 G2
Utsunomiya Japan 99 H6
Uvs Nuur *lake* Mongolia 96 E2
Uyo Nigeria 77 I8
Uzbekistan *country* C Asia 84 C5, 91 D7
Uzhhorod Ukraine 65 A10

V

Vaal *river* South Africa 71 F12, 80 D7
Vaasa Finland 49 F7
Vac Hungary 67 F10
Vacaville California, USA 27 B8
Vadodara India 93 B6
Vadsø Norway 48 H2
Vaduz *country capital* Liechtenstein 46 D6, 60 D5
Vah *river* Slovakia 67 F9
Valdecañas, Embalse de *reservoir* Spain 56 D5
Valdepeñas Spain 57 E6
Valdés, Península *peninsula* Argentina 43 E9
Valdivia Chile 43 C8
Valdosta Georgia, USA 31 I5
Valence France 55 H6
Valencia Spain 46 B7, 57 H5
Valencia Venezuela 38 C2, 40 D1
Valencia, Gulf of *gulf* Spain 57 H6
Valenciennes France 55 G1
Valentine Nebraska, USA 29 F5
Valera Venezuela 40 D1
Valga Estonia 64 C4
Valladolid Spain 46 B7, 56 D3
Valledupar Venezuela 40 C1
Vallejo California, USA 27 B8
Vallenar Chile 42 C4
Valletta *country capital* Malta 46 E9, 63 F13
Valmiera Estonia 64 C4
Valparaíso Chile 43 C6
Valverde del Camino Spain 56 C7
Van Turkey 89 F2
Vanadzor Armenia 89 F1
Vancouver British Columbia, Canada 23 C6, 24 B7
Vancouver Washington, USA 26 B3
Vancouver Island *island* British Columbia, Canada 23 C6, 24 A7
Vancouver, Mount *mountain* Yukon Territory, Canada 24 A4
Van Diemen Gulf *gulf* Northern Territory, Australia 103 E1
Vänern *lake* Sweden 46 E4, 49 C10
Vänersborg Sweden 49 C10
Vangaindrano Madagascar 81 J6
Van, Lake *lake* Turkey 89 F2
Vannes France 54 C4
Vanrhynsdorp South Africa 80 C8
Vantaa Finland 49 H9
Vanua Levu *island* Fiji 101 F6
Vanuatu *country* SW Pacific Ocean 100 E6
Varanasi India 93 E5
Varangerfjorden *fjord* Norway 48 H2
Varano, Lake *lagoon* Italy 63 G7
Varazdin Croatia 68 C2
Varberg Sweden 49 C11
Varde Denmark 49 A12
Varese Italy 62 B3
Varkaus Finland 49 H7
Varna Bulgaria 69 I4
Vasa *see* Vaasa
Vaslui Romania 69 H2
Västerås Sweden 49 E9
Vasto Italy 63 F6
Vatican City *country* S Europe 46 D7, 63 E7
Vatican City *country capital* Vatican City 63 E7
Vatnajökull *glacier* Iceland 48 C2
Vättern *lake* Sweden 46 E4, 49 D10
Växjö Sweden 49 D11
Veenendaal Netherlands 53 F6
Vega *island* Norway 49 C5
Vejle Denmark 49 B12
Veles Macedonia 69 F5
Vélez-Málaga Spain 56 E8
Veliko Turnovo Bulgaria 69 H4
Vellore India 93 D9
Velsen-Noord Netherlands 52 E4
Venado Tuerto Argentina 43 F6
Vendas Novas Portugal 56 B6
Venezuela *country* N South America 38 D2, 40 D2
Venezuela, Gulf of *gulf* Colombia/Venezuela 40 D1
Venice Italy 62 E3
Venice, Gulf of *gulf* NW Adriatic Sea 62 E3
Venlo Netherlands 53 G7
Ventspils Estonia 64 B4
Vera Argentina 42 F5
Veracruz Mexico 35 F6
Veraval India 93 A7
Vercelli Italy 62 B3
Verdalsøra Norway 49 C6
Verde, Costa *coastal region* Spain 56 D1
Verden Germany 58 D4
Vereeniging South Africa 81 E7
Verkhoyanskiy Khrebet *mountain range* Russian Federation 87 H4
Vermont *state* USA 33 I4
Vernon Texas, USA 30 D4
Vernon, Mount Illinois, USA 32 B7
Veroia Greece 69 F6
Verona Italy 62 D3
Versailles France 55 F3
Verviers Belgium 53 G10
Vesoul France 55 H4
Vesterålen *island group* Norway 47 F1, 48 D3
Vestfjorden *fjord* Norway 48 D4
Vestmannaeyjar Iceland 48 B3
Vestmann Islands *island group* Iceland 48 B3
Vestvagøy *island* Norway 48 D3
Vesuvius *volcano* Italy 63 F8
Veszprem Hungary 67 E10
Vetlanda Sweden 49 D11
Veurne Belgium 53 A8
Viana do Castelo Portugal 56 B3
Viareggio Italy 62 C5
Viborg Denmark 49 B11
Vibo Valentia Italy 63 H10
Vicenza Italy 62 D3
Vichy France 55 G5
Victoria *river* Northern Territory, Australia 103 E2
Victoria *state* Australia 103 H7
Victoria British Columbia, Canada 24 B7
Victoria Falls *waterfall* Zambia/Zimbabwe 71 F10, 80 E5
Victoria Island *island* Northwest Territories/Nunavut, Canada 22 E4, 24 D3
Victoria, Lake *lake* E Africa 71 G7, 79 H7
Victoria Land *physical region* Antarctica 21 C4
Victoria River Roadhouse Northern Territory, Australia 103 E2
Vidin Bulgaria 69 F3
Viedma Argentina 43 E8
Vienna *country capital* Austria 46 E6, 61 J3
Vienne *river* France 55 E5
Vientiane *country capital* Laos 85 F7, 94 C3
Vierwaldstätter See *lake* Switzerland 60 C5
Vietnam *country* SE Asia 85 F7, 94 D4
Vignemale *mountain* France 54 E8
Vigo Spain 56 B3
Vijayawada India 93 E8
Vík Iceland 48 B3
Vikna *island* Norway 49 C6
Vila do Conde Portugal 56 B4
Vila Nova de Gaia Portugal 56 B4
Vila Real Portugal 56 B4
Vila Real de Santo António Portugal 56 B8
Vilhelmina Sweden 49 E6
Viljandi Estonia 64 C4
Villach Austria 61 H5
Villahermosa Mexico 35 G6
Villa María Argentina 43 E6
Villaputzu Italy 63 B9
Villarrica Paraguay 42 G3
Villarrobledo Spain 57 F6
Villavicencio Colombia 40 C2
Villeurbanne France 55 H5
Vilnius *country capital* Lithuania 47 F5, 65 C6
Vilyuy *river* Russian Federation 85 G3, 87 H4
Viña del Mar Chile 43 C6
Vinaròs Spain 57 H4
Vincent, Gulf St *gulf* South Australia, Australia 103 F7
Vindhya Range *mountain range* India 93 C6
Vinh Vietnam 94 D3
Vinnytsya Ukraine 65 D10
Vinson Massif *mountain* Antarctica 21 B3
Virginia *state* USA 33 F8
Virginia Beach Virginia, USA 33 H9
Virgin Islands *US dependent territory* E West Indies 37 I5
Virovitica Croatia 68 D2
Vis *island* Croatia 68 C4
Visakhapatnam India 93 E8
Visby Sweden 49 E11
Viscount Melville Sound *strait* Northwest Territories/Nunavut, Canada 24 D3
Viseu Portugal 56 B4
Visoko Bosnia & Herzegovina 68 D3
Vistula *river* Poland 47 E5, 66 E4, 67 G7
Viterbo Italy 63 D6
Viti Levu *island* Fiji 101 F6
Vitim *river* Russian Federation 87 H6
Vitória Brazil 41 I7
Vitória da Conquista Brazil 41 I6
Vitoria-Gasteiz Spain 57 F2
Vitsyebsk Belarus 47 G4, 65 E6
Vittangi Sweden 48 F4
Vittoria Italy 63 F12
Vjose *river* Albania/Greece 68 E6
Vlaardingen Netherlands 53 D6
Vladikavkaz Russian Federation 86 A6
Vladimir Russian Federation 86 B4
Vladivostok Russian Federation 85 H5, 87 J7
Vlieland *island* West Frisian Islands 52 E2
Vlissingen Netherlands 53 C7
Vlore Albania 68 E6
Vltava *river* Czech Republic 67 B7
Vocklabruck Austria 61 H3
Voghera Italy 62 B3
Voinjama Liberia 76 D7
Vojvodina *cultural region* Serbia & Montenegro 68 E2
Volga *river* Russian Federation 47 G4, 86 B5
Volgograd Russian Federation 47 I5, 86 B5
Völkermarkt Austria 61 I5
Vologda Russian Federation 86 C4
Volos Greece 69 F6
Volta, Lake *lake* Ghana 71 C6, 77 G7
Volyn-Podolian Upland *hill range* Ukraine 65 D9
Vorkuta Russian Federation 86 D4
Voronezh Russian Federation 47 H5, 86 D4
Voru Estonia 64 D4
Vosges *mountain range* France 55 I3
Voss Norway 49 A8
Voznesensk Ukraine 65 E11
Vranje Serbia & Montenegro 69 F4
Vratsa Bulgaria 69 G4
Vrbas Serbia & Montenegro 68 E2
Vryburg South Africa 80 D7
Vukovar Croatia 68 D3

W

Waal *river* Netherlands 53 E6
Waalwijk Netherlands 53 E7
Wabash *river* N USA 32 C7
Waco Texas, USA 30 E5
Waddan Libya 73 I5
Waddenzee *sea* Netherlands 52 F2
Waddington, Mount *mountain* British Columbia, Canada 24 B7
Wadi Halfa Sudan 75 C5
Wad Medani Sudan 75 D8
Wagga Wagga New South Wales, Australia 103 I7
Wagin Western Australia, Australia 102 C7
Wah Pakistan 91 G9
Waiau *river* New Zealand 105 B12
Waidhofen an der Ybbs Austria 61 I3
Waigeo *island* Indonesia 95 I7
Waikato *river* New Zealand 104 G4
Waikerie South Australia, Australia 103 G7
Waimangaroa New Zealand 105 D8
Waiouru New Zealand 105 G6
Waipara New Zealand 105 E9
Waipu New Zealand 104 F2
Waipukurau New Zealand 105 H6
Wairoa New Zealand 105 H5
Waitakere New Zealand 104 F3
Wakasa-wan *bay* Japan 99 F6
Wakatipu, Lake *lake* New Zealand 105 B11
Wakayama Japan 99 F7
Wake Island *US dependent territory* SW Pacific Ocean 101 E2
Wakkanai Japan 99 I1
Walachia *cultural region* Romania 69 G3
Walbrzych Poland 67 D6
Wales *national region* United Kingdom 51 E10
Walgett New South Wales, Australia 103 I6
Wallis & Futuna *French dependent territory* C Pacific Ocean 101 F5
Walpole Western Australia, Australia 102 C7
Walvis Bay Namibia 71 E11, 80 B6
Walvis Ridge *undersea feature* SE Atlantic Ocean 45 G9
Wanaka New Zealand 105 C11
Wanaka, Lake *lake* New Zealand 105 B11
Wandel Sea *sea* Arctic Ocean 20 C4
Wanganui *river* New Zealand 105 G6
Wanganui New Zealand 105 G6
Wanxian China 97 G6
Warangal India 93 D8
Warburg Germany 59 D6
Warnemünde Germany 58 G3
Warrego *seasonal river* New South Wales/Queensland, Australia 103 H5
Warren Michigan, USA 32 E5
Warri Nigeria 77 I8
Warsaw *country capital* Poland 47 F5, 66 G5
Warta *river* Poland 66 D4, 67 F6
Warwick Queensland, Australia 103 J6
Washington *state* USA 26 C2
Washington D.C. *country capital* District of Columbia, USA 23 G9, 33 G7
Washington, Mount *mountain* New Hampshire, USA 33 I4
Wash, The *bay* England, United Kingdom 51 H9
Waterbury Connecticut, USA 33 I6
Waterford Republic of Ireland 51 C10
Waterloo Iowa, USA 29 J5
Watertown New York, USA 33 H4
Watertown South Dakota, USA 29 H4
Watford England, United Kingdom 51 H11
Watsa Democratic Republic of Congo 79 G6
Watson Lake Yukon Territory, Canada 24 B5
Watzmann *mountain* Germany 59 G12
Wau Sudan 75 C10
Wawa Ontario, Canada 25 G8
Weald, The *physical region* England, United Kingdom 51 H11
Weddell Plain *undersea feature* C Southern Ocean 45 E12
Weddell Sea *sea* SE Southern Ocean 45 D13
Wedel Germany 58 E3
Weert Netherlands 53 G8
Wei He *river* China 97 G6
Weinan China 97 H6
Welkom South Africa 80 E7
Wellesley Islands *island group* Queensland, Australia 103 G3
Wellington *country capital* New Zealand 101 F8, 105 F7
Wellington, Isla *island* Chile 39 C12, 43 C11
Wellsford New Zealand 104 F3
Wels Austria 61 H3
Wenzhou China 97 J7
Werra *river* Germany 59 E8
Weser *river* Germany 58 C4
Wessel Islands *island group* Northern Territory, Australia 103 G1
West Cape *headland* New Zealand 105 A12
Western Australia *state* Australia 102 C5
Western Desert *desert* Egypt 74 B4
Western Dvina *river* W Europe 47 F4, 65 D5
Western Ghats *mountain range* India 84 D7, 93 B7
Western Sahara *disputed region* Morocco 70 A3, 72 B6
Westerschelde *inlet* S North Sea 53 C7
West Falkland *island* Falkland Islands 39 E13, 43 F12
West Frisian Islands *island group* Netherlands 52 E2
West Indies *island group* Caribbean Sea 23 G11, 36 E2, 45 C6
West Mariana Basin *undersea feature* W Pacific Ocean 106 C4
West Palm Beach Florida, USA 31 J7
Westport New Zealand 105 D8
West Siberian Plain *physical region* Russian Federation 84 D3, 86 D4
West Virginia *state* USA 33 E7
Wetar *island* Indonesia 95 H9
Wetzlar Germany 59 C8
Wewak Papua New Guinea 100 C5
Wexford Republic of Ireland 51 D10
Weymouth England, United Kingdom 51 F12
Whakatane New Zealand 104 H4
Whangarei New Zealand 104 F2
Wharton Basin *undersea feature* E Indian Ocean 83 G5
Wheatland Wyoming, USA 28 E5
Wheeler Peak *mountain* New Mexico, USA 30 B3
Whitehorse Yukon Territory, Canada 24 B4
White Mountains *mountain range* Maine/New Hampshire, USA 33 I4
White Nile *river* Sudan 71 G6, 75 D8
White Sea *sea* Russian Federation 20 D5, 47 G2, 86 C3
White Volta *river* Burkina, Ghana 77 G7
Whitney, Mount *mountain* California, USA 23 C8, 27 D9
Whyalla South Australia, Australia 103 G7
Wichita Kansas, USA 29 H8
Wichita Falls Texas, USA 30 D4
Wick Scotland, United Kingdom 50 F3
Wicklow Mountains *mountain range* Republic of Ireland 51 D9
Wielkopolska *cultural region* Poland 66 E4
Wiener Neustadt Austria 61 J3
Wiesbaden Germany 59 C8
Wight, Isle of *island* England, United Kingdom 51 G12
Wilcannia New South Wales, Australia 103 H6
Wildon Switzerland 61 J5
Wildspitze *mountain* Austria 61 E5
Wilhelmshaven Germany 58 C3
Wilkes Land *physical region* Antarctica 21 D4
Willemstad Netherlands Antilles 37 G8
Wilhelm II Land *physical region* Antarctica 21 E3
Williston North Dakota, USA 29 E2
Willmar Minnesota, USA 29 H4
Wilmington Delaware, USA 33 H7
Wilmington North Carolina, USA 31 K4
Wilson North Carolina, USA 31 J3
Wilson, Mount *mountain* Colorado, USA 28 C7
Wiluna Western Australia, Australia 102 C5
Windhoek *country capital* Namibia 71 E11, 80 B6
Windsor Ontario, Canada 25 G9
Windward Islands *island group* E West Indies 37 J8
Windward Passage *channel* Cuba/Haiti 37 E4
Winnemucca Nevada, USA 27 D6
Winnipeg Manitoba, Canada 23 E7, 25 E8
Winnipeg, Lake *lake* Manitoba, Canada 23 E7, 24 E7
Winnipegosis, Lake *lake* Manitoba, Canada 24 E7
Winona Minnesota, USA 29 J4
Winschoten Netherlands 52 I2